Praise for Christopher Goffard and the *Dirty John* podcast

"This collection is journalism at its finest. Incisively reported and eloquently written, these stories reveal heartbreak and heroism and the frayed fabric of life. As gripping as any novel could ever be, every one of these stories cuts down to the bone. Christopher Goffard is a storyteller for these times."

—Michael Connelly

"Christopher Goffard is a master of literary journalism. His gracefully nuanced stories, full of feeling and finely observed detail, are always heading somewhere, always unfolding with an exquisite sense of narrative. They are about seekers and searchers—people who want something, who need something. Goffard wonderfully conveys their quietly desperate worlds."

—Barry Siegel, Pulitzer Prize–winning journalist

"Christopher Goffard, one of the world's most beguiling journalists, searches among the forgotten and the invisible for insights into how all of us live, how we die, and how we piece together whatever meaning we can along the way. His stories are so unforgettably vivid and heart-stopping that they refuse to let the reader go until the last word of the last sentence."

—Thomas French, Pulitzer Prize–winning journalist and author of *Zoo Story*

"Extraordinary and terrifying . . .This case has everything a noir drama ought to: suspense, deception and plenty of twists . . .Veteran reporter Christopher Goffard pursued the story with a rigor that other true crime podcasts simply don't have."

—*Time*

"A kind of journalism noir, blending entertainment and news in powerful, sometimes unnerving ways . . .The show's final episode is thrilling, horrifying, and expertly done, with a final scene like—well, like a bonbon with a core of arsenic . . .In the end, the series leaves you with a powerful set of thoughts and emotions about the darkest sides of the human need for love."

—*The New Yorker*

"This is as gripping and unsettling as true crime gets."

—*Esquire*

"More than a murder mystery—it's a portrait of a family fractured and how they put the pieces back together."

—*Entertainment Weekly*

"True crime hit a new high with the story of how Debra Newell's online romance with a charming man spiraled into horror . . .[Will have] you screaming: 'Noooo! Don't trust him!' into your device."

—*The Guardian*

"The immediacy of the story and the representation of the reporting in audio, print, and web formats helped it become another step in the evolution of podcasts as a valuable element of the modern journalistic landscape."

—*IndieWire*

"[The] *Dirty John* approach to true-crime storytelling doesn't limit expectations—it keeps them on their toes."

—*Rolling Stone*

"An epic story involving several generations of two families, with an incredibly juicy ending. For a podcast, you'll be as hooked as if you were watching the new *American Crime* Story or a documentary as crazy as *The Jinx.*"

—*Vogue*

"The audio equivalent of a page turner."

—*The Atlantic*

ALSO BY CHRISTOPHER GOFFARD

Snitch Jacket

You Will See Fire: A Search for Justice in Kenya

DIRTY
JOHN

AND OTHER TRUE STORIES OF
OUTLAWS AND OUTSIDERS

CHRISTOPHER GOFFARD

SIMON & SCHUSTER PAPERBACKS

NEW YORK   LONDON   TORONTO   SYDNEY   NEW DELHI

Simon & Schuster Paperbacks
An Imprint of Simon & Schuster, Inc.
1230 Avenue of the Americas
New York, NY 10020

First Simon & Schuster trade paperback edition November 2018

SIMON & SCHUSTER PAPERBACKS and colophon are registered trademarks of Simon & Schuster, Inc.

For information about special discounts for bulk purchases, please contact Simon & Schuster Special Sales at 1-866-506-1949 or business@simonandschuster.com.

The Simon & Schuster Speakers Bureau can bring authors to your live event. For more information or to book an event, contact the Simon & Schuster Speakers Bureau at 1-866-248-3049 or visit our website at www.simonspeakers.com.

Interior design by Carly Loman

Manufactured in the United States of America

10 9 8 7 6 5 4 3 2 1

Library of Congress Cataloging-in-Publication Data is available.

ISBN: 978-1-9821-1325-4
ISBN: 978-1-9821-1326-1 (ebook)

For My Parents

CONTENTS

INTRODUCTION

After college in the mid-'90s I had an English degree, no job, and a bed in my dad's apartment. I was trying ludicrously to get around Greater Los Angeles without a car, and increasingly convinced of the Harry Crews observation: "The world doesn't want you to do a damn thing."

I thought journalism would be a good job for someone without means to see the world. Reporters never had to apologize for their curiosity, and I always wanted to know more than it was strictly polite to ask. Night after night, I stood at Kinko's mass-photocopying application letters to newspapers around the country while speakers pumped easy-listening Muzak into the recycled air of the bright, empty room (a serviceable image of purgatory, it seems to me). No one wrote back.

I bought a 1978 Camaro for $300 and promptly destroyed the front half by running into other cars. Because it kept going, I kept driving it.

An accidental meeting at a YMCA swimming pool led to a job in Hollywood's nameless nether ranks. I fetched coffee. I photocopied script revision pages for a Pittsburgh-based cop drama (you will not have heard of it) in myriad obscure hues. I read a bad script a day, every day, and wrote "coverage" assessing its filmability. There was a porn publisher downstairs, which seemed a more honorable living.

I was encouraged to attend weekend parties and "make contacts in the industry," which is hard to do when you are parking your cracked yellow muscle car three blocks away so no one will see you pull up in it. I was out of my dad's apartment, but after a year I had made no contacts or friends and my brakes were so bad I started standing on them a half block from the stoplight, to avoid hitting any more cars.

In near despair I called the editors at my tiny hometown paper, the *Glendale News-Press*. No, they wouldn't hire me as a reporter. I lacked experience. "Experience is what I'm looking for," I pleaded. They had an opening they seemed a little embarrassed even to mention—as a typist. Readers would submit handwritten letters that needed to be typed up for the Letters Page Editor to peruse.

I took the job and looked at the harried, overcaffeinated, ill-paid young reporters hurrying around with skinny notebooks and wondered who they had interviewed that day and thought, I want to be them.

I begged for reporting assignments, which got me work at a small weekly, then a small daily, then bigger dailies, and—in the twenty-two years since that first job—access to crime scenes, courtrooms, judges' chambers, ERs, morgues, the living rooms and back porches of innumerable strangers, the makeshift genocide courts of Rwanda, the birth of a nation in South Sudan, the denizens of Skid Row and the Los Angeles River, death rows in Florida and California . . . and to the people you will meet in this collection.

When I interview people, I try to make myself small, colorless, forgettable, the better to channel *them*. The pronoun "I" makes no appearance in my stories; my interests are subordinated in the service of others' stories. This is, of course, a kind of illusion, in the same way no documentary film captures objective reality: every angle in every scene is a choice, a function of the artist's special obsessions. These stories are an oblique map of my own.

•

I call them stories because they are not "articles," which is what newspapers are known for. Articles are built to convey information, and they serve their purpose if they make you a little smarter about the world or embarrass people into doing their jobs or nudge crooks into jail or make your elevator conversation less empty. They depend on the professionalism of reporters who pester and cajole and browbeat their sources, who track rumors to their origin and triple-check the spellings, who sometimes risk assault and abduction and murder. Articles are the miracle of daily newspapers, without which the froth-speckled cadres of the punditocracy (who are too busy to do much reporting) would be helplessly lost. They are why reporters are among the first people dictators line up against the wall.

But articles don't care if you read them all the way through. They are resilient. They can be amputated at the knees and survive. They are designed that way, with the important stuff at the top. They don't work on mystery; they are meant to dispel it as soon as possible.

A story is a different life-form. A story is an experience. Like a movie or a song or a poem, the good ones allow you to live inside other people's skulls for a little while and to touch the quick of their terror and grief and longing. Stories care about textures, about the coldness of the jail floor, not just about the charges that put you there. They care about the courtroom smell that won't come out of your suits, not just about the verdict. If they work, they augment our reservoirs of empathy and make us a little less lonely in our skin and provide a frisson of recognition that is akin to telepathy.

Stories insist you finish them and hold you in a headlock until you do. They do this not by relying on pretty packaging, or digital razzmatazz, or fake gravitas, or appeals to good-citizen guilt, but because they withhold their mysteries, which means they don't make sense until you finish them, and the last paragraph—even the last line—is often the most important. The nitty-gritty is not promiscuously surrendered but cunningly withheld, and deviously parceled out.

Every barroom raconteur knows this instinctively. But it's easy to forget, working in newsrooms where we're trained to use the "inverted pyramid" (the five *W*s at the top) and to deploy "nut graphs" (the section meant to encapsulate, in a tidy acorn shell, why the piece is relevant and worthy of a reader's time).

Maybe it was reading Tom French's "Angels & Demons," or Tom Wolfe's *The New Journalism*, or Gay Talese's *Fame and Obscurity*. But I began to perceive that it is possible to write stories that are true in every particular, but partake of a novel's intimacy and immersiveness by borrowing some of its techniques (like scene-by-scene construction, point of view, and dialogue). I began dodging inverted pyramids and scuttling nut graphs, implicitly daring my editors to stop me. I was lucky: I worked at papers with rosters of narrative risk-takers like Tom French and Rick Bragg, Anne Hull and David Finkel, Barry Bearak and Barry Siegel, Bella Stumbo and J. R. Moehringer.

These stories involve nobody famous. They do not focus on policy makers and celebrities; they do not rely on news hooks or care much about "sweep." They are not polemics. They do not pound the table or raise a tin cup for a cause or aim to repair your flawed politics, though I hope they give some pain to ideologues.

They are about criminals and their victims, about people in the coils of faceless systems or their own obsessions, about the falsely accused and the born-trapped, about outsiders and the forms their desperation takes. They are sorties into the private psychic territory more commonly associated with fiction.

A pair of runaway kids huddled together against the onrush of adulthood. A Marine haunted by his father's desertion from

World War II. A mother who must leave her children to save them. An exile seeking redemption in a bus to the sea. A brave soldier whose memory has warped and twisted into a bludgeon to torture him. A lonely man in thrall to a childhood picture, building a boat to oblivion. A woman seeking love, who finds a predatory creature expert at its mimicry.

If you're familiar with that last one, which is the title story of this collection, it may be from the podcast I made or the TV series it inspired. A writer who claims to dislike unexpected attention is probably a lying writer. In this case, I'm mainly glad it brought you here.

DIRTY JOHN

THE ACCUSATIONS

PART ONE

He kept thinking that there had been a mistake, that he'd be out in no time. That the system, set into motion by some misunderstanding or act of malice, would soon correct itself.

That was before the detective informed him of the charges, and before the article in the *Ventura County Star*. "Man held after woman found raped and tortured," read the headline, and there was his name, along with a quote from a police officer: "In 19 years of police work, this has to go down as one of the most brutal attacks I have ever seen."

The sky was beautiful that afternoon. Louis Gonzalez III remembered it felt like spring.

He was standing on the sidewalk outside the Simi Valley Montessori School, having just flown in from Las Vegas, hoping to get a look at his five-year-old son's new kindergarten. Standing there, waiting for the door to open so he could scoop the boy up in his arms and fly him to Nevada for the weekend.

The first officer arrived on a motorcycle and headed straight for him. He did not explain the charges as he snapped on the handcuffs. As Gonzalez stood there stunned, he noticed little faces pressed against the schoolhouse glass, watching, and asked if he could be moved just a bit so his son didn't have to see.

Soon he'd surrendered all the items that tethered him reassuringly to the rational, workaday world. The BlackBerry he used a hundred times a day. His Dolce & Gabbana watch. His credit cards and photos of his son. His leather shoes and his socks, his pressed shirt and jacket, his belt and slacks and underwear. Naked in a holding cell, he watched his things disappear into plastic bags. He stepped into a set of black-and-white-striped jail scrubs, the kind his son might wear on Halloween.

A month passed in his single-bunk cell, and then another, and he had nothing but time to reckon all he'd lost. His freedom. His son. His job. His reputation. He had to wonder how much he could endure.

The other inmates in the solitary wing of the Ventura County Jail didn't talk about their cases, because anyone might be a snitch, but his charges were well-known on the cellblock. More than once, they warned him about what awaited if he were convicted and sent to state prison. With a sex crime on his jacket, he knew, he would be a target forever.

"Like you're waiting for death," he said. "Dying would probably be better."

•

Minutes before Gonzalez's arrest around 2:00 p.m. on February 1, 2008, Tim Geiges placed a frantic 911 call. By the account he would give consistently in years to come, he'd just returned from work and found his wife, Tracy West, naked and bound in an upstairs bedroom of their Simi Valley home in the 1900 block of Penngrove Street.

The dispatcher tried to calm him. "Sir, somebody beat your wife up?"

"Somebody tied her up, and I just got home—oh my God . . ." He was whimpering. "I just untied her head just now. She's crying. I need somebody, please!"

He managed to say that his wife's attacker would be at the Montessori School, a mile away.

"Who is this person?"

"Louis. Louis Gonzalez the Third."

When paramedics arrived at the house, they found West on the bed leaning forward, crying, with purple duct tape tangled in her hair.

•

Detective David Del Marto was on the other side of town, working leads on a robbery, when he heard the radio chatter about the attack. He has level blue eyes, a graying mustache, and the faultless posture of the Army MP he once was.

He found West, thirty-three, in the emergency room of Simi Valley Hospital and followed her across the street to Safe Harbor, a forensic facility where sexual assault victims are examined and interviewed. Her appearance suggested an attack of concentrated malice. Her face was swollen, her lip gashed, her hair torn out in chunks. A cord, found tied around her neck with a slipknot, had left an angry red line, and there were burns on her stomach and ring finger.

Later, Del Marto would remember how she looked away and pulled herself into a fetal position as she talked. It was the body language he'd seen in dozens of sexual assault cases.

West was unequivocal about who had attacked her. It was Gonzalez, she said. He was her ex-boyfriend, the father of her son.

Del Marto made his voice gentle. "I need to find out what happened and what to charge him with, OK? You know he's in custody, right? You don't have to worry anymore about him for now."

In a small, fragile voice that kept trailing off and lapsing into silence, West explained that she and Gonzalez, thirty, had been fighting over custody since their son's birth. She and Geiges were raising the boy, along with their younger daughter.

She said Gonzalez ambushed her in the garage, dragged her to an upstairs bedroom, hogtied her with her clothes, singed her with matches, and assaulted her vaginally and anally with a wooden coat hanger. Then, she said, he forced a plastic bag over her head and held it tight, and she feigned unconsciousness until he left.

4

"He told me he was gonna kill me," she said. "He told me that. Seven or eight different times."

"Did he have anything with him in his hands?"

"He had a bag. Like a little mini duffel bag."

During the attack, she said, she awoke from a blackout to find Gonzalez had placed mittens on her hands—she recalled drawstrings at the wrists—while he wore plastic gloves.

Del Marto thought this pointed to an uncommon level of sophistication—to a man who took extraordinary pains to avoid leaving fingerprints or traces of his DNA under his victim's raking fingernails. In his report, the detective noted another detail she gave: Her attacker had worn beige-colored overalls, as if to shield his clothes from evidence.

After the interview, West left with her husband. Del Marto followed them to their home on Penngrove Street for another examination of the scene. It was a placid residential block in one of California's safest cities. He watched for some time as she refused to leave the car and go inside.

Del Marto thought West was lucky to be alive. A twenty-three-year veteran, he knew custody cases bred a special sort of derangement, and he was confident he understood the outlines of what happened here: extreme rage mingled with extreme calculation.

•

A few hours after the arrest, Del Marto pulled the accused out of his cell. He was known as a low-key investigator who didn't raise his voice—"the epitome of the poker face," his supervisor called him—and this was his chance to clinch the case with a confession.

He studied Gonzalez. He saw no scratches on his face or hands, and thought: the mittens.

"What is the accusation?" Gonzalez asked.

"That you assaulted Tracy at her house."

"That I assaulted? At what time did this take place?"

Del Marto stopped him. He had to read him his Miranda rights, a delicate business he knew could end the interview fast. Gonzalez agreed to talk anyway.

Maybe he believes he's smarter than me, Del Marto thought. In the detective's eyes, the guy came off as a little arrogant, a little nonchalant, considering the situation. Gonzalez had an impressive title: senior vice president for business banking at the Bank of Las Vegas. He arranged commercial real estate loans. Del Marto thought: a salesman.

This is about a custody fight, Gonzalez said. "I always just assumed that she would lie and do things to get the edge in court. I don't know that she would go to this extent to get me in trouble. This is absurd. I mean, how can I possibly have done that?"

Gonzalez insisted he'd never been to West's house. Didn't even know the address.

"You work for a financial institution," Del Marto replied. "It's not hard to get a property profile on somebody."

The attack could have taken as little as fifteen or twenty minutes, he said, and it was just two or three minutes from West's house to the school where he was arrested.

"It's perfectly feasible for it to have occurred," Del Marto said. "Perfectly feasible."

What about evidence at the house? Gonzalez asked.

Del Marto thought of the gloves. "Somebody probably watches *CSI* quite a lot."

"Who, me?"

"You did things that reminded people of 'Hey, they do that on *CSI*' to try to prevent us from collecting evidence."

"I didn't do this," Gonzalez said. "I know you think I did it, but I didn't do it."

"I don't have a reason not to think you did it," the detective replied. "Yeah, I think you did it. I do."

Del Marto ended the interview after twenty-three minutes. He sensed he would not get a confession. He would have to build the case with other evidence. A forensics team was dusting door-knobs and plucking carpet fibers from the house. They were combing the black suit Gonzalez was arrested in, and the inside of the rented Dodge Avenger he had parked outside a hair salon near the school.

Super-criminals are fictitious, Del Marto thought. Even very careful ones leave traces.

•

If Gonzalez was presumed innocent under the law, the Ventura County Jail did not expect other inmates to honor that distinction. He was held in a segregated unit and received his meals through a slot in the heavy metal door. He wore a red-striped wristband denoting a violent offense. An hour a day, the doors opened so he could shower and make phone calls.

Now and then he could hear people going crazy in their cells, kicking their doors, screaming on and on until they had to be removed. He thought of himself as mentally sturdy, a survivor, but knew how easily anyone could crack. So he crammed every waking hour with routine. He read out-of-date newspapers and John Grisham novels and the Bible. He made a paper chess set and stood at the crack in his cell door, calling out moves to opponents down the corridor.

He listened to other inmates dwelling on the food they missed. One guy would say, "TGI Fridays, calamari," the others would groan, and it went on like that for hours.

He learned a rule about surviving lockup: Never take a daytime nap, no matter how tired you are. Because you might not sleep that night, and you'd be left for hours in the dark of a cold cell with only your thoughts and your fear.

He found himself replaying his whole life—every house he'd lived in, every deal he'd made, every girlfriend, including West.

They'd met in a finance-class study group at the University of Nevada in summer 2001. He was a high school dropout from the Bronx who had become a confident, career-minded student who wore pinstriped suits to class. She was smart, with brown hair and pretty hazel eyes, a vegetarian in flower dresses who spoke softly. He liked her air of West Coast bohemianism.

Their relationship was brief. They had been apart for months when, by his account, she called during a sonogram appointment. Suddenly he was listening to the heartbeat of their son.

In her fourth month of pregnancy, West met Gonzalez at a Denny's in Vegas. According to a police report, she said he became upset because she wouldn't go back to him. She said he slapped her and punched her stomach.

Gonzalez's version: They had gotten back together, and argued because she was seeing another man and lying about it. He admitted to breaking her windshield, but only after she "went nuts hitting him," the police report said. He was arrested on suspicion of misdemeanor domestic violence. The charge was dropped.

The family-court battle began before the boy's first birthday—an interminable gauntlet of judges, mediators, and psychiatrists as the two argued over custody and visitation.

Gonzalez's custody attorney, Denise Placencio, said West tried relentlessly to curtail his time with his son, accusing Gonzalez of domestic abuse and claiming the boy suffered "separation anxiety" when he was away from his mother. The campaign continued, Placencio said, after West married Geiges and moved to California with the boy.

The courts allowed Gonzalez two weekends a month with his son. He would pick him up from the Vegas airport on Friday, and they would have an intense couple of days together. They might go to the mall or the shark reef at Mandalay Bay. And then back to the airport on Sunday, a knife twisting in his stomach as he watched his five-year-old loping down the jetway, a gangly little guy with reddish hair glancing back uncertainly.

In January 2008, Gonzalez sent an email to West explaining that he wanted to see the boy's new Montessori School in Simi

Valley. He would pick him up there on February 1 and fly him back to Nevada for the weekend. He planned to take him to a Super Bowl Sunday barbecue.

West pressed for specifics. "What time are you planning on being here? Are you going to drive or fly?"

He would arrive by plane around noon, he wrote, and expected to get to the school around 2:00 p.m.

The email exchange soon descended into acrimony. All these trips to Vegas were taking a toll on their son, West wrote. "Having to tell him that he has to go despite his obvious distress, is not what I want. Having to sit with a crying child when he comes back because he doesn't want me to leave his side, is not what I want," she wrote. "I want a happy, healthy child. I have worked 24/7/365+ from the moment I knew of him, to do the best for him—not me."

Gonzalez answered that he hadn't seen these signs of distress—his son seemed happy to see him. "My focus right now is to make the best of what little time I have with him," he wrote to West. "I'm going to be thirty-one this year. A lot has changed since you last knew me." His whole life was his son, he wrote. "When he isn't with me the only thing I do is wait for him."

West replied by attacking him as a father, writing that he had "proven time and time again" that he did not put their son's needs above his own whims. "You are just not capable," she wrote. He had "mentally tortured" their son, she claimed, by telling him once that his plane would crash in bad weather.

If she believed he'd say that, Gonzalez replied, "then you need help."

It was hardly the nastiest exchange Gonzalez could remember. But he found himself replaying it in his cell, his thoughts racing. His hope of a quick release now seemed remote, considering the charges. If convicted of all counts—residential burglary, kidnapping, torture, attempted murder, anal and genital penetration with a foreign object—he faced five back-to-back life sentences.

"His goal was to degrade and humiliate her as much as humanly possible before killing her" and fleeing with their son, Ventura County Assistant District Attorney Andrea Tischler wrote in court papers arguing that Gonzalez should be held without bail. He committed "some of the most extreme possible crimes against another human being," Tischler contended, crimes "so heinous that they defy the imagination."

The judge ruled: No bail.

•

Looking at Gonzalez through the Plexiglas for the first time, three days after his arrest, his lead defense attorney, Debra S. White, was struck by his eyes, which she described as "these dark eyes, these piercing eyes." He looked distraught and tired and angry.

This is about the boy, Gonzalez insisted. She wants me out of his life. Nail down my alibi and get me out, he said. He recited a detailed list, mentally compiled over hours in his cell, of everybody who might have seen him around the time West said the attack occurred.

White called her sister, Leigh-Anne Salinas, her investigator on big cases. White has the clothes and looks of a lawyer in a prime-time drama. Salinas wears jeans and a T-shirt on the job. Her speech is salty and she's at ease both in gang neighborhoods and white-collar offices.

Salinas related to Gonzalez's businesslike, hard-edged manner—it reminded her of herself—but didn't think a jury would like him much. She is pessimistic about human nature, and on first meeting Gonzalez suspected he might be guilty. She thought: Wow, this guy really thought this out.

If there was any chance of proving his innocence, she knew she would have to move quickly, before memories faded.

Her task: verify Gonzalez's whereabouts in the hours preceding his arrest. West had accused Gonzalez of attacking her between 12:30 and 12:45 p.m. She knew the time, she told police, because she was about to leave to pick up her daughter early from school.

Salinas began retracing Gonzalez's movements, starting with his arrival at Bob Hope Airport in Burbank around noon that day. She walked into Enterprise Rent-A-Car on Hollywood Way, where employees remembered Gonzalez. He was the guy who needed a child's car seat and stepped outside for a cigarette as the paperwork was being drawn up. His receipt said 12:09 p.m.

Next, Gonzalez would have driven northwest to Simi Valley, a twenty-eight-mile trip. Salinas verified that Gonzalez was on his cell phone with another Nevada banker during the drive. They were discussing a loan, the other banker said, and Gonzalez was complaining about traffic as he approached his son's school. Phone records confirmed this call lasted from 12:43 to 12:48 p.m.

At the Montessori School at 1776 Erringer Road, Salinas's job proved tougher. School employees knew West—she volunteered regularly there—and Salinas sensed their reluctance to help the man accused of brutalizing her.

Salinas was polite and persistent. School workers remembered Gonzalez arriving between 12:45 and 12:50 p.m. He greeted his son and briefly toured the school. One lady joked that she felt underdressed alongside his suit and tie. They told him to return in about an hour to pick up his boy.

After leaving the school, Gonzalez said he walked to a bagel shop at an adjacent strip mall. Salinas retraced his steps and found herself inside John's Bagel Deli. The manager, Jung Soon Shin, recalled Gonzalez coming in around 1:00 p.m. to order a tuna sandwich on a sesame bagel.

When Shin explained that she didn't take credit cards, he patted his pockets—no cash—and promised to be back.

At the Wells Fargo a few blocks away, Salinas discovered, an assistant manager named Mercedes Saunders remembered Gonzalez coming in to make a withdrawal. They chatted, and she found him calm and pleasant. Surveillance cameras confirmed he was there from 1:14 to 1:38 p.m. They showed him waiting in line, resting his head on his palm, a bored-looking man in a dark suit.

Back at the bagel shop, Shin saw him return sometime before 2:00 p.m. with cash to buy his sandwich. She remembered him because he wasn't a regular, and because after he left she had to fish his reusable red sandwich basket out of the trash. And because he was so nicely dressed.

Salinas called her sister. West's story didn't hold up, she said.

"Wow," White said. "He actually may be innocent."

Del Marto, who had been talking to many of the same witnesses, was watching a case unravel against a man he believed guilty. Had Gonzalez cunningly timed the attack between periods he knew he would be seen in public?

Del Marto thought there was one thing that might solve the case: the duffel bag West said Gonzalez had been carrying. Had all the items Del Marto couldn't find—the mittens, the gloves, the overalls—been stuffed in there and discarded?

He'd looked in storm drains and sewers around West's house. He'd searched roofs, Dumpsters, freeway shoulders, anywhere Gonzalez might have tossed it. He'd even inquired at Simi Valley mailbox companies, in case Gonzalez had been calculating enough to mail it to himself.

No sign of the bag.

The detective needed proof that it had existed, something more than West's word. He needed a photo or video footage. He made a phone call. He made another. He waited.

PART TWO

In his single-bunk cell in the Ventura County Jail, on a concrete slab desk, Louis Gonzalez III found himself compulsively writing letters to his five-year-old son. They were a chronicle of their truncated time together. Telling him how they'd cheered for the Yankees. How his favorite toy had been a mechanical garbage truck. How he'd been a picky eater from the start, but crazy for Cheerios. He never mailed them.

He imagined his son in the cell with him, pushing around his Hot Wheels. In the silence and the isolation, his dream life had acquired surprising vividness. He could almost hear the little plastic wheels on the concrete.

He had a recurring fantasy. He saw himself in prison, ten or fifteen years from now, his conviction long since sealed, his appeals denied. His son, grown into a young man, would be his salvation, would take it upon himself to look into the case. He'd show up and say, "Mom admitted that she lied."

•

Doubts had been gnawing at Simi Valley Police Detective David Del Marto. In elaborate detail, Tracy West had told him that Gonzalez, her ex-boyfriend, had ambushed and sexually tortured her in her home between 12:30 and 12:45 p.m. on February 1, 2008.

To test that claim, Del Marto climbed into his car. He wanted to time the route between Bob Hope Airport in Burbank, where Gonzalez had arrived about noon that day from Las Vegas, and West's house in Simi Valley. Gonzalez was in California to pick up their son—a five-year-old he and West had been fighting over interminably—for a regular weekend visit.

Del Marto had picked a Friday just after noon for his experiment, to replicate the conditions Gonzalez would have faced. He pushed his car to 80 miles per hour. His partner held a stopwatch.

Even if Gonzalez had raced up the freeway, the detective discovered, he could not have arrived at West's house earlier than 12:42 p.m. And witnesses confirmed he was at the Montessori School, a mile away, right around then.

Del Marto called West. Was she sure about the time?

West, by the detective's account, replied that she had been guessing. She couldn't be sure.

Del Marto wondered: Did Gonzalez commit the attack after he left the school and before he was seen at a nearby bank? Or perhaps after he left the bank and before he was seen buying a bagel?

The detective concluded that each scenario would have given Gonzalez a narrow window of opportunity at West's house:

Six minutes.

Was that enough time for the attack she had described?

Enough time for Gonzalez to find her in her garage, knock her out, drag her up the stairs, put gloves on his hands and mittens on hers, and slip on protective overalls so that his suit would remain immaculate?

Enough time to strip her, tie her up, burn her with matches, sexually assault her with a coat hanger, and attempt to suffocate her with a plastic bag?

Enough time to dispose of all this evidence, along with a duffel bag she said he had carried?

Why did no one, before or after, notice that Gonzalez was nervous or out of breath?

The disarray at the house on Penngrove Street seemed to reflect the struggle West described: clumps of her hair, scissors discarded on the carpet, a spindle yanked out of the banister.

But Del Marto could find nothing to place Gonzalez there. No fingerprints, no DNA, no hair, no clothes fibers.

He remembered how West looked that day, bruised and traumatized. But the medical records seemed at odds with the sexual assault she described: They showed no internal tears or bleeding.

Maybe, Del Marto thought, the gloves, mittens, and overalls didn't exist. Maybe they were props in a story.

He withheld judgment until he could see the footage captured by the security cameras at McCarran Airport in Las Vegas.

Getting it required weeks of calls to the Transportation Security Administration. Finally, on March 11, 2008—thirty-nine days after Gonzalez's arrest—Del Marto and his partner were led to a private room in the bowels of Los Angeles International Airport and handed a disk.

Del Marto slid it into his laptop. He watched bodies shuffle through the security line in Vegas, taking off shoes, placing luggage on the conveyor belt. The detective trained his eyes on the screen for one thing in particular: the duffel bag West said was in Gonzalez's possession.

Of all the people who said they saw Gonzalez that day, West was the only one who remembered it. She said she'd heard him zipping and unzipping it during the attack. The airline said he hadn't checked bags when he flew to California. Had he carried the duffel bag onboard?

If he could find an image of that, Del Marto thought, it just might prove the case against him.

Three cameras captured Gonzalez walking through the metal

detector wearing a black suit, gray shirt, and patterned tie. On each angle, Del Marto froze the frame and leaned forward. Each time, he saw the same thing. Gonzalez's hands were empty.

Del Marto turned to his partner. "I don't know how he could have done this," he said.

•

The preliminary hearing in *State vs. Gonzalez*, to determine whether he should face trial, was weeks away, and Del Marto was expected to testify on West's behalf so she wouldn't have to. The detective did something rare in his twenty-three-year career: He called the prosecutor to say that he was uncomfortable testifying in his own case.

Ventura County prosecutors were not deterred by this, nor by the absence of corroborating evidence. They intended to put West on the stand to tell her story. There, she would face a defense team that had lined up ten alibi witnesses and was preparing to portray her as a pathological liar.

On April 21, 2008, the day before the hearing was to begin, prosecutors learned that West was in the hospital. They had obtained a note in what appeared to be West's handwriting.

"The DA asking me to relive my horror of Louis Gonzalez attack is more than I can bear. For them it is a case. For me it is my life shattered," read the note. "I died of Rx overdose—suicide."

Later, in family court, West would say she did not remember writing the note and blamed the hospitalization on drugs her psychiatrist prescribed.

At 5:26 p.m. on April 22, prosecutor Andrea Tischler sent defense attorneys a brief email: With West unavailable to testify, they were dropping the case. For now.

Jay Leiderman, one of Gonzalez's defense attorneys, hurried to the jail. To save a few minutes, he met his client through Plexiglas rather than face-to-face. Gonzalez was accustomed to odd-hours visits from the lawyer, but this time Leiderman's tie was loose, and he was smiling.

"You're going home tomorrow," he said.

Gonzalez's father, a retiree who had been watching his house outside Las Vegas and picking up his mail, was there to greet him when he walked out the next day. So was Gonzalez's mother, his brother, his sister, and his aunts, sweeping him up in a crush of family. After eighty-three days in a solitary cell, things felt wrong. All these people in one place, all this open air, made him dizzy.

He had his freedom. Now he wanted a French dip. Then he wanted to get as far away from Ventura County as possible and start figuring out how to reclaim everything else he'd lost: his son, his job, his name.

•

The job turned out to be the easiest. The Bank of Las Vegas valued his abilities, and three weeks after his release he put on one of the double-vented suits he'd had retailored to fit a frame that had shed ten pounds in lockup.

He pushed open the bank door and crossed the lobby toward his office, bracing himself for the questions, the strained expressions.

Lou, hey, welcome back. . . . So . . .

He got used to telling the story. He left out the worst details. It was all about the custody case, he said. She wanted me gone.

No one came out and said anything directly, but he sensed people were wary. Some clients avoided him. The woman he was dating before his arrest never called again. He felt a lingering mistrust. As if people figured some of it must be true—that he had hired a crack legal team and bought his way out of trouble. He knew certain things reinforced this perception: His accuser was walking free, after all, and retained custody of his son.

How come your ex isn't in jail? people kept asking.

He didn't have a good answer.

Soon after his return to work, he was sitting at a Cheesecake Factory in Vegas with two loan brokers and an underwriter. The lunch meeting passed in a blur of acute anxiety. His mind was on a restraining order West had filed in California, restating her claim that he attacked her and asking the court to keep him away from their son. He thought about how prosecutors might, at any moment, choose to refile charges. How tenuous freedom felt.

He was sure everyone at the table could sense his panic, that he was blowing it, fidgeting, speaking too quickly. Mercifully, the check came.

Don't worry, Lou, the underwriter told him afterward. You were fine.

•

Getting to see his son proved tougher. He missed his sixth birthday. A custody judge withheld visitation, concerned Gonzalez might still face criminal charges. Another complication was

West's restraining order, which hung over him for months after his release, until she withdrew it just as his legal team was preparing to attack it in court.

A judge awarded him $55,000 for legal fees he incurred fighting it, though West's subsequent declaration of bankruptcy made it doubtful he'd ever recover the money.

He was finally allowed to see his son—eight months after his arrest. It was a brief visit at the office of a family reunification specialist.

Soon after, on his day off, Del Marto gave a deposition to the family law attorney Gonzalez had enlisted to fight for full custody. All of the physical evidence had been processed, the detective said, and none of it implicated Gonzalez.

"Based on my investigation, I see no reason why he should not be able to see his son."

•

Winning back his name was hardest of all. Removing every trace of the taint would be impossible. Stories persist on the Internet. Once, a date told him she had googled him, and he had to explain.

Leiderman, one of his defense lawyers, thought it was not enough that the government dropped charges. He wanted the criminal justice system to recognize Gonzalez's innocence affirmatively.

There is such a thing as a declaration of factual innocence, he explained to Gonzalez. A judge can grant it. It is exceedingly rare—so rare that many cops and lawyers go a career without seeing one. It means not just that prosecutors couldn't make a case against you but that you didn't do the crime.

The case remained on the docket of Ventura County Superior Court Judge Patricia Murphy, who had earlier ordered Gonzalez held without bail. Leiderman petitioned the judge, trying not to get his client's hopes up. He laid out the case, pointing out the holes in West's story and the numerous alibi witnesses.

Prosecutors did not want Gonzalez declared innocent. They knew a jury wouldn't convict him but said they couldn't be positive of his innocence. James Ellison, Ventura County's chief assistant district attorney, later explained their reasoning: The attack West described was "improbable, but it wasn't physically impossible."

In January 2009, nearly a year after Gonzalez's arrest, Leiderman called him excitedly: The judge had sided with them. Gonzalez was soon holding a certified copy of the judge's order declaring him factually innocent.

He drove to the bank and put it in a safe-deposit box. He figured he would need it if he wanted to continue in banking, where the blot on his record would otherwise scare off future employers. It would help in his fight to win custody of his son.

But it hardly made him whole. It made it even more illogical, in his view, that West was free.

•

Asked why West hadn't been charged with filing a false police report, Ellison, the Ventura County prosecutor, gave this explanation: "We could not say with 100 percent certainty that Tracy West was lying."

To Gonzalez's attorneys, who have argued vehemently for West's arrest, the state's decision not to charge her criminally violates the most basic moral arithmetic.

Leiderman said he thinks the district attorney's office is embarrassed and wants the case to disappear. "No one wanted to believe a woman would make something like this up," he said.

Gonzalez sued West for malicious prosecution, and her insurance carrier settled the case on confidential terms. He did not sue Del Marto or his department. He doesn't blame the detective.

Del Marto can't say for sure what happened in that upstairs bedroom. He ruled out the possibility that West's husband, Tim Geiges, inflicted the wounds on her; his cell phone records proved he was elsewhere as she lay tied up.

Now and then, he found himself thinking of something he discovered on West's computer. It was a link to a sexual-bondage website that West had recently visited, Del Marto said. When he asked about it, she replied that a friend had sent it as a joke, the detective said.

The site featured men and women in elaborate restraints, and a depiction of a double-loop slipknot with a little eyelet on one end. To Del Marto, it resembled the knotted cord a nurse had removed from West's bruised neck on February 1, 2008.

The detective tried to imagine West hating her son's father enough to injure herself in such a methodical way. Tying the cord around her own neck, cutting off clumps of her hair, battering her own face, burning her own skin . . . and the other things. His mind strained at the effort.

He'd seen people give themselves a scratch or bruise to impersonate victims, but nothing like this. "My God," he said, "to this extent?"

Del Marto said prosecutors asked him whether a case could be made against her. His reply: Not without her confession. He prepared to confront her with the inconsistencies in her story. He planned to give her a lie detector test. He couldn't force her to cooperate, however.

"She stopped answering my phone calls," he said.

His supervisor praised his detective work, but Del Marto found the outcome unsatisfying. No one punished was a bad way to leave it.

When the department received the expungement order from the court, the recordkeepers dutifully deleted Gonzalez's name from the computers. They gathered up the evidence Del Marto had amassed in Case No. 08-04893—the warrants, the interview reports, the forensic results, the painstaking timelines—and began shredding.

•

As the custody battle staggered on, hearing by hearing, Las Vegas family court Judge Bill Henderson wrestled aloud with the implications of the criminal case. He didn't believe Gonzalez attacked West. But must he conclude, he asked, that she made it all up? Perhaps someone else attacked her?

No, testified John Paglini, the court-appointed psychologist who had interviewed West four times: Either Gonzalez attacked her, or she lied.

"She could have said, 'On February first I was attacked

by somebody, I don't know who it was,' but she picked this guy out, and she was very definite," Paglini told the court. "It couldn't be somebody else. She said, 'I heard his voice, I saw his face.'"

Asked about the events of that day during a deposition, West invoked her Fifth Amendment right against self-incrimination.

When she failed to show up for a hearing in the summer of 2009, Gonzalez was granted temporary custody of their son, but the case continued.

West's voice was soft, at times barely above a whisper, when she took the stand last June. Her straight, dark hair fell to her shoulders. She held her hands demurely in her lap, a still presence with an air of vulnerability.

She deserved her son, she said. She talked about how close he was to his little sister, how they belonged together in California, and her voice broke.

Her lawyer asked her about February 1, 2008. This time she did not plead the Fifth. Instead, she steadfastly insisted Gonzalez attacked her.

"Did you do it to yourself?"

"Absolutely not."

"Did you have somebody do it to you on purpose?"

"Absolutely not."

In her closing argument, Gonzalez's custody attorney, Denise Placencio, said West had been trying to divide father and son for years—attempting to change the boy's surname, moving him from Nevada to California, offering Gonzalez money to relinquish parental rights.

"The last resort was to frame Mr. Gonzalez and put him in jail," she said.

The judge concluded that West's insistence on Gonzalez's guilt "with no rational basis" was an attempt to remove the boy from his father's life.

"She continues to maintain that he's guilty of this heinous crime, and he's not," the judge said. "The court finds if mom is allowed to maintain primary physical custody, she's more likely to continue with this." She appeared to be a good mother otherwise, he said, and it was with "a heavy heart" that he awarded custody to the father.

The judge was not, however, prepared to accept the psychologist's either-or view of the case—that if Gonzalez didn't do it, she made it up.

What West believed about February 1, 2008, "remains unclear," and the possibility that she suffered a "delusion" had not been ruled out, the judge said.

West would stay in her son's life. She moved back to Nevada.

•

On Fridays and Sundays, Gonzalez and West exchange custody at a McDonald's or Starbucks. If possible, he waits in the car and sends his mother in to do it.

Sometimes Gonzalez wonders how much worse things might have gone.

What if he had grabbed breakfast in Las Vegas before boarding his flight? He wouldn't have needed that bagel in Simi Valley, so he wouldn't have gone to the bank for cash, and wouldn't have been caught on security cameras.

His alibi evaporates and he's in prison for life.

At the end of the day his mind automatically replays his movements, hour by hour, because it was his ability to do that that saved him. After his release he developed the habit of meticulously documenting his whereabouts, eliminating time gaps that might leave him vulnerable.

If he's in an airport or a 7-Eleven, he makes sure the surveillance cameras get a good look at his face. Anytime he can swipe his credit card and sign his name, even to buy a pack of gum, he does it.

He fills his wallet with receipts and the world with a conspicuous trail.

He feels most vulnerable when he is asleep, when, for six or eight hours a night, no cameras are watching, no witnesses are marking his presence, and no one but Louis Gonzalez III can say with certainty where he is.

HEALING SERGEANT WARREN

Jonathan Warren walks through the maze of corridors until he finds the little room. Anxiously, he puts on the earphones and adjusts the wraparound visor. The image before him is crude: road, desert, truck.

Describe that day, his therapist says.

We drove up in a Humvee . . .

No. Tell it as if it's happening now.

We are on a black route. The worst kind.

He isn't sure he can trust his memory. He knows he was in the commander's seat, right front. Scott Stephenson, his best friend, was sitting behind him. They had been inseparable since they enlisted two years earlier, the God-fearing California surf punk and the half-crazy Kansas street kid. They bunked together, drank together, learned to shoot together. They were lost boys reborn as hard Army muscle, shaved heads in Kevlar helmets, feeling as bulletproof as their steel-plated 12,000-pound truck.

Staring into the visor, Warren studies the computer simulation of gray pavement stretching before him. He knows what lies down that road, amid the flames and churning black smoke: the test his whole life was supposed to prepare him for. For years, he's fled the memory, drinking until he can't recognize himself, smoking pot until he's numb, swallowing pills until he can sleep.

Now, the therapist insists that he slow the memory to a crawl, uncoil it, examine it inch by inch.

He closes his eyes. His heart pounds. He sees it now, the worst part, the moment he glances back at the burning truck and realizes Scotty is trapped inside.

What do you see? his therapist asks.

A fireball.

What do you do?

•

In the dream from his boyhood, Warren and a younger brother are being chased through the woods by a swarm of vicious bees. His brother falls behind. To save him, Warren sacrifices his own body.

That was how he saw himself. His life made the most sense to him whenever he took a punch in a schoolyard fight for a brother, or threw a punch on behalf of an insulted girl, or played football with a dislocated arm because his high school team needed him.

"He was born with a savior complex," says his mother, Denise.

He grew up the oldest of three brothers in a five-bedroom tract home in Laguna Niguel, with evangelical Sunday school and a strong sense of God's personal disapproval. "You don't have permission to be a child. You have to be perfect," his mother says, ruefully now, of the upbringing she gave him. "There are only two options. You're either saved or you're going to hell."

In school he was popular, a good student, with light blond hair and broad shoulders, an image from a surf-wear poster. But his mother sensed a seething anger that he felt free to vent only when he was brawling or wearing a football uniform.

He started a fight club at a Christian college, where he lasted just two semesters. Boredom was suffocating him, making him do crazy things. He rode waves till 2:00 a.m. and led drinking trips to Mexico, where he danced with someone else's girlfriend and left the bar with his nose turned sideways.

He grilled cheesesteaks at Hooters. He mixed cocaine with Robitussin and saw demons. His parents braced for the late-night call informing them that he was in jail or dead.

He longed for the sense of warrior camaraderie he had seen in *Saving Private Ryan* and *The Thin Red Line*. He ached to do "something hard-core," like Denzel Washington's one-man stand against a kidnapping syndicate in a favorite film, *Man on Fire*.

He was angry about 9/11 and eager to fight in the war on terrorism, which he saw plainly as a war of good versus evil.

His father, a produce broker, found him at the computer one night studying an Army recruiting website. Tim Warren pleaded with his son to consider an easy paycheck in the family business.

Or, if he had to join the armed forces, why not pick a branch more remote from the killing and dying?

Warren heard fear in his dad's voice. It didn't matter. He could already feel the uniform.

•

November 25, 2006. They were lost, somewhere south of Baghdad. They sweltered in their ceramic armor and the Humvee's thick air. It was the end of a long morning patrol, and they were leading a five-truck convoy through the dangerous borderlands between Sunni and Shiite militias. At nearly noon, the sun was climbing toward its cruelest angle.

For the first time in longer than he could remember, Warren liked himself. He was twenty-four, a good soldier, cool under fire, a peacemaker among bickering troops, and, he believed, equal to anything. "Everything you want in a team leader," said his commander, who had promoted Warren to that job—which usually went to sergeants or above—even though Warren had just made corporal.

Because his middle name was Wayne, buddies in the 3rd Battalion, 509th Infantry, called him "The Duke." Just before he went to war, in an email to family and friends, he wrote of feeling "very excited and blessed to get to go over there and serve."

His first day on patrol, he narrowly escaped injury from a roadside bomb. He wrote with pride of his calm amid the mayhem, adding: "I am now officially a combat veteran!"

Of the four fellow soldiers in this truck, Warren felt closest to Stephenson—a twenty-two-year-old from small-town Kansas with a devilish grin, a professional rapper's wardrobe, and a vain regard for his good looks. They'd been together since basic training at Fort Benning, Georgia, day and night for two years, cutting up, surviving brutal drills from the Alaska tundra to the Thai jungle, always waiting for their moment at the heart of this war.

A former high school fullback, Stephenson couldn't pass a mirror without flexing. He would look at the smirking blue-eyed jock in his driver's license photo and declare: "Gorgeous." He had enlisted, at his mother's urging, to escape the drug scene in Atchison, Kansas, that she believed would kill him.

The other men in his squad nicknamed him "Oreo," because he was a white boy who freestyled hard-core rap and liked to slouch up to black women in bars, laying down a machine-gun street patter. He kept a closetful of flat-billed hats and meticulously matched sneakers, and worried so much about his clothes that buddies said he reminded them of their girlfriends.

Warren was ready to die for any man in this truck, but he felt a special protectiveness toward Stephenson. Maybe it was because he was so far from home and missed his two little brothers so intensely . . . maybe because Stephenson, two years younger, looked as though he needed a big brother . . . maybe because he wouldn't listen to anybody else . . . maybe because big brother was the role in which Warren felt most comfortable.

From basic training on, Stephenson had bristled at any sign of disrespect, running his mouth at commanders and accepting his punishment with defiant glee. He refused to look miserable when he was forced to do knee-bends around the base while shouldering his 17-pound machine gun.

"Scotty, I can't stop smoking you till you get the message," said Warren, who was supposed to oversee that particular punishment. His friend told him he didn't blame him and kept smiling.

Once, on a night Stephenson would spend in the drunk tank, he kept trying to squirm out of his handcuffs, yelling "It doesn't hurt!" at the cops who were Macing him outside a bar near Fort Bragg, North Carolina. Warren was there shouting: "Shut up, Scotty!"

For all that wildness, Warren saw in him an excellent soldier—the best machine gunner at the range. He thought so much of his abilities that he picked him for his squad. He was the reason Stephenson was on this road, in this Humvee.

Now Stephenson was sitting behind Warren in the saw gunner's seat, a photo of his one-year-old son in his wallet. Directly beneath him was the truck's diesel fuel tank.

Where are we going? The men were grousing, wondering whether their lieutenant—directing them by radio from the truck behind them—knew the way back to base. Along the road, Iraqi parents were hustling their children indoors at the sight of the Americans.

The radio ordered them to hang a right onto a narrow, nameless dirt road. It ran through waist-high grass along a canal. Nobody knew when it had last been swept for explosives.

The bomb, hidden beneath a thin layer of gravel, was made of 155-millimeter artillery rounds, probably leftover munitions from the disbanded Iraqi army. To maximize carnage, it was attached to a propane tank. It did not detonate the moment the truck's right front wheel depressed its pressure plate.

Warren passed over it, unaware he was experiencing his final moments as a personality he recognized. It exploded right below his friend, the fragments shredding the fuel tank and floorboards.

•

Warren woke to find himself in a furnace. He heard the shrill screaming of someone in terror. He realized it was himself. Fire ate at his neck and face.

He inhaled a scorching lungful of smoke. He shoved open the Humvee's heavy steel door and rolled into the dirt, extinguishing the flames on his body.

Stephenson was trapped inside, weighed down by his ceramic armor plates and bulging ammo pouches, drenched head-to-toe in diesel from the truck's punctured tank and propane from the bomb. He was being consumed.

Warren did what a soldier does, what he always expected he would do in such a situation: He raced to rescue his friend. The wall of flame repelled him. He couldn't will himself through it. Stephenson kept burning.

And then Stephenson was out, shambling blindly toward the reeds that flanked the nearby canal. His insides were ripped by shrapnel. His left arm dangled by tendons. His left leg was shredded. Warren screamed: Drop! Roll!

Stephenson heard him and tumbled, on fire, into the blast crater.

Now Warren was on top of him, patting frantically at the flames, heaping on fistfuls of dirt. Stephenson's uniform was burning, his skin was burning, his hair was burning, diesel was burning. The smell filled Warren's nostrils. Nothing worked.

Warren couldn't bear to watch. He staggered away. Collapsed. Crawled. Turned around.

Stephenson's voice was strangely calm:

Please help me, Jon.

The wait seemed interminable. Then Warren saw a pair of boots and knew it was the medic, rushing over with a fire extinguisher. Warren was on his feet again, unwrapping rolls of gauze to press against Stephenson's wounds, dragging his friend to safety while the Humvee's cargo of rockets and ammunition ignited.

Stephenson was conscious long enough to ask about his genitals. Were they intact? "Yes."

Then: "Am I going to die?"

No, Warren said. He held him until he heard the chopper and hunkered over him to shield him from rotor-whipped sand and debris.

They rode the helicopter thirty miles north to Baghdad Hospital in the Green Zone. Stephenson's chances of survival were put at 5 percent.

Of the truck, there was nothing left. A blackened shell. Collapsed roof. Naked rims where the tires had melted away.

Somehow, Warren had escaped with a concussion, a gash on his head, burns on his face and wrists. Somehow, three of the other four men had survived without critical injuries.

•

From his hospital in the Green Zone, Warren received fragmentary reports about Stephenson. He was in a drug-induced coma;

he was in surgery in Germany; he was fighting off infections; he was having his skull drilled; he was clinging to life at Brooke Army Medical Center in San Antonio.

He managed to reach Stephenson's mother, Luana Schneider, who had sneaked a cell phone into the ICU. Scotty's fighting, she said. She didn't say that he had already endured twenty surgeries, and that she recognized him only by the color of his eyes and the shape of his eyebrows.

She had the impression Warren had pulled her son from the flames.

"Thank you, thank you, thank you for saving my son," she said.

"I didn't. I didn't save him," Warren insisted.

He kept thinking of how he failed to charge into the flaming truck to pull his buddy out. Was it vanity that stopped him? Was he worried about his looks?

And why had he crawled away as his friend burned?

The Army gave Warren a Purple Heart and put him back on patrol. His eyes were hypersensitive. Daylight speared into his brain. He fought through headaches so painful they brought tears. At night his heart beat so hard, he thought he felt his bed shaking.

On patrol he popped Clonazepam, a sedative, to steady his nerves. Three soldiers from his company were killed in one twelve-day span. Shrapnel from a roadside bomb slashed his knee. The Army gave him another Purple Heart and made him a sergeant.

When he flew home on a three-week leave, his parents decked

their home in American flags and invited everyone they knew. People greeted him in T-shirts that read: JON'S OUR FREEDOM FIGHTER. They nibbled from cheese plates and veggie platters. He plastered a smile to his face and pretended he didn't want to scream.

"Promise you'll stay safe," his grandmother pleaded. He snapped: How could he promise that?

At a wedding, he stared down a twelve-year-old boy who asked: "Have you killed anybody?"

At night he binged on vodka. Once, his family found him in a delirium. He had flipped over a bedroom mattress, believing friends were trapped inside. He demanded a knife and cried: "I have to get them out!"

On the day before he returned to war, he flew to Kansas City and rented a car. He drove for an hour through bean and tobacco fields to Stephenson's hometown of Atchison. His mom had converted the living room of her three-story Colonial into a bedroom for Stephenson because he couldn't get up the stairs.

Warren wasn't sure what Scotty would look like, nine months after the explosion. He had always known him as cocksure, athletic, girl-crazy. Now he found him in a wheelchair, heavily drugged, seventy-five pounds heavier. Unable to regulate his body temperature, he had to stay out of the Kansas summer heat.

The bottom half of his face was scarred and crimson, as was 60 percent of his body. His left leg was gone below the knee. Doctors had removed his adrenal gland, a kidney, his spleen, and part of his pancreas, and were pessimistic about his chances of walking again.

His left arm was maimed. He had suffered three strokes and flatlined on two operating tables. He would become accustomed to people gawking; sometimes he snarled, "Five dollars for the freak show!"

His mother spent eight hours a day on his wounds, showering him, scrubbing dead skin away so vigorously that he bled, wrapping and unwrapping his bandages, enduring the bottomless rages of a young man who knew his former life was gone.

"This is never going to get better!" he screamed.

Warren and Stephenson had dinner at a riverfront restaurant, and afterward Warren pushed his friend's wheelchair into a bar. Stephenson kept asking about their squad; he wanted to go back and fight. They didn't talk about the bomb.

The friends drank more beer back at the house and played *Madden Football* on the Xbox. Stephenson balanced the joystick on his lap and delighted in beating Warren with his one good hand.

Long after midnight Warren carried him to bed, and Stephenson thanked him for coming all this way to be with him for just a few hours.

"Good night, brother," Warren said.

After Stephenson was asleep, Warren sat there listening to his friend's breathing. Somehow, compared to what he felt now, the demands of war were easy. At 3:00 a.m. he climbed into his rental car and headed back through the bean and tobacco fields in the dark.

•

Summer 2011. He'd been out of the Army for a year, surviving on disability benefits and the GI Bill. His war ran together as a blur of concussions, villages, dirt roads, checkpoints, bazaars, Humvee cabs, mess halls, bunkers, mortar attacks, raids, twenty-one-gun salutes, eulogies.

His knuckles went white on the wheel when he spotted a box or pile of trash discarded on an American freeway: That's where bombs hid. Selecting clothes for his civilian life, he made it to the changing room at Nordstrom before panic overtook him. At Wal-Mart, his hands turned clammy, his mouth dry; he abandoned his shopping cart.

He checked and rechecked the locks on his Costa Mesa apartment. He wrapped himself in a fog of pot and alcohol. He snapped at his parents until they were scared to approach him. He pushed away a girlfriend he had once longed to marry. Years of hard muscle melted off his frame.

To explain the feeling that lived inside him, he pointed to his midsection, where what he called "this crushing thing" resided like a great tumor.

"Like I know the reality about the world," he said, "and it's not good."

He was adept at hiding his torment. He had a level gaze, disarming smile, and easygoing charm, which he deployed like blast walls.

He looked for ways to fix himself. He bought a diesel-fueled Chevrolet Silverado, because the smell of diesel hurled him back to the horror of watching Stephenson burn and he was determined to make himself immune by constant exposure.

He enrolled in psychology classes at Vanguard University in Costa Mesa, hoping to understand his damaged mind. But he struggled to keep his voice from shaking in class. The former infantryman who had led men into battle now sat anxiously, watching the door, in a roomful of college kids.

When people asked about the war, he sounded like a man recounting a video game he just happened to have played. "We were driving," he would say. "We were hit. My buddy got burned up."

One day he volunteered to drive his seventeen-year-old brother, Logan, to the family's house on Lake Mead. His parents balked. They no longer trusted their binge-drinking son. He pushed his way out of the house and sat in his truck and shook.

•

In the years since the bomb, Stephenson had learned to walk on a prosthetic leg and gone through therapy for post-traumatic stress disorder. He and his mother traveled the country, talking about their experiences.

His anger and bitterness had abated. He had a quick smile and a mental encyclopedia of dirty jokes. He had girlfriends and a closetful of fedoras. His young son broke a leg off each of his G.I. Joes so they would resemble his dad.

Warren saw him maybe once a year, and they would fall into their old rhythms almost instantly, laughing, swapping infantry stories, trading lines from *Team America: World Police* and *Anchorman*.

But Stephenson could hear the despair creep into his friend's voice—a tone he remembered from his months in the Army hospital, where every day seemed to bring news of another suicide.

"Get help," Stephenson said.

Warren went to a Veterans' Center. They offered group therapy. He didn't want a roomful of ex-soldiers to see him broken and helpless.

He went to the therapist who served his college. The therapist had no training in dealing with post-traumatic stress disorder.

He went to the VA hospital in Long Beach. A staffer told him it would be months before he could see a PTSD specialist one on one.

He spotted a flier on the wall. It offered an alternative. He could volunteer as a test subject for a pioneering treatment. Veterans would be asked to throw themselves into their single worst memory, to relive every sight and sound with the help of full-immersion goggles and earphones . . . and then do it again . . . and again . . .

"How do I get started?" he asked.

•

Marya Schulte's closet-size office sits inside a maze of colorless corridors in the VA hospital's mental health wing. To add warmth, she has decorated it with gentle black-and-white photographs of Manhattan architecture.

A padded curtain hangs over a rear door, to muffle the bellowing of the Vietnam vets who meet next door. The VA has given her a converted storage room for a five-year study in the use of virtual reality in prolonged exposure therapy.

It is one of dozens of sites offering the treatment around the country, using simulations developed at the USC Institute for Creative Technologies.

For a generation raised on GameCubes, it promises a way to

lure reluctant soldiers into therapy. But it can be brutal for everyone involved. A patient must descend into his worst memory; a therapist must steer him into its grip, again and again.

It's March 2012. Warren studies the therapist's face, youthful and unlined. She hasn't experienced battle except in the stories of her patients. He wonders if she will understand.

She helps him adjust the earphones and visor. She hands him a joystick.

In the simulation, he sits in the passenger seat of a Humvee, looking over the hood. Before him, a paved road with a double yellow line runs through the desert.

The joystick moves him forward. Here and there, palm trees and Iraqi homes appear and disappear. He can turn his head and see another soldier, the driver, in the seat beside him.

Can he trust his memory? He is anxious to get it right.

Don't worry, she tells him. Narrate what happened on November 25, 2006.

"What do you hear?"

An explosion. Or maybe not. He can't be sure. All he knows is that he wakes to the sound of his own screaming.

Schulte hits buttons. His seat vibrates. His simulated windshield cracks. He sees black smoke billowing from the road.

"What does it feel like in the Humvee?"

Unbearably hot—a furnace. His face blisters. His neck burns. His wrists are singed as he forces open the heavy door and scrambles outside.

The simulation is imperfect. It cannot put him outside the truck. To relive that part, he closes his eyes.

Schulte hits buttons. He hears gunfire and chopper blades and radio chatter. More than the visuals, the sounds take him back five years and across 7,000 miles. Now his heart is racing.

"What do you see?"

Scotty struggling to escape the truck.

"What does he look like?"

A fireball.

"What happens next?"

He races toward his friend but is stopped by the wall of flame. For the barest instant he thinks, If I go in, what will I look like afterward?

"What happens next?"

Scotty is out and running toward a canal and Warren commands him to drop, and then he's leaning over Scotty in the dirt and pounding uselessly at the flames and then crawling away, defeated, until the medic arrives.

He feels helpless and worthless. What kind of soldier quits on his brother?

"I have nothing to help him with," he tells Schulte. "I should have come up with something."

The simulations last forty minutes. He feels raw. He thanks Schulte and weeps on the freeway drive home.

Warren can't shake the feeling that somehow, some way, Stephenson blames him for what happened. Because they don't talk about the bomb, Warren can't be sure.

If anyone asks, Stephenson will say Warren saved his life. It's the same thing Warren's mother always tells him: Scotty was lucky you were there.

Warren doesn't believe it. His memory has bent and twisted in strange, punishing ways. The chaos of that day has congealed into a narrative of his own incompetence and weakness.

He isn't sure he will return for another session with Schulte.

Then he thinks: What's the alternative? Pills, pot, blackout drinking? A lifetime of hiding in his darkened apartment?

He returns to Schulte's office, explaining that he feels no better. His flashbacks have not softened. The crushing thing in his midsection has not gone away.

That's normal, she says. She compares his war experience to a book that keeps popping open, no matter how hard he tries to close it. Things will get worse before they get better.

He puts on the visor. He grips the joystick. He goes down the road. The windshield cracks. The smoke churns.

He closes his eyes. His best friend burns.

"I'm not who I thought I was," he tells Schulte. "I didn't act how I thought I would act."

Why can he summon so many details of that day—the feel of the dirt, the smell of the blood—but not the image of Scotty's face as he was writhing? Maybe it is his brain's way of protecting him.

He enters the little room. He goes down the road. His best friend burns.

"Did you plant the IED?" she asks. "Did you set the vehicle on fire?"

Buried details are resurfacing. Now he can feel the intensity of the heat pulsing from the Humvee. He remembers the sensation of his face melting when he gets within ten feet of the truck. Remembers that his lips blister when he gets within five feet.

Slowly, he realizes that during the many times he's recounted the story—including the first few times he told it to Schulte—he omitted crucial details. It is as if he's forgotten everything that doesn't serve the story of his guilt.

Now he remembers that the bomb blasts him into the roof of the truck and tears off his Kevlar helmet.

That his ears are leaking cerebrospinal fluid.

That his own fire-dousing blanket is aflame.

That the interval between the bomb and the arrival of help feels like an hour, but is really only a minute.

That by ordering Stephenson to the ground, he might have saved him from scrambling blindly into the canal and drowning.

She asks him to imagine the situation in reverse—he is burning, and Scotty can't help.

Warren considers it. As a child in an evangelical Christian household, he was raised with a strong awareness of a God forever disappointed by his shortcomings. One day God would ask for a sacrifice, he knew, and he'd have to be big enough to give it.

Would you blame Scotty, if the roles were reversed?

That's different. God expects me to be perfect.

During his seventh session in the little room, Schulte asks:

"What if you do run into the burning Humvee?"

Warren thinks about his buddy laden with 120 pounds of armor, knives, bulging pouches, ammunition, and equipment.

He thinks about his own bulky armor.

He thinks about his disorientation and pain, and the chaos of the truck's interior.

And he realizes what would happen if he somehow got inside through the flames. He would prevent Stephenson from escaping. "We would have both died."

•

In the months after his therapy ends in the spring of 2012, Warren realizes that confronting November 25, 2006, might be only the beginning of healing. One night he pounds tequila and wakes up in the ER. One night police throw him in the drunk tank.

One night he stands in the center of the Dana Hills High School football field, bathed by floodlights, an honored veteran performing the coin toss before his brother Logan's final football game, and he knows the moment would have been impossible a year ago, even if he still needs the comfort of a Clonazepam in his pocket.

He is starting to attempt other things that were once inconceivable, like weekend trips with friends. He knows he will have to confront other terrible memories—such as the day his platoon called in rockets on the enemy and he found a dead girl and her dead mother amid the rubble.

He is crying when he asks his mother, "What did I accomplish over there?" He is still crying after she repeats the answer she always gives: that he saved Scotty, and it is enough.

RIDERS

Before dawn that morning, they clambered onto an empty box-car at the Union Pacific yard and rode it out of Bakersfield into the Tehachapi Mountains. There were six of them, a pack of drifters and runaways taking snapshots of one another and sharing bottles of McCormick vodka as the train climbed the chaparral slopes in the summer dark.

Traveling kids, they called themselves, a makeshift, ever-changing family that shared the hard floor of an empty junk train or the windy porch of a grain car before their journeys forked.

Adam Kuntz and Ashley Hughes, however, were inseparable. They had been riding together for eight months. He was twenty-two, tall and rangy, with a goatee, wild black hair, and a disarming smile. She was eighteen, with blue eyes and dishwater-blond hair. Crudely inked across her fingers was the word "sourpuss," advertising the side she liked to show people: the rebel and sometime dope fiend who bristled with free-floating anger.

But he saw another side of her too: the frightened runaway who, like him, found a tramp's dangerous, hand-to-mouth life less terrifying than the adult world.

They were curving through the Tehachapi Pass, seriously drunk, when a feeling overcame him. The words were unplanned, like everything else in their life.

Hey, you should be my wife, he said.

OK, she replied.

They slept through the night, curled side by side in their sleeping bags, and awoke about noon as the boxcar was slowing into the West Colton train yard. Everyone was thirsty and hung over. There was a Wal-Mart nearby where they could fill their jugs. They huddled along the edge of the boxcar, full of nervous excitement, the gravel moving slowly underneath. The train wasn't stopping. To get off, they'd have to jump while it rolled.

Naturally, it was Ashley who suggested they try it.

•

Trains run right through the heart of the American story, a symbol of industrial prowess and physical vastness and unfettered movement. For the broke and the discontent and the wanted, they are also a place to disappear, a mobile refuge where nobody cares where you're going or what your real name is.

Adam was a straight-F student at Ridgeview High School in Bakersfield whose stepmother suspected he had a learning disability. In his junior year he was kicked out after downloading pages from *The Anarchist Cookbook* about making bombs. Soon he was hitchhiking across the country. In Denver, he worked up the courage to hop a freight.

"The first time I ever got on a train—it's unexplainable," he says. "It's a feeling of, like, where I belong. You know how when you walk into a house where you're really comfortable?"

He came to relish the cat-and-mouse with the "bulls," or railroad cops. His gear was a backpack, sleeping bag, socks, a jug of water, ramen noodles, and a bandanna that he dampened and wrapped around his face through the long tunnels for protection against the trains' exhaust. The fastest ride, he discovered, was a cargo container, and the best hiding place was a crawl space in the front of a Canadian grain car.

Everywhere, he found kids like himself. In a new town, they could point out the best trash bins and missions. "You don't need money out there," he says. "You don't need anything. You have the greatest time in the world, but when it gets down there, it's really down there."

Boarding the wrong train in winter might take you into cold that went on forever. To prevent frostbite, you warmed your fingers over a piece of lighted cardboard curled inside a soup can. Squatter camps in cities like New York and Seattle were littered with junkies' cast-off needles, so you always wore your shoes. Tramps without backpacks were best avoided, because they would hurt you to get yours. A last-resort ride was called a "suicide"—the metal crossbeams of a freight car floor that put you so close to the rushing tracks you could reach down and touch them.

•

Snapshots of Ashley's childhood are drenched with sunshine. There she is, a smiling girl with blond bangs. Hugging Pluto. Kissing the family dog. Blowing bubbles in the backyard in Eugene, Oregon.

By her early teens, she was shuttling between divorced parents. She told outrageous lies. She cut her wrists with pens and picture frames. "She was not able to make friends," says her mother, Diane.

She kept slipping out her bedroom window. She'd be gone for weeks at a time. In her journals, she repeatedly wrote out the lyrics to "Nowhere Kids" by the band Smile Empty Soul, an anthem of family alienation. She longed for love and seethed with rage and thought of suicide. "I just get up and put a smile on my face every morning and pretend to be okay," she wrote.

In the summer of 2004, after taking an overdose of antidepressants, she was diagnosed with borderline personality disorder. She dropped out of school and jumped freights. She left her antipsychotic pills behind. She shot heroin.

In the company of ragged runaways, she found a surrogate family. At seventeen, she emailed home to say that she was the youngest in her pack of traveling kids. Many of the others, she acknowledged, had no homes to return to.

"There are some like me that are only out on the streets because they are rebellious and don't want to follow rules (me)," she wrote. "I hate sleeping outside. I hate sitting on the corner of the street begging for food every day. I hate not having anything productive to do with my time. I want to come home so I can graduate and take my time being a teenager."

Her dad brought her home with a Greyhound ticket, but her new focus was short-lived. Police picked her up for trespassing at a train station in Santa Maria, California; for hitchhiking in Redwood City, California; and for hitting a man—she claimed he was harassing her—back in Eugene.

She pleaded guilty to assault and received a thirty-day sentence. Soon, police booked her for heroin possession and for failing to check in with her probation officer. Letters from jail reflected an aching for innocence. She wrote that she missed her grandmother's blueberry pancakes.

"I thought I was invincible out there on the road," she wrote. "I was happy. But I know now that it wasn't a lasting happiness, only temporary." When she got out, she said, she wanted to stay sober and find a job. "I've thrown quite a few years down the drain."

Once released, she skipped town, blowing off a court-ordered drug program. When she could find a computer, she reached out to traveling friends and plotted meeting points. On her Myspace page, she rhapsodized about tramps and trains and said her religion had become "the countryside, the outdoors, the dirty folk."

In the grip of that vision, they weren't just lost, hungry kids but a band of noble outlaws rolling through a heartland that law-abiding Americans never saw.

"I don't want my life to go to hell," she wrote, "but the place I once called home is no more than a ghost and I have nowhere else to go."

•

Their tracks converged in the fall of 2006. Adam was walking with a buddy through the San Jose train yard. Ashley was sitting with a girlfriend.

"We'll trade you whiskey for water," she said.

"We don't have water, but we'll drink your whiskey," he said.

Two days later, Adam recalls, he got drunk and put his fist through a restaurant window. As the cops hauled him away, he handed her the leash attached to his puppy, Bumjug, an Australian shepherd mix.

When he got out a week later, she was waiting for him with the dog.

He called her Smashley. She called him Stogie.

He got her off heroin, he says, telling her he wouldn't lose her the way he'd lost so many other friends to the needle. Asked what he loved about her, Adam wouldn't hesitate: "Her wildness."

They tramped up the Pacific, hitched down to the Florida Keys, and rode the rails across the Southwestern deserts. Against everything the world demanded, they found a hideout in the sooty cubbyholes of diesel-electric behemoths.

Freedom to roam the country's 140,000 miles of freight track meant being at the mercy of a fixed grid. Once, they gambled on the wrong boxcar and found themselves stuck in Wichita, Kansas, in winter, a place so miserably cold they risked escape in a locomotive engine.

They ate from trash bins and begged on street corners. For shelter, they threw their sleeping bags under bridges and pried the plywood from the windows of abandoned houses. They shared three bottles of cheap whiskey a day. They found a stray husky they named Captain Morgan and a rabbit they called Dinner.

He says he didn't ask her about her family life or about the slash marks on her wrist. He figured it was her business.

"She was more scared than angry about life. She wanted someone there to tell her it was OK. She needed someone that told her they loved her," he says. "She hid it a lot, but she had a pretty big sweet side. She liked to cuddle and watch the scenery."

They were in Montgomery, Alabama, when he called his dad and learned that his biological mom had died. His father sent him a Greyhound ticket home to Bakersfield. Ashley made her way to California by herself, hoisting their two dogs onto freights state after state.

In Bakersfield, they stayed with Adam's folks. The house had tasteful wall fixtures, a handsome brick fireplace, and a big TV. This was the place where he grew up, the place he'd always felt the urge to flee. His dad offered him jobs repairing exercise machines. His stepmother, a manager at a Johnny Rockets, offered to get her work busing tables. The house felt claustrophobic and the city crushing, full of strip malls. Within months they were crazy to get out.

"Being in this house has really taken a toll on Stogie and I's relationship. Not saying that we're 'falling apart' or whatever but we do argue a lot more frequently. I'm so happy to be hitting the road again. Then things will go back to how they used to be," she wrote on Myspace. "It's almost intoxicatingly gross how in love we are."

•

June 3, 2007. After the nine-hour trip from Bakersfield—after the sloppy-drunk marriage proposal and the climb over the Tehachapi Pass—their boxcar was rolling west on the northern tracks of the West Colton yard, close to Interstate 10.

On a parallel track, the Amtrak Sunset Limited, carrying passengers on a three-day trip from New Orleans to Los Angeles, was barreling quietly around a blind corner at 60 miles per hour.

The traveling kids were hungover and thirsty. Wal-Mart had water.

They lowered their dogs to the gravel.

Adam jumped and scrambled to safety across the tracks.

Ashley jumped. She seemed to hesitate as she glimpsed the Amtrak, then tried to beat it across the tracks.

Adam heard her yell "Train!" and saw her body fly through the air into a ditch.

He found her on her back, her eyes open but cloudy. She was bleeding from a gash on her head, a bone protruding from her right arm.

Paramedics rushed her to Arrowhead Regional Medical Center. She had no ID. She died in the emergency room, with a wristband that said "Nomdeplume, Nancy 2316."

Adam felt numb on the long Greyhound ride to central Oregon, where he stood at her grave with a handful of street kids in T-shirts, studded leather belts, and bandannas. Ashley's mother asked church friends not to bring flowers but rather socks and sleeping bags to hand out.

Ashley's grandparents ordered a red granite gravestone etched with a train. Adam had a railroad crossing and the word "Smashley" inked on his arm. Within weeks he was riding again with his dogs. He thought it might be the only way to get her dying expression out of his mind.

"I would have lost two things that I love that day if I never got back on a train," he said.

•

Steven Kuntz, forty-six, reaches for a stack of envelopes piled on his desk: his son's citations, unpaid fines, and outstanding warrants stretching from San Luis Obispo to Liberal, Kansas. He's been making calls, trying to take care of them.

For years he felt guilty about Adam, wondering if he should have been less tolerant of bad grades, less a pal, more a parent. But he says Adam's younger siblings, raised under the same roof, loved just the same, are out earning paychecks and starting families.

Steven used to blow right past panhandling kids on the street. These days, he looks for signs they are travelers—filthy clothes, dogs, and backpacks—and stops to give them food. He admires his son's ability to get across the country with a smile and $2 in his pocket, but is pained at the thought of him begging.

After Ashley's death, Steven told Adam not to come home if he got on the rails again. Adam cried and said, "I can't have you not like me." Steven figured he would have to make peace with what his son did. He suspects that roaming the rails might be his son's way of coping with "tucked-away" emotions.

When Adam is home a few months a year, as he is now, Steven, who repairs photocopiers, throws some work his way. He encourages him to look for jobs.

Adam, with no degree and little experience, is quickly frustrated. He loves his parents, but home feels like a cage. He hears the train whistling by the house, hears it before others do. "It's like it's calling."

His new girlfriend, Kaley Chapin, is a twenty-two-year-old video store clerk, sweet-faced, eager to see things. Adam has been telling her stories of the rails, and she can't stop talking about it, even though she knows what happened to Ashley.

"In June, me and him are gonna take off," she tells Steven on a recent evening. They'll hop trains and scrounge change all the way to New York.

"You know how many people die on trains?" Steven says. "They're just as smart as you."

"You only live once," she says. "I think Adam will take care of me."

Adam isn't sure Kaley knows what's in store. How incredibly dirty she'll get. How it feels in a winter boxcar.

"It's so cold you can't even touch the metal," Adam says.

"That's a fun way to live?" Steven says.

"At least I can say that I've done that," Adam says.

"Believe it or not, life is pretty much the same everywhere you go," Steven says. "You get up and go to work and come home."

He keeps telling his son to think about the day when he can no longer drift on a young man's charm, when his dad's no longer around to bail him out.

But Steven Kuntz has given the lecture before. He knows that life in a squalid boxcar strikes his son as less intimidating than an adult existence of obligations and bills. He knows that nothing he can say will prevent his son from vanishing again soon, leaving home for the tracks that lead anywhere else.

THE $40 LAWYER

PART ONE

The day of his job interview, he pulls on his one good suit to find it no longer fits. The navy slacks and coat, bought off the rack from JCPenney, are uncomfortably tight. He stands in the mirror, practicing his answers. Around his neck goes the gold tie from Ross Dress for Less. Under his chin, a daub of Versace cologne that may or may not mask his desperation.

At twenty-seven, two years out of law school and a year out of steady work, Charley Demosthenous has been living in his father's spare Zephyrhills double-wide, minus heating. His diet is red meat, beer, *Seinfeld*. He has blanketed the private law firms with résumés, but no one's eager to hire an inexperienced attorney who finished near the bottom of his class and failed the Florida bar exam three times.

He's $17,000 in debt, surviving on bank loans and credit cards. His dad, fed up, wants him to apply at Lowe's. On the line that says "Education," he'd have the keen humiliation of writing *Juris Doctorate, University of Florida, Class of 2002*.

He has a standing job offer to inspect pavement for the state, which requires no degree, but he can't say yes. He imagines running into someone from law school, or one of those trust-fund darlings from his undergrad days at the University of Miami. Put a stake in him.

So today, in July 2004, he climbs into his dented, scratched-up Toyota Corolla and heads to downtown Tampa, toward the Twiggs Street office of the Hillsborough County Public Defender. He has rehearsed. He needs this.

They're waiting for him on the eighth floor, a roomful of the office brass. They sit him at the head of a long conference table. He sweats into his suit.

"Why do you want to be a public defender?" he is asked.

"The State Attorney's Office wasn't hiring," he answers.

He wanted to be a prosecutor. Everyone knows they get the respect, the prestige. Even his shrink told him so. Charley's view of public defenders reflects stereotypes of harried idealists and rumpled, inept clock punchers. For years, he wondered why anyone wanted the job.

"How do you feel about defending people you know are guilty?"

"It's not my job to prove they're innocent," he replies. "It's the state's job to prove they're guilty."

A good answer, untouchable, but he's far from a True Believer. He hasn't heard of *Gideon v. Wainwright*, the 1963 U.S. Supreme Court case that ensured free legal representation to the indigent. All he knows about the job he's asking for, really, is what most people know: You represent poor people accused of crimes.

"What you learn in three years here, it's going to take ten to fifteen years somewhere else," he adds. He has heard this, and it sounds good. It also happens to be true.

One of his interviewers scans his résumé, where his name is spelled in the original Greek, and wonders how it's pronounced.

"Charalampos Georgious Demosthenous," he says, making every syllable smolder exotically. He can't lose there.

Someone else is reaching for his law school transcripts. It's about to come, The Question.

"I see you've noticed my stellar grades," he says. "I think I've paid my dues for that. You can hold that against me, if you want. You can also look at the fact that I keep slugging through."

Over and over, people wrote him off. A biology teacher once said, You'll never be a scientist. An English teacher said, You're no writer. A law professor said, You don't have what it takes for this. During law school, he slept through class, played rugby, had girlfriend trouble, begged his professors for Ds.

Unknowingly, he tells his interviewers, he suffered from attention deficit disorder through law school and his three flubbed bar exams. His fourth try at the exam, he had medication that allowed him to focus. He was prepared to give up if he failed again. He scanned for his results online. When he saw PASS, his cheek sank into the keyboard. He squeezed his eyes shut.

"It doesn't matter what my past was," he says now, "as long as I do well here."

The bosses at the Public Defender's Office love an underdog. They know the qualities that make a good PD are more elusive than what a test can measure. Besides, the job burns lawyers out so fast—they stay about three years, on average—that they need a constant stream of new ones.

They take a chance on Charley Demosthenous.

•

He finds out who Clarence Earl Gideon is.

His new employers plant him and another rookie in front of a VCR to watch *Gideon's Trumpet*, the 1980 TV movie. Henry Fonda plays the Florida handyman who is busted for breaking into a pool hall and is too poor to afford a lawyer. His crusade to get one, waged from behind bars, leads to the creation of the office of the public defender.

Charley feels like he's supposed to weep patriotic tears. But Gideon doesn't strike Charley as much of a hero, not someone he'd particularly want to represent. He's mulish, cantankerous, wretched.

Charley already understands what a PD is expected to say: that it's not the charmed and well-adjusted who need you. And if you pressed him, he'd say he believes it. More or less.

The son of a Cyprus-born refrigerator mechanic, Charley is the first in his immediate family to attend college. Now he's a working member of an ancient and venerable profession. A lawyer. What people want their kids to be, next to doctor.

As a beginning PD, his salary is $38,000.

He's going to need some suits.

"You have to feel like an attorney for once in your life," his shrink says, and tells him to max out his credit cards if he must.

At Men's Wearhouse, they run the tape over him and send him to the dressing room. He studies himself. He's big-shouldered, built for rough sports. His pudgy cheeks carry a perpetual five-o'clock shadow. His eyes are hazel, puckish. Something about him gives girlfriends the urge to pull up his socks and fix his collar.

He rotates in the mirrors, thinking, Lawyer, lawyer, lawyer. He's immature in too many ways to count, but right now he looks like someone to reckon with. He can successfully impersonate an adult. No one has a reason to laugh at him now, at least until he opens his mouth. He fears he will stammer.

The courtroom, he already knows, will not conceal the flaws of a fledgling adult. Most people get to shed their callowness out of the spotlight. Most people don't do what he's about to do.

He leaves the store with a nice blue suit and a nice gray. A good start, but they're just extra skin, really, holding together a walking welter of anxieties. The clothes don't eliminate his sense of being an impostor. He isn't sure what will make that feeling go away, or if it ever will.

•

Before dawn, he pulls into the parking lot outside the Orient Road jail. Inside, he places his picture ID on the counter and waits nervously for the guards to unbolt the first of several heavy metal security doors. He has never been inside a jail.

Suddenly, he's standing among hundreds of men in shackles and orange jail scrubs, struggling to answer their questions. This is First Appearance Court, and these are the just-busted, all lined up and waiting to appear via video link with a judge who will apprise them of their charges.

There are hard-core muggers and sad-eyed vagabonds, barroom brawlers and businessmen who hit their wives. There are crackheads stripped of their pipes, pores oozing poison. They are tired and irritated and foul-breathed and demanding to be let out and are convinced, somehow, that their twenty-seven-year-old assistant public defender should be able to do more about it.

Soon, many of them will empty bank accounts or mortgage homes to hire private defense attorneys. Many others, if they're poor enough or lie about being poor enough, will pay a $40 application fee and be assigned a PD.

Rookie PDs pay their dues here. Charley's job is to prevent clients from blurting out confessions, and to persuade the judge to reduce their bail enough so they can go home.

He wears his best I-know-what-I'm-doing face, tries hard not to stutter. When he's nervous, the words get tangled up in his mouth. On days he forgets to take his ADD medication, it feels as if his thoughts are ricocheting off the jailhouse walls.

The judge hands Charley his first small victory, agreeing to reduce a client's bail. Then it happens again, and again. After six weeks, when he begins to feel like he knows what he's doing, his bosses transfer him to his first real courtroom. He's relieved to escape the jailhouse stink and clamor. Everyone is.

Juvenile Court, Division A, Courtroom 26, mid-September 2004.

A sliver of Tampa skyline shows through the window, but the courtroom feels like a dungeon and reeks of mildew. Lawyers get one or two good uses out of their suits, even dousing them with Febreze. There are TimeMist boxes mounted behind the state and defense tables, which now and then spurt jets of fruity perfume, discoloring the nicked wooden benches below.

Charley inherits 186 cases, a whole stack of green folders filled with legal notations he hasn't yet learned to read.

His supervisor, Anthony Lopez, explains the nature of the game.

"These kids aren't going to prison," he says. "At the very worst, they're put on probation or put in a residential commitment program for delinquent juveniles."

Lopez, a veteran PD in his late thirties, has a neatly trimmed black goatee, a perpetually hurried air, and a reputation as a harsh, hypercritical boss. Charley has been warned about him.

"This is the perfect training ground to try cases," he tells Charley, "because you're not putting your kids at extreme risk."

Still, he explains, there are stakes in keeping felonies off juveniles' records. When they are charged with felonies as adults—and many of them will be—their recent juvenile felonies count and can send them to prison.

On the day of Charley's first trial, Lopez is sitting to one side of him. On his other side, biting a finger, sits the client, a thirteen-year-old boy with sneakers and dreadlocks. He's charged with felony theft of a motor vehicle.

The prosecutor is Joel Elsea, who is not even a lawyer yet, just an intern waiting to pass the bar. He has stylishly shaggy hair and an air of suave self-possession that Charley finds disconcerting, considering the jangled state of his own nerves. It would be humiliating to be beaten by an intern.

As the trial begins, a gray-haired man with Coke-bottle glasses testifies he came upon Charley's client, and another boy, using a screwdriver to try to steal his motor scooter.

Next, the investigating detective takes the stand. He mentions an unnamed tipster who told him the accused had reported borrowing a screwdriver.

Charley knows enough to object. Hearsay! He's not so sure how to follow that up, though.

"I move to strike that statement from the record," Charley's boss whispers to him.

"I move to strike that statement from the record," Charley tells the judge.

"Based upon hearsay," the boss says.

"Based upon hearsay," Charley says.

In defending the case, Charley's options are scant. He can't plausibly claim mistaken identity. So, for his closing argument, he walks to the lectern with a law book under his arm.

"Under the statutes, a scooter is not a motor vehicle," Charley says. "I would ask the court grant a motion for dismissal."

Elsea, the state intern, notes that the vehicle in question starts with a key and has a gas engine.

"My little brother has a Tonka truck that starts with a key," Charley counters. "I don't think that qualifies as a motor vehicle either."

Charley sits down, trying to keep a poker face. He is wearing an $8 haircut from a Latin barber. Dark stubble rides his chin and cheeks, because Hurricane Jeanne has knocked out his bathroom light.

The judge, Richard A. Nielsen, has a sharp-boned face and a grave, phlegmatic manner. Here in juvenile court, where there are no juries, his word is everything. In his slow, deliberate way, he walks through the evidence and concludes Charley's client is guilty—but only of petty theft, a misdemeanor punishable by probation.

Charley can count it a victory, but he can't really call it his own. Reading the statute was his idea, but Lopez is still coaching him heavily, feeding him lines. "People think I'm Anthony's puppet," Charley says, "and it pisses me off."

•

Charley doesn't remember much from law school, but a few things stick:

A tort is a civil action.

Don't sleep with your clients.

Neither is particularly useful in his current work.

There is another:

Lawyers are zealous advocates for their clients.

Which doesn't tell him anything about how to negotiate day-to-day relations with judges and prosecutors he must see regularly.

Prosecutors keep pressuring him to make their lives easier. They want him to stipulate, for instance, that the chalky white powder found on his clients is cocaine. If he stipulates, they won't have to bring in a state chemist to prove the obvious.

Early on, he decides not to cut prosecutors any breaks. Let them prove it's not baking soda.

These first few weeks, he quickly learns to analyze statutes, negotiate pleas, pick apart witness statements. He also learns to turn the system's glut of cases to his advantage.

To stymie the state, Charley deliberately clogs the court docket. When he gets a case he knows he can't win—misdemeanor shoplifting, say—he sets it for trial and demands a speedy one. This forces the state to exhaust resources on petty crimes, reducing its ability to fight more serious ones. This increases the chances, Charley figures, that the state will come through with generous plea offers.

In such ways, Charley delights in torturing the young prosecutors. At the same time, he frets constantly about what they think of him.

"They don't like me, do they?" he asks Chris Chapman, a thirty-one-year-old PD in his courtroom who regards the prosecutors as friends.

"No, man, no," Chapman says, trying to spare Charley's feelings, though he knows the state is griping.

Chapman is bald and chatty and an improbable presence, grandson of former Tampa Bay Buccaneers owner Hugh Culverhouse. He wanted to be a fighter pilot or, failing that, a prosecutor. He hates the long hours at the PD's office but wants the job on his résumé. His rich-kid hobbies—horseback riding, fencing, piloting prop planes—seem alien to his cash-strapped colleagues.

Chapman thinks Charley's courtroom approach is short-sighted and self-sabotaging. Chapman tries hard not to irritate what he calls "my state attorney people." He thinks being nice gets him better deals.

Plus, he figures he'll be in private practice soon and may be working with some of them. "I'm looking ahead," Chapman says. "If you ask any state attorney over there about their favorite public defender, I bet they'd say me."

Charley knows his life would be easier, and relations with the state less tense, if he were more accommodating. But he cannot abide an image of himself as a pushover, a suck-up. In court, he has the instincts of a back-alley scrapper. If he sees a broken beer bottle, he's picking it up.

It's not that he has become a True Believer overnight, imbued with high mission, a savior of delinquents. He's not like Lily McCarty, the apple-cheeked twenty-four-year-old PD in his division who hugs her clients and cries for their terrible upbringings. This job was her Plan A, a way to practice social work with a law license.

Charley's different. Yes, he fights for his clients' future. But with every trial, every argument, his own future feels at stake. In his mind, the options remain stark: Be somebody, or be nobody.

What's more, he realizes, he just hates losing. He takes it personally. He has had enough for a lifetime.

•

After work one Thursday, Charley heads home in his Corolla, the one no lawyer should be driving. The passenger side of the car has been keyed—he suspects an ex-girlfriend—and he can't afford a new paint job, much less a new car.

At home he cracks open a Rolling Rock, trying to unwind. Since August, he has been living in a noisy, bug-ridden, $525-a-month apartment and pinching pennies to afford furniture. There is an empty space in the kitchen alcove where the dining room table will go, when he gets one.

He eats his meals on the living room couch, watching a TV propped on a Wal-Mart entertainment center. His one indulgence is a wood-frame bed set. On his nightstand there's a small statue of an accidentally decapitated Lady Justice, her little head at her feet. He dropped her.

His girlfriend, Kristin, arrives just before 7:00 p.m. She's blond, pretty, shy, a student in her early twenties. They've been dating about a year. She loved him when he looked like a hopeless case, jobless and living in that Zephyrhills double-wide.

"What do you want to do tonight?" she asks.

"I've got to get up super early tomorrow," he says.

Wrong answer. She gives him a look that makes him feel guilty. He backpedals.

"We can still do stuff," he says.

But it will be an early night. The green folders on his desk keep piling up. There will be no respite, as long as he's in juvie, and no money, until he can make it to the felony division with its $50,000 salary.

With luck, it will take two or three years to get out of debt. Then maybe he can start taking Kristin to nice dinners. Right now, that seems a long way away.

•

From the defense side, it's easy to despise what seems an air of privilege and hauteur around the opposing table. The young prosecutors believe God is on their side. They relish their power over delinquent kids only slightly their juniors. They possess the sheen of the effortlessly charmed, of straight-A students and future politicians. They aren't driving to work in ratty cars.

Or at least that's how it feels from across the room. It doesn't help that whereas PDs look like ordinary people, by and large, their state attorney counterparts are uncommonly good-looking, the kind that used to make classmates feel weird or fat or gangly. Beating the state becomes sweet on so many levels.

Some months back, in another courtroom, a young female prosecutor struck the PDs as particularly snooty and unreasonable. The PDs decided to teach her a lesson. They swamped her with depositions, besieged her with motions, double-teamed her at trial. They kept up the barrage until, one day in open court, she dissolved in wretched sobs. Point made. And even if it wasn't, it felt good to do it.

In late November, facing another young prosecutor in trial, Charley is swinging his sledgehammer, objecting to everything that is remotely objectionable. His client, another teenage boy, is accused of yelling in the face of a Hillsborough County sheriff's deputy. The charge: obstructing a law officer.

Charley believes his aggressiveness is having an effect on the twenty-five-year-old prosecutor, Stefanie Morris. Studying her face and voice, he senses she is becoming flustered, angry. Incredibly, she strikes him as even more frazzled than he is. The worse she looks, the bolder he feels. By the end, the prosecutor's voice sounds small and tentative.

Charley argues that mouthing off to a cop is free speech. Result: Not guilty. Charley makes an exultant fist.

After that, he feels different. He senses he has learned something crucial, though he's not sure exactly what. Maybe that he doesn't need Anthony Lopez whispering in his ear. Maybe that the other side may be as raw and scared as he is.

"I knew before that I could beat private attorneys," he says after trial. "Now I think you can look at me and know I'm a good attorney."

He's beginning to feel more like a lawyer worthy of the name.

•

In late December, the court hosts a holiday party for everyone in juvie.

The PDs pool their money for a cake. Charley, in a prankish mood, wants it to read "J.O.D.," for "Judgment of Dismissal." His coworkers vote to skip gratuitous digs at the state. The frosting says "Happy Holidays."

Judge Nielsen wears a nativity tie. Judge Mark Wolfe, who runs the other juvie courtroom, regales the young prosecutors with jokes. They rollick along obligingly.

The PDs and prosecutors sit on opposite sides of the room, munching chicken wings and cookies, like vaguely hostile relatives at a family reunion.

•

In the hurly-burly of juvenile court, Charley's triumphs prove transient, his stutter steps toward confidence undercut by the unforgiving workload.

Often, with a young client's fate in his hands, he still feels like he's fumbling blind through a labyrinth. The relentless Anthony Lopez keeps barking in his ear, reminding him of every misstep.

He barely has time to sleep, much less clean his office. Fungus is growing on the bottom of his coffeepot. One of the law books on his shelf sits upside down.

In January, his desk calendar still says December, and a coffee stain covers a whole week. His courage is bleeding away. He dreams he's losing his hair. His girlfriend wants more time. His clients don't say thank you. The green case folders keep piling up. What's it going to be? Somebody, nobody.

PART TWO

On his desk, veteran attorney Anthony Lopez keeps a row of mounted baseballs charting the evolution of their form. Left to right, they run from the lumpy prototype to the aerodynamic modern model. At the Hillsborough County Public Defender's Office, he presides over a similar transformation of formless law school grads into game-ready attorneys.

One of the rookies, Charley Demosthenous, sits across from him now, confessing a litany of self-doubt. As one of the office's last-chancers, Charley came desperate for a job and burning to prove himself. Now, midway through his first year, Charley wonders how much longer he can stick it out.

His workload is crushing. His learning curve has no top in sight. He worries that his clients are ill-served by his fumbling hands. And there seems no escape from juvenile court, where prosecutors dislike him and clients distrust him.

Beneath it all, Lopez hears the young lawyer confiding a familiar fear: Can I hack it in the world of grown-up lawyering?

The veteran regards him carefully. He has been trying to break Charley of his bad courtroom habits: fidgeting with his pen, speaking in a condescending tone, pumping his fist when he wins. Once, he rebuked Charley for placing one of his Lady Justice statues on the defense table, mocking the state.

Lopez thinks Charley's a little scatterbrained, a little excitable. But he also sees a young lawyer who cares enough about his clients to fight for them. Lopez knows it's easier to rein in an overzealous rookie than to instill fire in a passionless one. He tells Charley that self-doubt plagues every young lawyer. That he's coming along fine, for now.

Charley leaves feeling better. Enough to hang on awhile.

•

Early January 2005. Division A. Public defender Lily McCarty is cooing maternally over a shackled teenage client. "He tells me he's doing well," she says. "He's learning to lay tile!"

Today, Charley is representing a less hopeful prospect, a lanky teenage boy with tired, red-rimmed eyes and a long record. The client, already in high-risk lockup, slouches in chains and a red detention jumpsuit. He has new charges of car theft and burglary. He belongs to what the PDs call their All Stars, their handful of incorrigible return clients.

When they first met, Charley tried to reach him. "You don't stop this," he said, "you're gonna go to prison for the rest of your life."

"Fuck you, cracker motherfucker," he snapped back.

About three of every four clients Charley handles are African-American. Charley figures he looks like just the latest of a long line of Caucasian authority figures to distrust. The same government that is paying their lawyer, after all, is trying to put them away.

By the end of a long day, All Star agrees to plead out to a lesser charge, get it over with. He's going back to lockup anyway.

"How much do you want in restitution?" Charley asks Ron Campbell, an employee of the plumbing company the client burglarized.

Campbell seems to regard Charley's question as stupid.

"How you going to get any money out of someone who's going to be incarcerated?" Campbell replies sharply. He considers Charley a moment and decides he's happy to be a plumber. "If I had his job," he says to no one in particular, "I'd a done killed myself."

Charley lets it pass, sitting quietly with weary eyes. The loop on the back side of his gray tie has gone missing. The tie flops around.

"How long you been a public pre—" Campbell continues. "How long you been a public defender? I was gonna call you a public pretender."

The client, who has been holding his head tiredly in his hands, livens up enough to chime in: "That's what I call him too."

"About six months," Charley answers stoically.

It feels much longer, like he's aging in dog years.

•

Early that month, Chris Chapman, one of the PDs Charley started with in juvie, turns in his resignation. From the start, he didn't feel like he belonged in a place that drew such a motley pack of underdogs.

"Here I was, a white guy with a bald head from an upper-class family," he says. "They might disagree, but that's three strikes against me."

A few months back, he put in an application with the State Attorney's Office. They wouldn't hire him.

Chapman thinks the courtroom has turned Charley into a cutthroat. No wonder he kept prosecutors' teeth on edge. "He made them nervous enough that they'd do their job maybe a little better," Chapman says. "They never knew what he was going to do."

•

A burly man with a mullet is standing at the receptionist's window, indignant. "You guys expect us to pay $40 to get you guys' help," he says one April morning. "Meanwhile, you guys ain't helping."

For months, Charley has been taking similar abuse from clients, from strangers, from everyone. He tries to suck it up like a pro. Increasingly, though, his temper has been on a hair trigger. In court, he overhears a private defense attorney bad-mouthing PDs to a prosecutor. At least, it sounds that way to Charley.

He's not about to take it today. Charley jumps in the defense attorney's face and snarls a few words. The guy backs down, a little bewildered, insisting he meant no disrespect.

When Charley became a PD, he was queasy with ambivalence. Now he calls his juvenile clients "my kids." Some tug at him. Like the Hollow-Eyed Boy, the scrawny kid whose husky stepdad choked him and threatened to feed him glass. The boy was taken to the Crisis Center on suicide watch, where the stepdad slapped him in the parking lot. The boy punched back, and was charged with battery.

Sitting next to Charley in court, his client exuded hopelessness. Charley kept thinking, He's got nothing. Nothing. Charley felt like his job mattered, like it might even be noble. He made a case for self-defense, but the law is the law. Guilty as charged. Charley told the Hollow-Eyed Boy to call him if he needed anything, but he never did.

"You're the only lifeline they have. You're all that's standing between them and spending the rest of their life in prison," Charley says. He's still not Lily McCarty, his True Believing colleague. But he isn't who he was, either.

"I guess," he says, "I believe in what I do now."

Still, his frustrations are crystalizing right along with his convictions. By mid-April, after eight months in juvie, Charley has already seen two other rookies promoted ahead of him. "I'm just done! Done!" Charley says. "Someone's gonna be moved up to misdemeanor in the next two weeks. It better be me."

Next week, he gets word: He's going to misdemeanor adult court. No raise, but a step on the way to felony adult court, his ultimate goal. He's ecstatic.

He can't go yet. First, he must defend a boy accused of throwing a pregnant teenager to the sidewalk. "We're going to lose," he tells Lopez, asking half-seriously if he can fob it off on another attorney.

"Oh no, you're keeping this one," Lopez says. "This is your swan song. This is your baby."

The state's star witness is the accuser, a tall, sullen-looking nineteen-year-old woman. When the case is finally called, Charley learns she has left for a doctor's appointment.

Without her, the state can't proceed. Charley asks the judge to throw out the case, saying that, to his knowledge, she won't be back.

The judge informs him the trial has been rescheduled for the afternoon, when she returns.

Alex Lau, the division's supervising prosecutor, glares at Charley. He seems to think Charley knew the witness would be back but was trying to trick the judge into scuttling the case.

Later, Charley recalls Lau's words:

"I can't believe how dirty you are."

The spat continues in the crowded hallway. Charley insists it was an honest mistake. But Lau believes he's getting a taste of what his prosecutors have complained about for months: Charley's wiliness.

A crowd witnesses what happens next. "You're a liar!" Lau shouts at Charley.

Charley shouts back, returning the insult. The hall buzzes about it for an hour. To some, the confrontation appeared on the verge of a fistfight.

Suddenly, to Charley, it feels like there's something very personal at stake. The other side has questioned his honor, in front of his client and coworkers and everyone. To cap that humiliation, he must now walk into court, where Lau and another prosecutor are waiting to thrash him in an ugly case he cannot win.

Charley's client is a bony, dreadlocked eleventh-grader with plucked, pencil-thin eyebrows. Waiting in the lobby, he sings in a jazzy falsetto and holds a purse that reads, in faux diamonds, BABY FAT. He tells Charley he confronted the pregnant woman only because her dog, a chow, was mauling a neighborhood child.

"And she slapped you and you put her down?" Charley asks.

"I put her down."

"And you didn't know she was pregnant at all?"

"At all!"

On the witness stand, the accuser testifies she was standing outside her home when the defendant, a stranger, confronted her and slammed her to the ground, apparently for no reason.

"I told him not to hit me or he'd go to jail, 'cause I was six months pregnant," she says.

Charley calls Baby Fat, who repeats the story of the dog, the slap, and his insistence that she didn't appear pregnant. "She smoked a cigarette," he says.

As Charley rises to deliver his closing, Lau watches from the state table.

Charley's voice thunders with outrage.

"This is the woman whose dog was viciously attacking a child! This is the woman who was six months pregnant and smoking a cigarette in front of her house!" Then, in a lower voice calculated to convey suspicion: "She's hiding something."

Judge Herbert Baumann considers. The state, he concludes, has not proved the defendant knew she was pregnant. He tosses the felony charge, gives him probation on a misdemeanor.

"I feel like I'm on cloud nine," Charley says. "I feel like I just lost my virginity."

•

Judge Nick Nazaretian, who presides over misdemeanor domestic violence cases in Division F, has hung his courtroom with portraits of Abraham Lincoln and George Washington, aiming for an old-fashioned feel.

"The fish on the wall that's mounted—that mouth is always open," he likes to lecture people who talk too much. "What does that tell you? Keep your mouth shut."

Charley, fresh from the cage-match battles of juvie, enters his new assignment in early May primed to fight. He's burning for a jury trial. But most of the ostensible victims—women accusing husbands or boyfriends of attacking them—refuse to pursue charges.

One day in late May, prosecutor Nicola Papy is at the back of the courtroom, engaged in a wearily familiar ritual.

"If you testify," she tells a tired-looking, red-haired woman, "there's at least a chance—"

"There's no protection for me," the woman replies, sobbing. "None."

•

At the jail, Charley always sits near the panic button.

There are just too many stories of clients who attack, the mean ones and the insane ones and the ones who think it will get them a new lawyer. In Charley's old juvie courtroom, a bailiff carries a photo of a PD with a pencil impaled in her cheek.

The little red button on the wall will summon guards. Charley isn't taking chances.

Especially not today, with a client as volatile as the skinny, drug-addled guy with the Grim Reaper tattoo. He is accused of battering his girlfriend, and furious at having been in jail a month and a half.

"Did you hit her?" Charley asks. "If I tell the judge you didn't hit her, I want to be telling the truth."

"This is not even my MO," Grim Reaper says in fury. "I sell drugs. It's not me."

Back in court, prosecutors drop Grim Reaper's charges for the usual reason: His girlfriend now denies she was attacked.

Charley tries to tell the judge the accuser has been harassing his client, but the judge cuts him off. When the charges are being dropped, why say anything to risk undoing that?

Charley: "To dispel—"

Judge: "What did I tell you about the fish on the wall? There's a reason it got caught."

•

All morning, Charley's clients come into the jailhouse interview room with the same sense of outraged innocence, the same stories of crazed, greedy, vengeful women.

"I feel like the victim here," says a man with pudgy cheeks and a linebacker's build. "I lost my job. She done took the furniture. She done took the vehicle."

The next guy is a pizza deliveryman with rotten teeth and a skull on his forearm.

"She says you pushed her," Charley says.

"This is her way of getting me out of the house," Skull says. "She's ornery. Mean. She beats on walls."

When he started, Charley believed a lot of what his clients told him. By now, he knows a PD hoping only for innocent clients, or even a handful a year, is in the wrong line of work. What he's defending, after all, is the presumption of their innocence. Still, it would be nice if they didn't talk to the one guy on their side as if he were an idiot.

The next guy has a baby face and bright smile and wants to know why he can't go home.

"I been in prison two times already," he says. "I'm not trying to go back on no battery charge."

"Well," Charley explains, "your girlfriend says you choked her till she passed out."

"I wasn't even there, man!"

The crawling pace of domestic violence court is making him crazy. All of May passes, and most of June, and still he can't find a jury trial.

The towering test of his chops as a criminal lawyer, of how far he has come from the scared, stumbling neophyte who couldn't even read a case folder, will be how well he performs before that panel of ordinary Hillsborough County citizens.

"That's what I wanted to do since I became an attorney," Charley says, "to see how good I really am."

Not negotiating pleas, not arguing before a judge, not drafting motions—no, in the hierarchies of criminal law, the jury trial is the first and last index of achievement.

A jury trial is an infinitely complicated beast, demanding mysterious and unquantifiable talents never measured in the many law classes Charley botched or the bar exam he repeatedly flubbed.

In June, eleven months into the job, he takes over a client from another division: an ice deliveryman accused of flashing a woman from his van. He insists he was set up. Charley takes a look at him—a reedy little bald guy with a goatee, jutting ears, and sunken eyes—and figures he probably did it.

Trial day arrives, and prosecutors still won't budge with an acceptable deal.

"I gotta know what happened," he tells his client. "Straight up, did you flash this girl?"

"I whipped it out," he finally confesses. His excuse: She flipped him off in traffic.

Members of the jury pool file into the courtroom, filling the first four rows. Charley must pick six to decide his client's fate. He takes a breath. He stands up.

PART THREE

Four rows of Hillsborough County citizens stare up at him, looking as nervous as he is. They don't know, he reminds himself. They don't know it's my first time.

"My name is Charalampos Georgious Demosthenous," he says. "That's a fancy Greek way of saying Charley George Demosthenous."

He knows people love to hear his name, in the original. On a date, it's one of his trumps. Right now, he feels like an eager suitor on a date with sixteen strangers. He apologizes in advance if he butchers any names—rest assured, he has been there. From the jury pool: some appreciative half-smiles.

For Charley, nearly a year's apprenticeship as a public defender—brutal, arduous, and often humiliating—has pointed to this moment, this courtroom, this pack of faces. More than any other challenge, a jury trial is where criminal lawyers make their bones.

He walks over to his client, a seedy-looking ice deliveryman accused of flashing women from his Ford van. The guy has dirty fingernails. Charley introduces him, touching him on the back. He wants to show he's not repelled by his client. People pick up on things.

As he questions potential jurors, Charley tries hard to be

personable, quick to smile. He invokes his favorite TV show, *Seinfeld*—the episode where the supermodel thinks she sees Jerry picking his nose in a car—to demonstrate that people do things in cars they wouldn't ordinarily do.

To select their panel, Charley and his co-counsel, Logan Lane, must rely on gut impressions, guesswork. They want working-class types and they want guys, nobody squeamish or moralistic. Right away, they eliminate three middle-aged women they think will torpedo their client:

A secretary, because she looks like a prim and proper Baptist. A Realtor, because she sells every day and will sway other jurors. A librarian, because the wrinkles around her lips make Charley think she purses them a lot.

Charley would also like to bump a retired schoolteacher who reminds him of someone's cookie-baking grandmother, but their peremptories are exhausted, so she stays.

Otherwise, Charley likes the final panel:

A quiet, docile-looking Wal-Mart stocker. A gray-haired civil attorney. Three other blue-collar guys, including a mechanic and a limo driver. And a former hairstylist, who Charley thinks might be okay because he once dated a salon receptionist and knows they love bawdy gossip.

•

The accuser is a twenty-two-year-old woman with long dark hair. In April 2004, after the Flasher's van cut her off in traffic, she flipped him off. By her account, he followed her to her apartment complex, summoned her over, and exposed himself.

Because of a flaw in the charging documents, prosecutors can try the Flasher only on this incident. But to prove it was no accident, they want to call other victims—two who were flashed on the Howard Frankland Bridge in June, and a third who was flashed at International Plaza in July.

Four young white women, three exposures, a three-month span.

"There is no common scheme whatever, your honor," Charley argues. "They are totally different fact patterns."

If the other women testify, Charley knows, his first jury trial is sunk.

The judge decides jurors should hear them.

One after another, the women take the stand to implicate the Flasher. Charley has no witnesses. Confronting a factually hopeless case, he opts for smoke and mirrors. For his closing, Charley brings up a big placard with the Florida statute at the top:

798.02: ADULTERY; COHABITATION

The statute makes it a second-degree misdemeanor 1) for unmarried people to have sex, and 2) for people to engage in open and gross lewdness.

Only the second part applies here, but Charley hopes jurors will focus on the antiquated—and irrelevant—first part.

"Adultery," he tells jurors, grasping, "and cohabitation."

He can't really deny his client exposed himself, so he casts the act as one of road rage, done not for sexual kicks but in retaliation for being flipped off. He invites jurors to consider whether dogs mount each other for sex or for dominance. He compares prosecutors, in their presentation of the evidence, to incompetent fast-food clerks.

"You have received your Big Mac. You have received your supersize Coke. But where's the supersize fries?"

The jury deliberates just six minutes. It must be some kind of world record. Barely enough time for them to hustle into the little room, sit and vote. The Flasher is guilty as charged, one count of misdemeanor lewd and lascivious behavior.

No one looks surprised, not even the Flasher. He gets thirty days.

Michelle Florio, who has supervised Charley since he left the juvenile division, is impressed with the fight he put up. She knows right away whether a lawyer has the chops for trial work. This one does. She sees presence, fire.

"He has no fear," she says. "I truly believe he's going to be one of the great ones."

•

Mid-July 2005 marks Charley's one-year anniversary with the Public Defender's Office, and it flashes by without his notice. He's too busy arguing motions, visiting jail, working up cases.

He sounds egotistical in one breath, quiveringly insecure the next. Comparing himself to other attorneys his age, he thinks he's better than most. Then he thinks of all he still doesn't know, the vast forbidding terrain of trial work.

His first crack at a jury, humbling though it was, only intensified his desire. Day after day, he asks coworkers if he can take their trials.

Late July, he gets one. The case involves a Wal-Mart stocker accused of battery. The trouble is, Charley has budgeted poorly this month, so he can't scrape together the $25 to refill his attention deficit disorder medication.

On the day of jury selection, over lunch in downtown Tampa, his goofy, manic side is running amok. He's speaking in foreign accents, calling people "lad" and "chap" with exaggerated cheerfulness, and swigging his coffee like water.

"When you have ADD, drinking coffee calms you down," he tells Lily McCarty, but his thumb keeps twitching. He spills his coffee, yelping. The server brings napkins.

Logan Lane, Charley's co-counsel, looks worried.

Charley inspects his ham and Swiss, announcing: "What is this travesty of food before me?"

Florio, his supervisor, watches him across the table.

"You're not giving me a lot of confidence at this point," she says, "because you're a little high-strung."

Charley promises he'll calm down.

After lunch, Charley grabs his case files from his office and carries them down the back stairway of his building toward the street. As he walks, he listens to his footsteps, trying to will away his twitchiness, master his nerves.

In his head, he goes somewhere he calls the Happy Place. He pictures himself standing by a willow tree, one he remembers from Chicago, where he spent his early childhood. He pictures looking out at a field of tall grass, the one in the 1998 World War II film *The Thin Red Line*. He hears the wind rising and falling and the grass rustling, silence and then rustling, the rhythm of the wind and the rhythm of his footsteps synching as he goes down the steps of his building, into the sunlight, toward the courthouse.

•

"My name is Charalampos Georgious Demosthenous, which is a fancy Greek way of saying Charley George Demosthenous," he tells the jury pool, looking confident, not at all scatterbrained. "So if I mispronounce your name, I empathize, I sympathize, and I apologize."

His line clunks. He looks at a sea of unsmiling faces. He digs himself deeper. To make a point about reasonable doubt, he speaks of leaving the house with the fear of leaving the stove on.

"I imagine you like to bake?" he asks an overweight woman, but receives only a blank stare.

The jury picked, Charley finds himself uneasy. It looks like a hostile bunch. He lets his nervousness slip in front of his client.

"You have to exude confidence," Florio rebukes him later. "Act like you know what you're doing, even if the world is falling apart."

And don't insult the jury pool.

"You said, 'You look like you bake,'" she says. "That is your bias against heavyset people, and if you do it again, I'm really gonna kick your ass."

The woman Charley insulted is on the panel. So is a young woman who, Charley is convinced, is smitten with prosecutor Joel Elsea, he of the sideburns and stylishly shaggy hair.

The next day, trial day, Charley finds a single white pill remaining in his bottle of ADD medication. He rattles it, debating. It will calm him down, keep his thoughts from ricocheting like pingpong balls. But it will also leach away a little bit of his fire, and he thinks he'll need it today of all days. He leaves the pill in the bottle.

If he didn't care much for the Flasher, he sympathizes with the woman he's representing now, a Wal-Mart stocker who is forty but looks much older. She has an addled, worn-down look, puffy eyes, and a tight slash for a mouth. Every time she visits Charley's office, she smells of beer. She mutters to herself. She works nights, helping to support a teenage stepdaughter. The stepdaughter is surprisingly bright, sweet, and well-spoken. As far as Charley can tell, she's the most hopeful thing in the Stocker's bleak life.

The accuser is tall, blond, and skinny, a twenty-four-year-old Brandon woman with a pouty mouth and a cop for a dad. To Charley, she looks like a conceited party girl, every cold princess he has ever known.

The trouble started last August when the Stocker left her van double-parked outside her apartment complex. The Princess, just home from Tia's Mexican restaurant and about to head to Ybor, left a note: "Learn to park, asshole."

The Stocker's fifteen-year-old stepdaughter, who found the note, claims the Princess hurled curses and threatened to fight her. The Princess says she was leaving in her roommate's Toyota when the Stocker kicked the car and reached over the window to punch her.

Charley knows his job. He must destroy the accuser's credibility. Calmly and methodically, he cross-examines her, looking for openings. He forces her to acknowledge that she was frightened of his client. Then he springs the trap, asking: "Even though you were terrified, you decide to open the window to talk to her?"

The Princess looks uneasy, eager to get off the stand. Charley makes her hold out her arms, to show she has a much longer reach than the Stocker's stepdaughter. He reminds her she was cursing.

"What obscenities were you throwing?" Charley asks.

"I called them white trash."

"So you were throwing racial epithets?"

The state objects. Charley withdraws his question. He has made his point.

Charley calls the stepdaughter, who describes the Princess as the aggressor.

"She was just cursing," the stepdaughter says. "She said. 'You wanna fight me?' I said, 'I'm fifteen years old, you'll go to jail.' "

The stepdaughter wears a crucifix around her neck. She's a good witness, soft-spoken and likable. Her testimony helps. So does the fact that the accuser and her roommate waited two days to contact police. And that the roommate, who was in the car, never saw the alleged punch.

The Princess didn't want any trouble, Joel Elsea tells jurors.

"The last thing she wanted that night was a physical fight,"

Elsea says. He borrows Charley's fast-food metaphor to demonstrate the elements of the statute have been satisfied.

"Supersize? We got it. No doubt."

As he listens, Charley makes quick notes, picking his forehead.

In court, psyching himself for battle, Charley often thinks of his favorite Japanese animation series, *Dragon Ball Z*. One scene in particular: A young man, good-hearted but unimposing, witnesses a friend's murder. He goes berserk. His rage unleashes latent superpowers. Lightning flashes around his head. Muscles explode from his arms. Suddenly he's fearsome, unstoppable.

Charley has studied the scene over and over. Just thinking about it is like intravenous caffeine.

Elsea finishes. Finally, Charley rises. His pill is in the bottle, back home. Time to go berserk. He stands at the lectern, looking squarely at six Hillsborough County citizens.

"Ladies and gentlemen," he tells them. "You have the victims saying they were scared. Scared victims don't roll down windows to hurl curse words at someone beating the back of the car.

"Victims don't wait several days to call the police.

"Victims don't write, 'Learn to park, asshole.'"

His words used to get jumbled up so easily, hurrying off his tongue. Right now they launch themselves quickly and smoothly, his voice rising, his argument building toward its conclusion: It doesn't make sense, what the Princess and her roommate say. What makes sense is a fabricated story, born of contempt.

"'Let's get this white trash in trouble,'" he says. "They take a couple days to craft a story, to create one."

He tells jurors that they may have a drink, and they may even have a burger, but they don't have a supersize meal.

"There most certainly is not a fry," he says, "much less a large fry."

The Stocker could receive a fourteenth-month sentence if convicted as charged. Charley doesn't want her stepdaughter to go home alone.

The jury takes thirty-five minutes to return.

The verdict: not guilty of battery, but guilty of a lesser charge of criminal mischief for kicking the car. The Stocker gets probation.

As she listens, there isn't much change in her hard expression, barely a flicker in her puffy eyes. This isn't going to save her life. This isn't going to keep her off the bottle. But at least she won't have to sleep in jail.

Charley squeezes his fist. Discreetly.

•

Most of Charley's growing up this past year has been painfully public, a messy, stumbling journey through the Hillsborough County courts, under the eyes of judges and mentors and co-workers and clients.

From the start, the forum exposed and amplified his every flaw, every sophomoric tic and twitch. Where he was dumb and green, he had to get smart and savvy. Where he was scared, he had to get brave.

Nothing scared him as much, however, as what he's about to do now in early August, quietly and privately.

He has to find his mom. At the heart of his family, for as long as he can recall, there has been a void. His parents divorced when he was seven, a kid growing up in Chicago. His dad, a Cyprus-born refrigerator mechanic with little formal education, took him to central Florida, making a clean break.

He didn't see his mother after that. It was like she had vanished.

When he thinks about her, it's tough to conjure specific memories. Mostly, he remembers how he felt when he was with her: safe, cared for, protected.

Tough and hard-driving, with Old World views on the rearing of children, Charley's dad pushed him to make the most of his education. In elementary school, Charley bawled when he got Bs, knowing how furious his dad would be.

"Life is not the rose, it is the thorns" was his dad's favorite saying. Part of why Charley slacked off in law school was rebellion against his dad's firm hand. But in the end he knew he was daddy's boy. Stubborn, scrappy.

These days, they live just an hour apart. Charley doesn't visit him much.

Charley's dad always told him his mom was too soft to raise a boy as he ought to be raised, hard enough for the world. But Charley always wondered what his life might have been like had he stayed in the Midwest, had she raised him.

In recent months, he has been thinking about her a lot. He'd like to have a mom. He wonders what she looks like now, twenty-one years later.

His shrink has been telling him to find her, but it seems too big a thing to confront. He has been avoiding it, in the same way he avoided studying for the bar. He doesn't know where she is.

Now, he decides to find out. Maybe it's the self-confidence he has wrested from the courtrooms over the past year. Maybe it's the extra courage he reaped from the Stocker trial. Maybe he just feels that his adult self, so close to assuming shape now, can't begin to walk upright otherwise.

He knows his mother operates a tollbooth somewhere in the Midwest, so he scatters messages around the big toll authorities.

That night, he's on the phone with her.

She's in Hammond, Indiana, married to a tree surgeon.

He tells her he's a lawyer.

"Ooh," she says, "you wear a suit."

He puts a round-trip plane ticket on his American Express card and flies to Chicago.

As he pulls his rental car into Hammond, the smell strikes him through the open window. The whole area has an oil refinery reek, mingled with other nameless industrial stenches. He's glad he didn't grow up here. It already feels like a place to escape, not come home to.

His mom answers the door of her house. She embraces him.

"My baby," she calls him, over and over. "I knew this day would come."

"You have no idea how much I missed you," he says.

They talk forever, catching up. She shows him a picture of himself as a boy, with pudgy cheeks and curly locks. She's gentle and warm and loving and as nervous as he is. She's so glad he found her. She was frightened to reach out, too.

His mom shows him off to the extended family. He meets an aunt who is surprised how good he looks, since she remembers him as a short, chubby kid. Even then he had an air of small promise.

"I'm shocked you're a lawyer," the aunt says.

He wants to talk about being a PD, everything he has seen and done in the last year, but no one shows much interest in the particular kind he is. They just know he wears a suit.

He meets a cousin, a dockworker in his thirties who still lives with his parents. Charley thinks: That would be me. He sees an entire town with these might-have-been versions of himself.

His mom gets around in an old car with a broken odometer. She hardly has any furniture. No couch, so Charley sleeps on the floor through the weekend.

It's a tough, paycheck-to-paycheck life. Charley senses a pall of resignation, of fatalism, hanging over the family, like hard luck and wretched-smelling air were just burdens to be endured. Like you couldn't ask for better cards.

"See," he tells his mom, "I wouldn't be what I am today if you'd raised me."

"No," she says, "you'd do it anyway."

But he's sure she's wrong. Absolutely sure.

Over the past year, he has made sporadic attempts to get in shape. When he gets home to Tampa, he devotes himself to the South Beach Diet. Something about Hammond convinces him of the necessity.

•

In October, the bosses send him to felony.

They give him a raise to $50,000. They move him from a colorless office on the fourth floor to a colorless office on the more prestigious fifth floor, where the brass dwells. He takes his nameplate off the old door and slips it into the slot on the new one. He brings his brass Lady Justice, too, to plant on his new desk.

This was his goal, from the start. Some of the PDs he started with are already gone, long before making it this far.

When he calls his girlfriend to tell her the good news, she sounds inexplicably subdued. She's breaking up with him. He hasn't been the most attentive boyfriend in the last few months. She needs someone who makes her feel wanted.

Charley has no argument to make, no defense to mount.

It cuts him badly. He suffers, and then he's okay.

He's a lawyer, young, single, with a closetful of nice suits that fit him and his own place and even some furniture. Plus that smoldering Mediterranean thing. He'll be all right.

•

It's a whole different feeling, walking into court now. He doesn't feel like a guest on another team's home turf. Young lawyers look to him for advice. His words don't collide like a train wreck.

Now and then he still feels the twinge, the old ambition to be a prosecutor. That's what he wanted more than anything, during those rock-bottom years after law school. To run with the top dogs. Then he thinks about it and feels sort of disgusted with himself, that he'd even consider changing sides, because he has discovered that so much about being a PD suits him.

He was never part of the in crowd, never preordained by money or pedigree or looks to succeed. He still doesn't get many "thank-yous" from clients. He doesn't get cards and flowers, the way Lily McCarty does. But he likes being a thorn in authority's side. He likes swinging a sledgehammer for the accused. Some of his clients are bad people, plain and simple. But he was never under the illusion that he couldn't be where a lot of them are, save for a fork or two in the road.

•

The catcalls erupt as soon as he enters the jail pod.

"You don't want to talk to no pretender! You know what they say, you pay for what you get!"

It's October 2005. Inmates are sitting on bunks and clustering around tables, playing cards, stewing in the dead air. They don't even know him, and they hate him.

Charley's client is a young woman in on drug charges. She needs to get out. She looks at him uncertainly. She has heard the stories about PDs.

"I was going to get a private attorney," she says, "but if you can do it . . ."

Can he? Even now, he hears the question too many times to count. Coming from clients, it makes him defensive, makes him want to scream.

But not today. Today, he replies without hesitation:

"I can do anything a private attorney can do, and I can do it better."

The client could be forgiven for thinking her PD believes it, believes it completely. Methamphetamine is starting to waste the young woman, but there remains a trace of sweetness in her face. At this moment, her lawyer is watching it brighten hopefully.

THE CHOICE

She woke before dawn in the cramped apartment in Istanbul. She kissed her three children as they slept, and decided not to wake them. She might lose her courage if she did. She said goodbye to her husband and stepped into the chill of the dark street, under the towering minaret of the mosque next door. It was drizzling.

At forty-four, Sawsan Ghazal could not recall a day she had been apart from her children. A small woman with a dulcet voice, she had always been resourceful, always found a way to protect them, whether from bombs or the mayhem in their genes.

As a girl, she had seen little of her own parents. They had divorced when she was young. When she grew up and built a family, she promised herself, she would never abandon them to that kind of loneliness.

Now, in February 2014, she was convinced that the only way to save her children was to leave them, crossing the continent with a man whose real name she didn't know. She had an assumed identity and a fake passport.

She had memorized her role. She would be an English-speaking Turkish nurse on vacation, not just another Arab Muslim fleeing Syria's interminable civil war. The smuggler was waiting.

•

They had been dressmakers in Aleppo, Syria's bustling commercial hub. She had never lived anywhere else, and took an outsized pride in her city's history. It had endured millennia of strife and shifting rule—the Romans and Byzantines, the Mongols and Ottomans, plague and war.

Aleppo had, to her, an eternal quality. Her earliest memories were of her grandmother, who mostly raised her, taking her by the hand through the Old City. They explored the noisy labyrinth of the great bazaar, the tables teeming with dates and spices and gold.

As an adult, she came to search out fabrics for the small garment factory she ran with her husband, Ourwa Alaraj. She would lead her own children—her son Abdulsalam, and daughters Joud and Cidra—through the clamor of the ancient maze.

They vacationed on the Mediterranean shore at Latakia. When she returned from a trip, the city's smell—a compound of the earth, the trees, and the flowers—greeted her like an embrace.

Syria was a police state. But it was possible for a nonpolitical family like theirs, part of the Sunni Muslim majority, to live comfortably. Street crime was rare and harshly punished; she had always felt safe.

More important, there was health care for her two oldest children, Abdulsalam and Joud, who had slight, brittle bodies as a result of thalassemia, a genetic blood disorder. Because their bodies didn't make hemoglobin normally, they needed regular transfusions to live.

Every two weeks, all through their childhood, she had packed them into the family Volkswagen for a four-hour ritual at the hospital. The siblings lay side by side, often asleep, as blood dripped through a tube into their bone-thin arms.

She told them the disease did not need to define them. Their bodies might be weak, but their minds were strong and capable. She had always tried to shield them, to explain hard realities in a way that left room for hope, but there was little she could do when doctors ran tests and learned they had contracted hepatitis C from bad blood.

By then they were old enough to understand that hepatitis could eventually kill them, and that it probably made their one hope of a thalassemia cure—a bone-marrow transplant—too dangerous to try.

•

They did not want to leave Syria. They clung to it as long as possible, even as it crumbled around them. She and her husband were sure the antigovernment protests that erupted in early 2011 would be short-lived.

They believed it possible to wait out the chaos, even as the street-by-street fighting reached Aleppo and rebels carved out large chunks of the city and her children learned to dive to the floor of the car if she turned down the wrong street.

They believed it even as they became accustomed to warplanes overhead, and as Cidra called weeping from school to say militants had scrawled threats on the walls: If you send your kids to school, we will kill them and send back only their bags.

They believed it even as they learned to leave the windows slightly ajar so they wouldn't shatter, on nights when they could feel explosions trembling through the carpet of their ground-floor apartment.

Somehow, the children were able to sleep through the encroaching war. She and Ourwa would carry them into the central hallway, farthest from the windows, and tell themselves: If death comes, at least we will be together.

In early 2012, they closed the dress factory. Supplies of cotton and linen and chiffon had been cut off. They rented a shop and sold shoes.

Blood became harder to get. Soldiers needed it. She pleaded with friends and neighbors to donate, so her children could get blood in return.

That winter the hospital lost power, and finally she was bringing the blood bags home for Abdulsalam and Joud and swabbing their arms to insert the intravenous lines herself. She had seen it done hundreds of times. She kept them warm with blankets and told stories of the Old City.

Abdulsalam was a bright, curious, ambitious boy, a social magnet. He was instantly likable. He picked up languages quickly. He had taught himself English watching American movies. He had the high cheekbones and fervent eyes of a pop star. Thalassemia had arrested the aging process. In his late teens, he looked like a much younger boy.

His mother was working in the shoe store in January 2013 when a customer asked if she'd heard about the bombing at Aleppo University. It was the first day of exams, so she knew Abdulsalam would be on campus. He was a first-year geology student there, in a government-controlled part of the city.

She tried frantically to call him but couldn't get through. An hour passed, and then another, and she thought she might go crazy.

Finally he called to say, "Mom, I'm OK." He was alive, but he wasn't OK. He said he had been nearby when the blast tore through the Department of Architecture.

The facades of buildings were sheared away. Smoke poured from the husks of cars. Glass was everywhere, twisted beams, rubble, bodies. More than eighty people were killed, some of them his friends.

Witnesses had seen a warplane overhead, which pointed to a government attack. Had the military targeted the school because it was known as a site of antigovernment protests? Had the real target been rebels, encamped just a few blocks away? Each side blamed the other; nobody took responsibility.

"At that moment I said, 'No, I can't stay here anymore,'" she would say. "I could lose them."

. She saw her son change. He said almost nothing for three days. He became withdrawn. He would refuse to talk about what he saw. He refused to return to school.

And so in April 2013, in the third year of the war, they left Aleppo. They were luckier than many other Syrians, who became stranded in refugee camps. They had some jewelry and a car to sell.

A hired driver took them to Beirut, a plane took them to Istanbul. The Turkish government gave them ID cards, with a stamp forbidding them to work. They found a small second-floor apartment in a dense hillside neighborhood on the city's European side, next to a towering concrete mosque whose loudspeaker filled their living room with the call to prayer.

She and her husband found low-paid, under-the-table factory work to pay for rent and food and blood transfusions, but it quickly became clear their options were meager.

Her husband had slipped disks in his back, from a lifetime of bending over garment-cutting machines. Turkish factories wanted younger, fitter workers.

She had always admired her husband, a talented dress designer and a tireless breadwinner. "An amazing man," she called him. Of the many men who sought her hand in marriage as a young woman, most wanted her to abandon any ambition beyond caring for the kids, but Ourwa respected her independence.

He was from a poor family, and had worked double-shifts for years at other people's factories before he could open his own, and he had had to leave it all behind. "Everything he built is gone," his son said. "His only future is to see us living a normal life."

Abdulsalam tried to make some money for his family. He found jobs as a waiter, but got fired because he needed to sit. He worked in garment factories, but his arms were weak and he dropped things.

Nor could he get an office job, because that required perfect Turkish and English. "When I say I am Syrian, they say, 'No,'" he said. "They want to avoid problems with other Turkish people who think we're stealing their jobs."

His sisters stayed in touch with friends from home on social media, but he decided to sever ties with Syria. He kept getting word his friends were being killed. He didn't want to know.

When he closed his eyes and tried to remember the Aleppo where he grew up—his school, his street, where he played, the way home—he drew a blank. He had a theory.

"It's like a firewall. If I think about this, maybe I'll miss Syria. And I don't want to. I don't want to look back, so I can go forward," he said. "I turned my back to everyone I knew. I think that's the most evil thing I did, trying to protect myself."

In some ways, Turkey proved generous. When Sawsan found a bureaucrat willing to listen, the government paid for transfusions. This would at least keep Abdulsalam and Joud alive, though they were getting no treatment for hepatitis C.

She had a half brother who had made a new life in Sweden. Of all the places they might try to reach, it seemed the most hopeful—a stable government, big northern forests, human rights. That was its image, at least. It was granting Syrians automatic asylum, teaching them Swedish.

•

It would be a 1,300-mile journey with the smuggler.

The family managed to borrow $10,000, the fare for just one of them.

After touching down in Sweden and getting a residency permit, the plan went, one of them would send for the others.

It couldn't be Cidra, fourteen, who was so anxious she held her mother as she slept. It couldn't be Joud, eighteen, or Abdulsalam, twenty—their illness made it too risky.

That left her and Ourwa. Usually, the man went. But Ourwa's back pain might debilitate him, and someone needed to stay behind to protect the children.

Plus, authorities would be looking for Syrian men, which improved her odds of success. And she spoke better English than her husband, so she could fake a non-Syrian identity.

"I have to be a strong woman," she would say. "I have to be the strong one."

And so, on the drizzly morning in February 2014 when she left Istanbul, she squeezed into the back of the smuggler's covered truck for a daylong ride to Athens. She counted thirteen others in the crush of bodies, mostly Syrian men.

Soon she was in a security line at the Athens airport. She knew nothing about the smuggler except his first name, Mohammed, and she figured that was probably as fake as the one on the passport he'd given her.

She was supposed to be a Turkish nurse on a ski vacation, but she spoke no Turkish. So if anyone spoke to her, she had to remember to reply in English, rather than give herself away with Aleppo-inflected Arabic.

She and the smuggler boarded the plane, careful not to look at each other. They landed in Copenhagen, and he drove her into the southern Swedish city of Malmö and left her.

She would stay with her half brother in Ljusdal, a small country town in central Sweden, a few hours north of Stockholm.

It was night when she arrived. There was snow on the big open fields and snow on the trees, and the lakes were frozen. Lanterns glowed from the windows of red farmhouses, a sight she found welcoming and beautiful.

The town was a postcard of bucolic Sweden, tidy and sleepy and forested, with one movie theater that closed in the summer. A massive lumber pile greeted visitors at the train station.

The Swedish government had no room for refugees in the big cities and was scattering them across the vast, thinly populated countryside, in dorm-like camps and repurposed apartment buildings and gone-to-seed hotels, some as far north as the Arctic Circle. In one well-publicized case, a group of newly arrived Syrians, aghast at the remoteness and coldness, refused to get off the bus.

But she found much to like about Ljusdal. There were hiking trails through deep woods of spruce and pine. There was a public library with a shelf of Arabic books and a geography room, where she studied Swedish atlases until closing. Socially, she quickly learned, it was nothing like the Middle East with its overcrowded cafés, big extended families, spontaneous meals, fast friendships.

Swedes were kind and polite, but reticent and hard to approach. It was difficult to make friends.

Six months, she thought. At most, her family would be joining her within six months.

•

She was one of 30,583 Syrians to apply for asylum in Sweden in 2014. Despite the deluge, the government was processing some cases relatively fast. By summer she was in her own apartment, with a residency permit, which allowed her to apply for permission to bring her family.

Her husband and youngest child had a strong case, according to Swedish Migration Board policies, but Abdulsalam and Joud were over eighteen. The board would give permits to adult children only in "special cases," the website said.

Months passed, and she told herself not to panic.

But how could she not, considering the news her family was giving her—sometimes reluctantly—from Istanbul?

One morning, her husband woke to find dirty footprints in the kitchen. Thieves had climbed through the window at night and stolen their mobile phones, and the last of the family's cash.

There was little police could do, or cared to do. As much as the theft, the official indifference left the family feeling vulnerable. It chilled her to wonder what would have happened if they had awoken to find the thieves. Would they be alive?

Shortly afterward, her family related another frightening incident. Two Syrian men had appeared at the apartment. They spoke in the accents of the Aleppo countryside.

They had orders from their boss to kill Abdulsalam, they said, but would spare him for $10,000.

Again, the Turkish authorities were no help. Someone must have informed the men that they had been a prosperous family, and still had money. For all they knew, it was someone in the neighborhood they saw every day.

•

Her face appears on their smartphone in their Turkish living room. Their faces appear on her Samsung tablet in her Swedish kitchen. They spend hours that way, in a melancholy simulacrum of togetherness. Often they don't talk at all, just watch each other's routine chores.

She watches Abdulsalam and Joud in their living room sipping cups of water mixed with Exjade, the iron remover they need to survive. She watches Ourwa unroll his prayer rug in the corner and face Mecca.

It is how they celebrated Ourwa's fiftieth birthday. It is how she teaches her daughters things they didn't have time for in Syria, like how to prepare the Middle Eastern dish *kousa mahshi*, zucchini stuffed with rice and meat.

"I'm trying to make them feel I'm still with them," she says.

Often, she and her husband talk about what they will do when they are reunited in Sweden. They talk about opening a shop together. Importing clothes from Turkey, and handbags from Italy. She tells him he will have a chance again to be the man he once was.

The government sends her monthly checks of about $1,200,

about half of which goes for rent. The rest she sends to her family and uses for bills.

She lives alone in a small third-floor apartment, amid woods. Her window looks out on a well-kept courtyard with a playground and slide. She knows her neighbors only enough to say hello.

Her closest Swedish friend is Gunhild Carlbom, a seventy-eight-year-old pensioner, who found her alone at a folk-dancing festival and befriended her. She helped her buy a wooden kitchen table, and gave her a rustic green one-speed bike, still sturdy in its fifth decade.

"She's a very lovely person and she has had a very hard life," Carlbom says. "I don't understand how she can bear it."

She keeps a Koran on a shelf above photos of her family that are arranged like a shrine. During Ramadan this summer, she found it impossible to keep the fast required of Muslims during daylight hours, because just about all the hours were daylight hours in summertime Scandinavia. When night came, it was like a hand passing quickly over your face.

Like many Syrian refugees in Sweden, she can't find a paying job. She's willing to work anywhere—in a restaurant, a hotel, a shop. She has worked her whole adult life, and prolonged periods of enforced idleness are grinding.

As part of the government's effort to acculturate her, she puts in a few unpaid hours at a perfume shop in the downtown mall. She struggles to understand the labels. She misreads Swedish menus and has to pick ham chunks out of her salad.

She takes Swedish classes, where they watch American movies and TV shows like *Welcome to Sweden,* a sitcom finding mirth in the cultural idiosyncrasies of Swedes.

But how can she focus, when every second thought is about her family?

Nobody will tell her how long it will take to process their case. About 74,000 more refugees, from Syria and elsewhere, are expected to reach Sweden this year.

Her greatest fears are for Abdulsalam and Joud. How long will blood supplies last, now that Turkish soldiers are in harm's way in the fight against the Islamic State?

"Nothing can make me happy here," she says. It is a feeling of being amputated; half of her is somewhere else.

Every spare moment, she Skypes her family. She teaches them basic Swedish phrases. *God morgon.* Good morning. *Mar du bra?* Are you OK? *Hej då.* Goodbye.

More than once, she has had to remind them to study the language. They will need it when they get here.

•

There is no chance of going home. On her tablet, she calls up photos of Aleppo—what it was, what it is.

The great mosque, its minaret smashed.

The great bazaar, burned.

The Old City where she grew up, rubble.

"Even I can't understand what's happening. It will take a generation to repair," she says. "My life is just a memory. I carry it on my tablet."

There is a little Syrian grocery store behind the language

school, where she buys thick Syrian coffee, grape leaves, olives, spices, falafel mix. There were only a few Syrians in town when she arrived, but more seem to be coming all the time.

One of them is another refugee from Aleppo named Amar, a pharmacist, who wears a stricken and baffled look when he talks about what Syria has become. On his smartphone he calls up footage of Islamic State militants beheading a man in the desert.

The victim was a family friend, he says, accused of working for the Syrian government. His throat spills blood into the sand. Sawsan looks away.

•

For her daughters, Cidra and Joud, the apartment in Istanbul is a kind of prison. It is plain, the walls bare. There is no air-conditioning in the brutally hot summer months.

Their father does not let them out of the house unescorted. They aren't enrolled in school. They play Candy Crush on the smartphone, and draw elaborate cartoons based on Japanese anime.

Her husband, a proud man, left the core of his identity in Syria. "My husband feels like a destroyed man," she says. "He used to support the family, and now he can do nothing."

He likes to say that it is all in God's hands. "Whatever happens, we believe destiny has been written," he says.

His temper is quick to flare. He buys cheap bags of hand-rolled cigarettes, twenty for a dollar, which he methodically deposits in an empty pack of Gauloises Blondes, the more expensive brand he smoked back home.

Fate in its mystery has somehow brought him full circle, from a poor man to a comfortable man to a poor man, now without even a country.

He carries a plastic bag full of butts and ashes from the living room to the trash can. This is what he does now, he says ruefully. This is his job.

Then there is Abdulsalam. He sleeps through the day's heat and stays up late smoking and streaming *Agents of S.H.I.E.L.D.* and other TV shows on his smartphone.

He is determined, somehow, to make it to Sweden. He'll walk, if he has to. "It may take a lot of time, but I'm going there," he says.

It is unwise to speak Arabic too loudly in public, he says, because there are enough people in Turkey who don't like Syrians to make it dangerous. Once, he says, men attacked him at a train station and shocked him with a Taser.

He reads psychology texts online, to understand human motivation. He thinks of it as a matter of survival, a way to protect himself. He has read that raising your elbows when you speak disarms people, as does a big smile, so he practices these.

"I give the friendly signs, so people don't think of me as an enemy, so I don't have to fight, because physically I'm weak," he says. "Because I'm Syrian, I'm always in danger. My muscles don't get enough blood, so I can't fight."

He studies psychology, too, because he knows he hasn't recovered from the day the bombs hit his school.

"The light inside me is broken, and I need to find a way to fix it," he says.

All day long she checks the migration board's website for the status of her request to bring her family over. When she wakes up. At lunch. After school. Before bed. It is always the same:

Decision pending.
Decision pending.
Decision pending.
Decision pending.

She emails the United Nations refugee agency, writing "Save my family" in the subject line.

The UN refers her to the Red Cross, which refers her back to the Swedish Migration Board, which replies with form letters when she sends pleas to consider her children's illness and expedite their cases. The letters send her into the woods on her old bike, pedaling furiously to outrace her growing desperation.

Her mind races. The war goes on and on. The deaths have passed 200,000. The news is full of Syrian refugees decomposing in trucks and vanishing in the Aegean and washing up on beaches.

She thinks of flying to Turkey and bringing her family back herself, by land or sea, whatever the risks.

"Maybe if I die, I could find peace," she says.

Twice, she has been back to visit them, and it is terrible to say goodbye. But Sweden is where she lives now. It is where she is laying the groundwork for a future she is struggling, more and more, to make them believe in. It is where they are going to live together and tease each other about the difficulty of learning a strange, brand-new language. It is where, every Wednesday, she walks to the government building across the street from the downtown mall to see the migration authorities.

She waits amid wall murals celebrating Sweden's pastoral glories: big farmhouses, picture-book fishing villages.

The young official who greets her today, Zlatko Powicevic, listens politely as she explains that she's been here more than a year waiting for her family. That she keeps emailing the case officer, but gets no reply.

"What shall I do?"

"You can email her again," he says, but seems doubtful that would help. Unaccompanied minors seeking asylum have been contributing to the backlog. "There's a heavy flow of kids now, so they're prioritizing those cases."

•

"I kind of lost hope."

This is Abdulsalam, his face appearing on her tablet one day this summer.

"After two years now, I don't feel like I'm going anywhere," he says. "That's killing me."

He speaks with a despair that she knows she cannot afford to surrender to, and so she sits at her kitchen table telling her son what she has told him many times before: "But I will win it. I will do it."

"You can't win every fight."

"You don't know what the heart of a mother can do."

He is alive, he says, but not really living, because "only breathing doesn't count." He believes that if Sweden were going to approve their case, it would have happened.

"I just think this is going nowhere," he says.

They talk for a while, and then it is time to sign off.

"*Hej då*," she says in Swedish.

"*Hej då*," her son replies.

She covers her face. Her eyes are wet. She has always found shreds of hope where others couldn't. Right now, it is in the language he spoke when he said goodbye.

THE HIDDEN MAN

An American soldier sits alone in a wooden box in the desert, trying to erase himself. Off comes the Velcro patch that says CAPTAIN. Off comes the name tag that says HILL. He positions the camera so it will show nothing to betray his identity: just a chin, a mouth, and the words U.S. ARMY on the breast of his combat fatigues.

The box is a ten-by-ten-foot room made of quarter-inch plywood, which counts as officers' quarters at this combat hospital in northern Iraq. He takes care not to show any of the personal touches on the walls. Not the taped-up note that reads, *I love you. I'll never be able to show, say, write or send anything that can ever truly show you.* Not the pinned-up chew toy bearing the teeth of his dog, Macho, or the stuffed *Super Mario Bros.* doll.

It is September 2011, in the waning months of the Iraq war. The soldier has duct-taped every crevice of his room, to keep out the harsh light and the endless gusts of desert grit. He still has a cough from Desert Storm, exactly half a lifetime ago. Because the walls are thin, he has chosen for his task an early-morning hour when he knows the soldier in the adjoining box will be away on duty.

He squares himself before his Sony laptop and hits record. The camera's tiny green light comes on. He swallows and begins talking. He stops, erases, starts over. He does it again and again, until he has a take he can live with.

Fear is a habit, and during his twenty-three-year Army career he has seen what happens to soldiers who are careless. He clicks a button and sends off his thirty-four-second message under a disguised email address. Maybe, he thinks, that will do the job. Maybe he can stay hidden in the lightproof, dustproof box.

•

Stephen Hill joined the Army just out of Upper Sandusky High School in north-central Ohio. He hoped to pay for college, because in the Hill family you paid your way. And he hoped to win the respect of his father, a former Marine who had come home from Vietnam with scars from the sharp elephant grass, and a hundred stories of peril and friendship. When he put on his father's combat helmet, it swallowed his head and his large ears.

In basic training at Fort Sill, Oklahoma, people knew Hill as the spindly, guarded kid who quoted Scripture and never cursed.

One night he found himself on fire watch with another recruit, who began to cry and confessed that he was gay.

Hill didn't know any gay people, but he knew they were definitely not tough enough for the US Army, and so he said, sternly, "You can't be here." Soon after, the gay soldier was gone.

More than anything, Hill wanted to love women and have kids. He'd dated some girls, but had never kissed anyone with passion, nor experienced anything resembling romantic love. He believed in the Bible he carried, but it was also a good way to deflect questions.

"God, let me be normal," he prayed.

They made Hill an artilleryman in Desert Storm. From his armored truck, he sought out enemy positions and called in the coordinates.

Sometimes, he thought about how easy it would be if he stuck his head out of the truck and an enemy bullet just erased him. He'd be written up as a hero in the *Daily Chief-Union*, his hometown paper, and his parents would have no cause for shame.

One night, during the brief land war in February 1991, an artillery shell landed to his left, very close, and then another to his right, just as close. He braced for oblivion. When the danger passed, he thought, I never would have loved anyone.

A few months later, as a freshman at Ohio State University, he listened intently to a speaker who claimed the power of prayer could help one surmount homosexual tendencies. He seethed. He had tried.

He sat outside a gay bar in downtown Columbus, watching people come and go, until he worked up the courage to enter.

The bartender handed him a Diet Coke and touched the straw, which made him fear he might contract AIDS. He drank from the rim, head down, and left fast.

He came out to his parents, terrified of losing their love. His mother had sensed his distress and was relieved that it wasn't something worse. His father wondered if his son was under the influence of a campus cult. Then the former Marine said, "This is not a big deal," and embraced him.

One day, he argued with a boyfriend outside a coffee shop. A drunk called him a faggot and snarled a threat. He was accustomed to absorbing ugliness. But now he was a war veteran, trained in hand-to-hand combat, and this was a public street in a country he nearly died for.

He confronted the drunk and let him throw the first punch. Then he knocked him to the ground, pinned him facedown, and pummeled his spine. It would have been easy to cripple or kill him. His friends blinked in shock. He walked away frightened of himself. He'd never allowed himself to hit someone in anger.

He got a master's in dietetics and went to work for the Columbus Public Health Department. He gave two weeks a year to the Army Reserve. When he showed up for duty, he tried to peel the pink triangle sticker off his car. He had to scrape it with his fingernails, strip by strip.

The Army drills were easy—by now he could outrun and outlift many of his peers—but the loneliness was hard. He invented girlfriends and endured endless talk of the female anatomy. Every year, for two weeks, he encased himself in a shell to survive. "Like dipping myself in concrete," he would say.

He followed President Clinton's attempt to lift the ban on gay service members. One senator promised that this would "destroy the greatest Army that the world has ever known." The military brass spoke of the harm that would be done to the "cohesion" of combat units. Some warned of violence against gay soldiers.

The debate yielded "Don't Ask, Don't Tell," which was billed as a compromise but would result in the discharge of more than 14,000 gay service members over the next eighteen years.

For Hill, it prolonged a double life of tension and hiding. The fortress of lies he'd constructed had to be ironclad. A soldier didn't have to broadcast that he was gay to lose his career. Someone noticing was enough.

•

I want so badly to one day have a family of my own with my soul mate, he wrote in his journal.

I really wonder if that's possible. I know you are out there. I know you think about me too. I am so hungry for compassion, not sex. I fall asleep every night and hug my pillows so tight pretending it's you. I don't have any idea what you look like. I don't care. How do I know what to say to you when I see you? How will I know it is you? I am so lonely waiting for you that I want to be extremely careful not to be blinded by someone pretending to be you.

Josh Snyder was instantly likable, with an effortless smile and blue eyes that matched his own exactly.

He met him at a party in summer 2010, after nearly a decade of dead-end liaisons. Snyder was as outgoing as Hill was reserved. He worked for a big Columbus bank and wore dark, conservative suits.

He liked video games. Hill invited him over to play on the arcade-sized machine he had jury-rigged from spare parts. They spent hours tearing through the games of their childhood. *Frogger, Pac-Man, Super Mario Bros.*

There were innumerable tiny humiliations. At the Columbus fair, Hill spotted another soldier from his unit and yanked his hand from Snyder's grip. If anyone asked, they were brothers.

That summer, Hill learned his unit would be sent to Iraq by year's end. He would be gone 408 days. He knew deployments killed relationships, and he told Snyder that he wouldn't blame him if he wanted to break up.

At the airport, they watched soldiers embracing their families, saying goodbye. Hill and Snyder were hunkered under an escalator. "Like little rats, hiding," Hill would say.

He climbed on an airliner with three hundred other soldiers. His life would be in their hands, in a land where many people wanted them dead.

"Don't Ask, Don't Tell" had been in the news again, as Congress debated its repeal. A jokester grabbed the intercom and announced the in-flight movie would be *Brokeback Mountain*. The line provoked raucous laughs.

Hill's throat went dry. When the plane door closed, it felt like the shutting of a tomb, leaving him with "one of the sickest, emptiest feelings you can have."

"I can't do this. I can't do this," he sputtered over the phone when he landed. His voice had a desperation Snyder had never heard before.

•

A mattress, a TV, a broken chair. His tiny wooden room has the amenities of a cell, but affords more privacy than the communal tents. It smells of the duct tape he has plastered everywhere. It's a prison, but also a sanctuary, the place where he retreats to make secret phone calls.

He must survive a year at Contingency Operating Base Speicher, a makeshift city in northern Iraq encircled by concrete blast walls. His fellow soldiers know him as the spirited diet guru and fitness instructor who screams at them in the gym, a forty-year-old who can run harder and lift more weight than men half his age.

None of them knows.

He jogs amid the rubble of Saddam Hussein's reign. A bombed-out soccer stadium. A high diving board from which, he is told, one of Saddam's sons made people jump into a drained pool.

All day and night, through the plywood walls, he can hear choppers bringing the wounded from hundreds of miles around. Lying on his bunk, he looks at the flimsy ceiling and knows how easily an enemy mortar round could crash through it.

Snyder sends him a chew toy gnawed on by Macho, his beagle-pug mix. It reminds him of home. He sends him a *Super Mario Bros.* doll, which reminds him of their hours together. He sends him a handwritten love note, which bears his initials, J.S. If anyone asks, the *J* is for Jessica.

Snyder will text, "Are you free?" before initiating a conversation, just in case. Once, Hill's smartphone auto-corrects "I love you" as "Oliver," and that becomes their favorite word.

Sometimes mortar rounds hit the base while they are Skyping. Hill gropes for his flak vest, helmet, and M16, and scrambles to the concrete bunker, leaving Snyder blinking in panic at a blank screen.

Hill doesn't want to make him worry, so he leaves a lot out. He doesn't tell him about carrying the shrapnel-impaled victims of suicide bombings on a stretcher. Or having to collect the personal effects of a soldier who walked into a latrine and shot himself in the head.

Or trying to coax food into the mouth of one who had given up and was determined to starve himself to death. Or calculating the stomach-tube formula for another, whose .50-caliber rifle had accidentally blown off half his face.

Many mornings, Hill awakens to voice mail messages from Snyder. He is careful to listen to them on a headset.

I love you. I miss you. You're one day closer to getting home. You're my hero.

He is home on leave in May 2011 when they decide to get married. Ohio will not perform the ceremony, so they drive to Washington, DC. He returns to war wearing a titanium wedding band.

Jessica, he says. For his screensaver, he uses the image of a lesbian friend.

September 2011 should be a month for celebration. The military brass have retreated from their objections, and "Don't Ask, Don't Tell" is officially ending.

Maybe it is all the years of hiding and paranoia, but for Hill the victory feels like it could be snatched away in an instant. It is election season, President Obama looks vulnerable, and some Republican candidates have vowed to reinstate the policy if elected. If that happens, he could lose his career. His uniform. His pension. His identity as a soldier. His honorable discharge. Everything.

He learns that Google and YouTube are hosting a nationally televised debate in Orlando, Florida, for the nine Republican presidential candidates. They are accepting questions.

He closes his door. He strips his name and rank from his uniform. He hides his face. He would like to disguise his voice, but he doesn't have the technology.

"I am a gay soldier, and I am currently serving in Iraq," he says to the camera. "The repeal of 'Don't Ask, Don't Tell' is going to be taking place in six days. Then it will be legal to say, 'I'm gay, and I'm here.' I wanted to know what the rights of gay people will be under a presidency of one of you, and if you'll try to repeal any progress that's been made for gay people in the military."

He sends it in and waits. YouTube likes his question, but they have a request. Could he please do it again without the "six days" line, so it won't seem dated if it airs?

He closes his door. Instead of his combat fatigues, he wears a

T-shirt that says ARMY. It is less official, he reasons, and therefore less likely to get him in trouble if he is discovered. It also displays his gigantic biceps, which he has not spent twenty years developing so he can hide them.

His face, he hides.

"I'm a gay soldier and there's been a lot of progress made in the military with the abolishment of 'Don't Ask, Don't Tell.' My question is that under one of your presidencies would you try to change what's been made for progress for gay people in the military?"

He sends it in and waits. Viewers are allowed to vote on potential questions, and he is informed that his question is a hit. But now YouTube has another, much scarier request:

Would you consider revealing your identity? Hill doesn't need time to consider. There's no chance. He has too much to lose.

Snyder reminds him that they are now married, and that it would not be hard for his command to discover this, and that if the ban is reinstated, he will be kicked out anyway.

He wakes for his 5:00 a.m. run. The blast walls seem closer than they were a week ago. The base is shrinking as America ends its nine-year occupation. He has survived his second war, and soon he will fly home, the same furtive, frightened man who arrived.

He thinks of the gay recruit he helped drive from the Army. He thinks of the drunk he might have killed. He thinks of how he clawed the pink sticker off his car. He thinks of hiding under the escalator.

In the subject line of his next email to YouTube, he writes: *I have reconsidered.*

•

On September 22, 2011, Captain Stephen Hill appears on the big screen at the Orange County Convention Center in Orlando, and on TV and computer screens across the world.

The camera is angled upward, revealing the features of the buzz-cut soldier. His muscles are almost comically swollen, bursting through the Army T-shirt. He speaks for fifteen seconds. Midway through, his voice cracks.

"In 2010, when I was deployed to Iraq, I had to lie about who I was because I'm a gay soldier and I didn't want to lose my job. My question is, under one of your presidencies, do you intend to circumvent the progress that's been made for gay and lesbian soldiers in the military?"

There are boos. It might be only two or three people in the audience. But everyone will remember it.

Former US senator Rick Santorum gets the question, and says, "Sexual activity has no place in the military." Allowing gays to serve openly "undermines" America's ability to defend itself. The crowd applauds enthusiastically.

Seven thousand miles away, before dawn in Iraq, Hill watches in his plywood box. It is not the booing that devastates him but Santorum's response, which frames the whole issue in terms of sex.

He turns off his TV. Because of the early hour, it is possible most of the soldiers have missed the debate. Somehow, he harbors the hope that he can escape with his anonymity and melt back into the ranks.

He lines up for breakfast in the chow hall. There are jumbo TVs mounted all over the walls. His face is on every one of them.

•

At a dinner speech, President Obama remarks on the Republican candidates' silence amid the boos: "You want to be Commander in Chief? You can start by standing up for the men and women who wear the uniform of the United States, even when it's not politically convenient."

On *Face the Nation*, Senator John McCain—who fought fiercely to keep "Don't Ask, Don't Tell"—says: "We should honor every man and woman who is serving in the military."

On *The Daily Show*, Jon Stewart flashes an image of Hill and says: "If this guy turned into the Hulk, his arms would stay the same size. They would just turn green."

On HBO's *The Newsroom*, a fictional news anchor says: "The only president on the stage last night was Stephen Hill. God-speed, Captain Hill, and come home soon. A grateful nation is waiting to say thank you."

•

The C-17 transport idles on the tarmac, and Hill looks out the window at what is left of Contingency Operating Base Speicher. The PX and the gym have been shuttered, the shops with the bootleg DVDs boarded up.

He is going home. It is October 2011, just weeks after he asked his question.

Some soldiers told him they were surprised, some said they

kind of suspected, and some confessed to leading their own secret lives. The initial awkwardness has been replaced, mostly, by a sense of exhilaration and possibility. He knows there must be soldiers mocking him, but the dynamic has shifted, and now they are the ones hiding.

Before boarding the plane, he empties his plywood hiding place and strips away all the duct tape. The light filters through the cracks into the empty shell.

THE PRISONER

Shawn Jason Derrick, the dreamer, never lets his mind wander into the little room where they kill boys' fathers.

He knows there is such a place, there in one of the houses of brick and razor wire that have been his weekend home since he learned to crawl, the place where guards used to search his diapers for drugs and blades.

When his imagination starts skittering down those dull gray corridors toward the glassed-in rectangle of bright light, Shawn stares hard at the ceiling above his bed to make the nausea pass, to make his mind empty again.

He prefers the other dream, the one in which the courts tell his father, "You can go home now." He pictures bringing his dad to school, showing him off, a strapping 6 feet, 207 pounds, big like his son, a free man in a free man's clothes. He pictures the two of them under the hood of a '57 Chevy, their hands filthy with grease, his dad teaching him how to fix something, maybe an alternator. The two working quietly into the night.

But then he wakes, on the bunk he shares with his kid brother, amid his Hot Wheels and Florida Marlins pennants, under walls pinned with prison Polaroids and the sketch his dad sent home of their dream Chevy with flames licking the sides.

He wakes and he's back, a lonely thirteen-year-old facing a protracted version of every kid's direst dread—the prospect of a parent's death—with this special torture: He knows who will do it, and how.

•

Shawn works the console of his Sony PlayStation, running cops off the road, the best part of the game *Driver*, in which he gets to be an underworld wheelman. "I hate them," he says, pixeled police cruisers screeching and crashing on the screen.

He lives in a sleepy town called Eustis, near Leesburg, and until recently sang in the Sunday kids' choir at the Sorrento Christian Center. He wants to be a rapper, or a cartoonist, or maybe a Christian rock star, depending on which month you ask.

At school, they call him Big Tank, a nickname Shawn loves because it refers to how fiercely he charges on the football field, where a 220-pound eighth grader is awesome and fear-inspiring.

In the halls, it just means getting called fat, though that's only the second meanest nickname he hears.

He loves his mom, Cherie, who is raising him alone on her Wal-Mart salary. He loves his seven-year-old half brother, Kyle. And he loves his dad, Samuel Jason Derrick, who lives three hours north in Raiford, in a cage at Union Correctional Institution. Shawn lists his idols as Michael Jordan, Jeff Gordon, God, and Prisoner No. 097494.

When he spots his dad's initials on the letters that come from prison, his heart moves a little with pride. S.J.D. They're his initials too. He inherited them, the same way he inherited his size, and what to think of cops.

Shawn's bedroom is a shrine to his father. It's also a private dreamscape. In the posters of ballplayers, he sees the games they'll go to together. In the Hot Wheels he arranges and rearranges lovingly on his dresser, he sees the speedsters and hot rods and antiques they'll tinker with together. Maybe when they open that NASCAR shop they've talked about.

Shawn used to take it for granted that all those things would be possible, someday. For as long as he can remember, his parents told him what he ached to hear: It's only temporary; there's been an awful mistake; we'll be a family again soon.

They were his parents; he believed them. Believed them, too, as a youngster, when they told him "Daddy's at work" to explain why they piled into the Corolla before dawn and drove and drove, then passed under coils of razor wire just to see him for a few hours.

Continued to believe, a few years later, when they told him why Daddy couldn't leave this place: He's in trouble for running into a telephone pole.

He was nine when he learned the truth. Rummaging through a cabinet, looking for something or other, he found Mom's hidden stash of news clippings. He started reading. It was a murder story.

The setting was Moon Lake, then a backwater of pitted dirt roads and sagging mobile homes in Pasco County, where Shawn's parents used to live. The victim was a man named Rama Sharma.

He was fifty-five, the owner of the Moon Lake General Store, an immigrant from India with no local family. He had closed up the night of June 24, 1987, and headed home with $360 in store receipts. A passerby found him the next morning, with stab wounds covering his face, neck and body, thirty-three cuts in all, twenty of them in his back. The money was gone.

There, in the clips, was a photo of the man the cops identified as the killer, a fresh-faced twenty-year-old described as an unemployed high school dropout who had been in and out of trouble for years.

Shawn read that a friend as well as a jailhouse snitch had implicated the suspect. Under interrogation, he confessed how he lay in wait in the bushes to rob the store owner, but Sharma recognized him and started screaming . . . so he stabbed him and stabbed him to shut him up, then sank the double-edged knife and his own bloody shirt in a lake. The jury gave him death.

When Shawn finished reading, he was quiet for a long time. The killer had Shawn's initials, a younger version of his dad's face . . . except the boy couldn't connect the man crouched in the bushes with a knife to the man he knew, the one with the big smile who scooped him up in his arms every weekend.

Shawn's mom was angry that he had found the newspaper clippings. You're still too young, Cherie Derrick said, you shouldn't have read them.

It's my right, Shawn insisted.

His dad settled it: Our son should know.

Shawn learned that he was twenty-nine days old when his dad was arrested. He learned that Pasco sheriff's detectives never got his dad's confession on tape, never found the submerged knife or the bloody shirt—gaps in the evidence that didn't seriously trouble prosecutors, judges, and jurors, gaps that Shawn embraced as proof positive of a frame-up.

There were details Shawn didn't learn. That his father rode with detectives to the murder scene and showed them where he lay in wait for Sharma, that he led them through the woods in search of the discarded items. That he wept when he confessed and told detectives: "I'm an animal."

For a sixth-grade English assignment, Shawn made a ten-page colored picture book titled "Innocent Man on Death Row." The cover shows the scales of justice, defaced by a diagonal slash. One drawing shows the Moon Lake General Store, crossed with crime scene tape; another shows a shadowy, martyred figure trapped behind bars.

"So please, when you talk about how much you hate your father, remember that not everyone can play catch, or ask their dad for advice," Shawn read from the book to the class. "I hope you will take this story seriously and not taunt me, because of where my father is."

It mostly worked, this plea. Classmates showed respectful curiosity, even solidarity. But there also came the nickname that cut so much deeper than being called fat: The killer's kid. Don't get on Shawn Derrick's bad side—his dad might get out and murder you.

He's careful now whom he confides in. Even friends aren't safe, because he never knows when they'll turn the knowledge into a weapon. An argument gets bad enough and they poke at the one subject guaranteed to wound him.

"I tell them my dad shouldn't be there, and they better keep quiet," Shawn says, balling his hand into a fist. "The kids know not to go as far as my father. Because when they go as far as my father, I get really mad.

"They don't know how wrong they are."

•

A father on death row has to choose between two bad options. One is to distance himself from his kids, sparing them pain later. The other is to stay involved in their lives, knowing a death warrant awaits. Is it better to have a father whose extinction hovers on the horizon, or to have no father at all?

If Samuel Jason Derrick has wrestled with this question, he doesn't show it. Nor did he worry that his son would turn on him when he learned the real reason he was in prison. "I never even gave it no thought," Derrick says in his rough drawl. "Because before that, he would know that Daddy is a good guy."

Now thirty-three, Derrick is tall and powerfully built, his face harder and thicker than it was fourteen years ago.

"I ain't never been to school," he says. "Things I know how to do I learned myself. I ain't had nobody teach me how to do things. That's what troubles me with my son—he ain't got nobody to teach him how to do things."

In the death row visiting room, on a cheap plastic board, Derrick teaches his son chess. "He gets mad at me. I think he expects me to let him win," Derrick says. "If I just hand it to him, then he's going to expect that in life, and I don't want him to expect things like that in life."

Hunched over the board, game after game, they talk about the girls Shawn likes, basketball and football stats, the Bible, cars, the status of Derrick's case—everything except what happens if his appeals fail. Derrick stokes his hopes with news that his state-appointed lawyers in Tallahassee haven't given up.

In the visiting room, some of the faces Shawn became accustomed to growing up are gone now, and with them some of the kids he used to play paper swords with.

"Can any child really understand, even if you explain it to him, the concept of death row?" Derrick says. "I don't know if he'll be able to accept it or not. He's awfully young. Maybe if he was an adult and didn't need me in the sense of how a young boy would need his father, it might be easier for him."

Derrick is trying to prepare his son for that day, supplying the arsenal of essentials he figures a boy ought to have. Things like: Be good to your mom. A family's just like a baseball team: Everyone needs to do his part. Never hit girls. If someone tries to hit you, hit back: It gains respect.

Of course, it's easy to be a perfect father when you are not a daily father. Derrick has never had to ground his son or endure an hours-long screaming jag. A wild twenty-year-old when Shawn was born, Derrick already had convictions for forgery, burglary, and theft. "In reality I wasn't ready to be a father."

But now, he says, "I try to teach him how to be a man. To me, I don't consider a man just a male who's an adult. A man is psychological, it's not physical. That's what I'm trying to teach him, how to be a man psychologically."

Then it's time to say goodbye for another week or month or two months. Derrick returns to his six-foot-by-nine-foot cage, where he sits on his bunk filling notebook after notebook: more of what his son will need to know to be a man, should he find himself alone later in life. Derrick hasn't told his son about these notebooks, but he intends for him to get them if his death warrant is signed.

Shawn returns to the daylight, to home, to school, his dad's words a drumbeat in his head: They lied about me. Witnesses, cops, prosecutors—they lied to put me here. But I'll be going home with you one of these days.

Shawn does what he's always done when it comes to his dad, does what he can't help doing. He believes him.

•

About 3,700 people are on death rows across the country. The children of the condemned, in some important ways, are like other children. They believe in their parents, something that has little to do with the objective sifting and weighing of evidence.

The case of Anthony Bryan is a lesson in such faith. By the time the state of Florida executed him last year, Bryan had stopped denying that he had marched an elderly night watchman to a creek in Santa Rosa County, stolen his wallet, and shot him in the head.

Still, his children couldn't fathom him doing anything so savage. They remembered him as the captain of a big, steel-hulled shrimp boat, with its fish smell and tangle of nets.

"I can't picture that man actually putting a shotgun to a man's face and blowing his head off," says Bryan's son Timothy, who is twenty now. "I never asked him. I pretty much always believed he didn't do it."

Nor did he believe, as he stood on the grassy pasture across from Florida State Prison in Starke praying for a last-minute stay, that his father's sentence would be carried out. "Even up to the last two minutes, I thought it wouldn't happen."

"People want so much to hope," says Margaret Vandiver, a professor at the University of Memphis who studies the family dynamics of death row inmates. "And what's the alternative to hope? 'They're going to kill your father one of these days'? How do you bring up a child telling him that?"

Parents don't. Instead, they hammer home this message: Just hang on. Death doesn't necessarily mean death. Over and over—twenty-one times since 1972—people have come home from Florida's death row, for reasons ranging from outright innocence to severe legal errors. That fuels the belief that however long the odds, anyone can come home.

The children of the condemned are snared between mutually hostile worlds: the world of the parent they need in a thousand simple and complicated ways, and the world of murder, evidence, and the official stamp of condemnation by judge and jury.

"How can a child understand his own position in society when his loyalty to his father puts him at odds with society and the state?" Vandiver says. "There are two separate realities here, and there's no way to reconcile them except by saying, 'My father is innocent.' But what if the evidence is overwhelming that he is not innocent?"

Shawn Derrick goes a little crazy every time the news carries word of another execution. The same month that Florida sent Bryan to the death chamber, Texas did the same to Betty Lou Beets. "I was on a warpath at school that day," Shawn says. "I was mad. I was depressed. I told my teachers to stay off my case, because I'll blow up today."

Another bad day—one of the worst—came when Shawn learned the length of the average stay on Florida's death row: just over eleven years. "My dad's been there thirteen years," he says. "My dad's time is up."

•

Mike Halkitis, the prosecutor who persuaded a judge and jury to send Samuel J. Derrick to death row, has four kids of his own. He sympathizes with Shawn, he says, but what is there to do? As long as people murder, their families will suffer, capital punishment or no capital punishment.

Halkitis doubts that sentencing Derrick to life in prison would make things any easier on his son. "Which is more hell? It's like if you have cancer. Would you rather go down, or spend the next year whittling down, dying?"

What obligation does the state have to the children whose parents it undertakes to execute? Does society owe some kind of help to the innocents who live in the psychological wreckage of the death penalty?

Halkitis considers the question carefully. The state provides psychological help for families of crime victims, he says; maybe it could provide help for families like Derrick's.

"I think it's one flaw in the system. You have no counseling for Derrick's wife or child. If they can't afford it, they can't get it. The problem is, the taxpayers foot the bill."

Clint Vaughn, one of the detectives who coaxed a confession out of Derrick, doesn't blame the system for damaging Shawn. Derrick did it—first by murder, then by lies. Vaughn believes that Derrick, and only Derrick, can rescue the boy: by looking him in the eye and saying, I did it. This is what I don't want to happen to you.

•

Shawn's mind has been taking him to dark places.

There was that dream, not long ago, in which he saw himself and two friends burst into the school bathroom and open fire on classmates. Not that he believes he's capable of anything like that, but it spooked him, so he told his mom. She banned video games involving guns from their house.

So he plays them at Lake Square Mall arcade. In one game, he plays a police sniper; in another, a gunman mowing down wave after wave of zombies. "You've just got to kill 'em all," Shawn says, squinting into a sniper's sight.

His temper frightens him, especially because he knows his size. There was the sixth-grade girl he tried to choke last year when she accidentally bonked him in the head with a plastic ball. He's not proud of that. Dad says not to hit girls. "It scares me that one day I'm going to blow up and hurt somebody really, really bad. I'm real easy to set off. It's like someone pushes my button and *bang*."

Cherie Derrick senses the rage building in her son, and it scares her: the after-school suspensions, the hallway scuffles with other kids, the obscene rap lyrics Shawn can rattle off in whole chunks, the way he seems angry at everything, especially her. The thirty-two-year-old mother can't say how much is just adolescence and how much is the legacy of that night in Moon Lake nearly fourteen years ago.

"All he ever wanted was for me and his dad to be together again. He's really afraid that I'm going to fall in love with someone else," especially lately, since she started dating a coworker at Wal-Mart.

"He has this perception of his father being home and everything being normal. That I didn't keep my end of the bargain."

For years, she says, she thought of Derrick as her true love, even as he went to death row, even as she divorced him and moved in temporarily with the man who gave her Kyle. But now there are no more predawn drives with Shawn to prison. Cherie refuses to go. Shawn has to get other rides.

Cherie tells her son, gently, that he shouldn't put his life on hold, that the odds against his father are long.

Should she have encouraged his daydreams for so long? She saw no alternative to hope, but hope, she has learned, can impale you like a stick; she has been feeling much better since giving it up. If she doesn't warn her son now, who will?

"I guess it's something I should have been more open about through the years," she says. "Of course, Jason's not going to tell him he's never coming home."

When Shawn's mother began dating her coworker, Shawn decided immediately that he loathed him. Grumbled when his name came up. Stalked off when she mentioned him spending the night. Let his mom know in no uncertain terms where he stood on this. Kept asking: What are you going to tell Dad when he gets home?

FRAMED

PART ONE: THE CALL

The cop wanted her car keys. Kelli Peters handed them over. She told herself she had nothing to fear, that all he'd find inside her PT Cruiser was beach sand, dog hair, maybe one of her daughter's toys.

They were outside Plaza Vista School in Irvine, where she had watched her daughter go from kindergarten to fifth grade, where any minute now the girl would be getting out of class to look for her. Parents had entrusted their own kids to Peters for years; she was the school's PTA president and the heart of its after-school program.

Now she watched as her ruin seemed to unfold before her.

Watched as the cop emerged from her car holding a Ziploc bag of marijuana, 17 grams worth, plus a ceramic pot pipe, plus two smaller EZY Dose Pill Pouch baggies, one with eleven Percocet pills, another with twenty-nine Vicodin. It was enough to send her to jail, and more than enough to destroy her name.

Her legs buckled and she was on her knees, shaking violently and sobbing and insisting the drugs were not hers.

The cop, a twenty-two-year veteran, had found drugs on many people, in many settings. When caught, they always lied.

Peters had been doing what she always did on a Wednesday afternoon, trying to stay on top of a hundred small emergencies.

She was forty-nine, with short blond hair and a slightly bohemian air. As the volunteer director of the Afterschool Classroom Enrichment program at Plaza Vista, she was a constant presence on campus, whirling down the halls in flip-flops and bright sundresses, a peace-sign pendant hanging from her neck.

If she had time between tasks, she might slip into the cartooning class to watch her ten-year-old daughter, Sydnie, as she drew. Her daughter had been her excuse to quit a high-pressure job in the mortgage industry peddling loans, which she had come to associate with the burn of acid reflux.

No matter how frenetic the pace became at school, the worst day was better than *that*, and often afternoons ended with a rush of kids throwing their arms around her. At five feet tall, she watched many of them outgrow her.

Peters had spent her childhood in horse country at the foot of the San Gabriel Mountains. She tossed pizzas, turned a wrench in a skate shop, flew to Hawaii on impulse and stayed for two years.

She mixed mai tais at a Newport Beach rib joint. She waited tables at a rock-'n'-roll-themed pasta house. A married lawyer—one of the regulars—grew infatuated with her and showed up at her house one night. He went away, but a sense of vulnerability lingered.

In her mid-thirties she married Bill, a towering, soft-spoken blues musician and restaurateur who made her feel calm. She spent years trying to get pregnant, and when it happened her priorities narrowed.

"I became afraid of spontaneity and surprises," she said. "I just wanted to be safe."

In Irvine, she found a master-planned city where bars and liquor stores, pawnshops and homeless shelters had been methodically purged, where neighborhoods were regulated by noise ordinances, lawn-length requirements, and mailbox-uniformity rules. For its size, Irvine consistently ranked as America's safest city. It was 66 square miles, with big fake lakes, 54 parks, 219,000 people, and 62,912 trees. Anxiety about crime was poured into the very curve of the streets and the layout of the parks, all conceived on drawing boards to deter lawbreaking.

For all that outsiders mocked Irvine as a place of sterile uniformity, she had become comfortable in its embrace. She had been beguiled by the reputation of the schools, which boasted a 97 percent college-admission rate.

The muted beige strip malls teemed with tutoring centers. If neighboring Newport Beach had more conspicuous flourishes of wealth, like mega-yachts and ocean-cliff mansions, the status competition in Irvine—where so many of the big houses looked pretty much alike—centered on education.

Plaza Vista was a year-round public school in a coveted neighborhood, and after six years she knew the layout as well as her own kitchen. The trim campus buildings, painted to harmonize with the neighborhood earth tones, suggested a medical office park; out back were an organic garden, a climbing wall, and a well-kept athletic field fringed by big, peach-colored homes.

Around campus, she was the mom everyone knew. She had a natural rapport with children. She could double them over with her impression of Applejack, the plucky country gal from the *My Little Pony* TV series. She would wait with them until their parents came to pick them up from the after-school program, but she couldn't bring herself to enforce the dollar-a-minute late fines.

The school had given her a desk at the front office, which provided an up-close view of countless parental melodramas. The moms who wanted the seventh-grade math teacher fired because their kids got Bs. Or the mom who demanded a network of giant umbrellas and awnings to shield her kids from the playground sun.

Smile, Peters had learned. Be polite.

That afternoon—February 16, 2011—the karate teacher had texted her to say he was stuck in traffic, and would she please watch the class till he arrived? She was in the multipurpose room, leading a cluster of tiny martial artists through their warm-up exercises, when a school administrator came in to find her. A policeman was at the front desk, asking for her by name.

She ran down the hall, seized by panic. She thought it must be about her husband, who was now working as a traveling wine salesman. He was on the road all the time, and she thought he'd been in an accident, maybe killed.

Officer Charles Shaver tried to calm her down. He was not here about her husband.

•

On a normal shift, Shaver could expect to handle barking-dog calls, noisy-neighbor calls, shoplifters, and car burglaries, maybe a car wreck or two. He was a sniper on the Irvine Police SWAT team, armed with cutting-edge equipment that was the envy of other departments, but had never needed to pull the trigger. He was forty, a former NCIS investigator with the Marines.

He had been seven hours into an unmemorable shift when, at 1:15 p.m., a man called police to report a dangerous driver in a school parking lot.

"I was calling because, uh, my daughter's a student at Plaza Vista Elementary School," said the caller. "And, uh, I'm concerned one of the parent volunteers there may be under, uh, under the influence or, uh, using drugs. I was, I just had to go over to the school and, uh, I was, I saw a car driving very erratically."

The caller said he had seen drugs in the car. He knew the name of the driver—Kelli. He knew the type of car—a PT Cruiser. He even knew the license plate, and what was written on the frame—"Only 4 the Groovy."

•

People were drifting in and out of the school with their kids, watching, as the policeman led Peters into the parking lot. His patrol car was blocking her PT Cruiser.

He told her about the caller's claim that she had been driving erratically around 1:15 p.m.

That's impossible, she said. She had parked her car and was inside the school by then.

Did she have anything in her car she shouldn't have?

No.

Could he search her car?

Absolutely.

The drugs were easy to find. They were sticking out of the pouch behind the driver's seat.

He put them on his hood, and she begged him to put them somewhere else. Her daughter might see. Anyone might see.

Someone must have planted them, she said. Sometimes, she left her car unlocked.

Shaver put the drugs in his trunk and led Peters back inside the school to a conference room. He peered into her pupils and checked her pulse. He made her touch her nose. He made her walk and turn. He made her close her eyes, tilt her head up, and count silently to thirty. She passed all the tests.

At some point her daughter arrived, as did her husband. She did not know what to tell them.

Shaver could have arrested Peters. Possessing pot on school grounds was a misdemeanor. Possessing narcotics like Vicodin and Percocet without a prescription was a felony. She could do time.

He could take her to the station, clock out by the end of his shift, and be home in time for dinner. Instead, he kept asking questions.

He was patient and alert to detail, qualities ingrained in a sharpshooter trained to lie atop a building for hours, studying a window through a rifle scope.

He interviewed school administrators, who confirmed what Peters had said. She had arrived at the school office around 12:40. This meant the caller, who claimed to have just seen her at 1:15 p.m., had waited thirty-five minutes to report her, a gap that puzzled Shaver.

He tried to reach the number the caller had given. It was fake.

Shaver asked Peters if he could search her apartment. She agreed, reluctantly. If someone could plant drugs in her car, why couldn't they do the same at her apartment?

She drove her PT Cruiser to her apartment about a block away, while Shaver and another officer followed. The apartment had a Jimi Hendrix print above the living room couch, and her daughter's art hung on many of the walls.

They had lived here since moving to Irvine, more than a decade back. They had found themselves consistently outbid in their attempt to buy a home. Money had been tight since she quit her job. She ran a small business called "Only 4 the Groovy," painting tie-dyed jeans, but it didn't pay the bills.

Now they were permanent renters, a condition she didn't much mind, though she noticed how embarrassed neighbors became when acknowledging they were apartment dwellers, not owners. "This is only temporary," they insisted. In affluent Irvine, your relation to the real estate you inhabited was one of the invisible class lines.

She watched as Shaver searched the kitchen cabinets, the bedrooms, the drawers, the couches, the patio. He was looking not just for drugs and drug paraphernalia but for baggies that said EZY Dose Pill Pouch. He found nothing to link her to the drugs in her car.

By now, the case had lost its open-and-shut feel. In Shaver's experience, no one left a bag of pot halfway out of a seat pouch, as if begging for it to be discovered. People typically hid their drugs in the glove box, or under the car seat. And for some reason—he didn't know why—pot smokers didn't typically keep their pipes inside the stash bag itself.

Peters was convinced she would be spending the night in jail. But after he had finished searching the apartment, Shaver told her that he was not going to take her in. The forensics team would be coming with the long Q-tips to take cheek swabs from her and her daughter, to take their prints and to scour the Cruiser for evidence.

If her DNA turned up on the drugs, she could still be charged.

The next morning, Shaver sat in the police chief's conference room surrounded by department brass and detectives, walking them through a case that had quickly seized the interest of the command staff.

It seemed a much stranger scenario than a suburban mom with a pot-and-pill habit.

He had asked Kelli Peters:

If the drugs aren't yours, how did they get in your car?

"I have an enemy," she said.

PART TWO: THE POWER COUPLE

The lawyers lived in a big house with a three-car garage and a Mediterranean clay-tile roof, on a block of flawless lawns and facades of repeating peach. The couple had three young children, a cat named Emerald, and a closetful of board games. On their nightstand were photos of their wedding in Sonoma wine country.

Kent and Jill Easter were in their thirties, and wore their elite educations on their license plates: Stanford and UCLA Law School for him, Berkeley Law for her. Experts in corporate and securities law, they had met at a Palo Alto law firm.

She had quit her practice to become a stay-at-home mom in Irvine, and by appearance her daily routine was unexceptional: play dates at the community pool, sushi with girlfriends, hair salons, Starbucks, yoga. He was logging sixty-hour workweeks as a partner in one of Orange County's biggest law firms, with a fourteenth-floor office overlooking Newport Beach.

The story Kelli Peters told police about them, in February 2011, was a strange one. She was scared, and her voice kept cracking. A year earlier, the Easters had campaigned unsuccessfully to oust her from the school where she ran the after-school program. The ordeal had shaken her, but she thought it was over.

Now, after a phone tip led police to a stash of drugs in her car, she thought of the Easters. She thought, They got me.

It had started over something so small.

February 17, 2010, had been a Wednesday, which meant it was one of the busiest afternoons of the week at Plaza Vista elementary in Irvine.

A tennis class had just ended on the playground behind the main administrative building, and Peters—volunteer director of the Afterschool Classroom Enrichment program, called ACE— had the task of rounding up the kids.

She would lead them into the building through the back door and hand them off to parents waiting on the sidewalk in front of the school.

The Easters' six-year-old son had been left outside briefly, waiting at the locked back door for someone to let him in. The man who ran the tennis class had found him and walked him to the front desk.

Jill Easter thought her son seemed upset and demanded to know what had happened. Peters explained that the boy had been slow to line up, that he tended to take his time, so this wasn't unusual. She said she hadn't noticed he was missing when she scooped up the others.

"I apologized over and over," Peters wrote in her account to school officials. "I gave him a hug and I thought she looked like she was OK with everything."

Easter was not OK. She seemed fixated on the tennis coach, by Peters's account, and wondered whether he had touched her son. Wasn't it strange that the coach had brought him to the front? "I kept saying no, it's not strange, a lot of my instructors bring the kids up," Peters wrote.

The conversation made Peters uncomfortable, and she

wanted to end it. "She made a comment as I walked away that she wondered how I could sleep at night with the way I treat people. I went inside and started crying I was so upset," Peters wrote. "But the weird thing was she never changed her facial expression. It was always the same weird smile."

•

The day after the confrontation, Jill Easter complained that her son had been "crying hysterically" after being locked out of the school building for nineteen minutes. She wanted Peters gone.

"She told me that she blames my son because he is slow and he often gets left behind because it's hard to wait for him," Jill Easter wrote to school officials. "For the record, my son is very intelligent, mature and athletic and has successfully participated in many ACE classes. He is receiving good grades and has earned many awards this year. He is not mentally or physically slow by any standard."

The district ACE director, in her own reports on the incident, wrote that she'd interviewed the coach, as well as the Easters, and concluded that "nothing happened" to the boy, who had been left outside for "closer to 5–8 minutes."

What, then, could account for Jill Easter's ire? It seemed to boil down to a single word, misheard as an insult. The director wrote that Easter thought Peters had called her son "intellectually slow, not pokey slow."

Peters adored the Easters' son. She knew him as a quiet kid, smart, prone to daydream, a participant in the school arts program that she had worked hard to keep alive. He would race up to her, proud of his drawings. "I thought he was amazing," she said.

Peters's friends suggested that maybe the boy's attachment to her played some role in engendering the mother's rancor. Peters did not know. "Maybe he'd go home and say, 'Ms. Kelli, Ms. Kelli, Ms. Kelli,'" she said.

School Principal Heather Phillips talked to Jill Easter by phone the week after the incident. Easter said that she "didn't want other children to be hurt," Phillips wrote. "She mentioned that both she and her husband are attorneys."

Phillips had learned that Easter was approaching parents on campus to rail against Peters. This could be construed as harassment, the principal told Easter. The school had a rule about civility.

"She stated that what she is doing isn't harassment, that she is fully within her rights and that she is going to continue until Kelli is gone," Phillips wrote. "She also stated that she might be making a sticker or sign for her car stating what Kelli had done."

Peters, who had volunteered for years without controversy, was badly shaken. She worried how the attention might affect the school.

If you want me to leave, she told the principal, I will.

Of course not, the principal replied.

Jill Easter demanded that the Irvine police look into it. They did. There had been no crime.

She requested a restraining order, claiming that Peters was "harassing and stalking myself and my six-year-old son," and had threatened to kill her. The court threw it out.

Then came the civil suit, filed by Kent Easter, claiming his son had been the victim of "false imprisonment" and "intentional infliction of emotional distress." He had suffered "extreme and severe mental anguish," the suit claimed. "The acts of Defendant PETERS alleged above were willful, wanton, malicious, and oppressive, and justify the awarding of exemplary and punitive damages."

The Easters dropped the suit. As a result of their complaints, the school required a head count before children were released from the after-school program. And the Easters got a refund on their ACE tuition. Otherwise, the power couple lost. The school stood by its longtime volunteer, and in early 2011 she was elected president of the PTA.

•

Peters struck Detective Mark Andreozzi as genuinely scared. Alerted by a mysterious caller, police had searched her car in the school parking lot on February 16, 2011, and found a stash of marijuana, a ceramic pipe, and painkillers in baggies labeled EZY Dose Pill Pouch.

Peters told police something she recalled Jill Easter saying during their original confrontation: "I will get you."

The drugs had appeared nearly a year to the day since that incident—the third Wednesday of February—and Peters did not think the timing was coincidental.

Still, she could not be positive the Easters were behind the drugs in her car. She told police there was another possibility— a forty-three-year-old dad who lived across the street from the school and had a reputation for bizarre behavior.

Police knew him well. They had responded to complaints about him wandering onto campus without permission, ranting at school staff, heckling the crossing guard, and videotaping the crosswalk as kids moved through it. At least once, he showed up in a Batman costume, masked and caped, to pick up his son.

He made parents nervous; Peters had felt sorry for him. But now she recalled how he'd wanted her PTA job, how he'd even asked her for copies of the bylaws. Maybe he had studied them, and knew that drug possession would disqualify her from her position.

Cops have an informal phrase for such people, who do not quite meet the requirements of a 51-50, the code for an involuntary psychiatric hold. They are 51-49½, vexing but hard to do anything about.

At the Irvine Police Department, some cops thought, It has to be him. He seemed a likelier culprit than two lawyers they had never heard of.

•

Andreozzi was a former highway patrolman who had worked narcotics for years. He wore plain clothes, a beard, and a half Mohawk. As the lead detective on the case, he had been given carte blanche. Safety and schools were the twin pillars of Irvine's pride.

He couldn't rule Peters out for drug possession just because she came off as sympathetic. He checked her record. It was clean. He asked about her at the school. "Everyone loves her," the principal said.

Andreozzi played the call that had summoned police to the

school on February 16, 2011. When the dispatcher asked for his name, the caller had said, "VJ Chandrasckhr" and spelled it out. The caller claimed to have a daughter at Plaza Vista, but the school had nobody by that name.

Andreozzi listened to the call again and again. He noticed that the caller stuttered nervously, and volunteered more information than a typical caller did, as if following a script.

Andreozzi noticed, too, that while the caller started off speaking in standard American English, he inexplicably acquired an Indian accent midway through the conversation—a faint, half-hearted one—as if suddenly deciding the name he'd given required it.

Some of Andreozzi's colleagues believed it was Peters's PTA rival, trying to disguise his voice. They traced the call. It had been placed from a wall-mounted phone in the ground-floor business office at the Island Hotel, an elegant high-rise resort in Newport Beach.

Detective Matt McLaughlin went to the hotel basement to study surveillance footage. On the screen, people moved in and out of the lobby. He was looking for the PTA rival, a five-foot-eight Asian man in his early forties. There was no sign of him.

There was, however, a tall, lanky figure he did not recognize—a man in a dark suit who walked calmly toward the business center just before the call.

"It looks like Kent Easter," the school principal said, when shown the footage.

•

Andreozzi's team began following the Easters, learning their habits.

They learned that Kent Easter's office was just a few hundred feet from the Island Hotel.

They discovered that the couple's home on Santa Eulalia Street in Irvine was about a mile from Peters's apartment.

They discovered that Kent Easter carried a BlackBerry, his wife an iPhone, and that between 2:37 a.m. and 4:21 a.m. on February 16, 2011—early on the day the drugs turned up in Peters's car—the phones had exchanged fifteen texts.

The iPhone had been pinging off the cell phone tower nearest the Easters' home. The BlackBerry was pinging off a different tower, the one near Peters's apartment complex, where her PT Cruiser had been parked in the outdoor lot.

The lot had a code-activated gate, but was easy to infiltrate for anyone patient enough to follow another car in.

•

Every time Kelli Peters talked to police, she had a powerful guilty feeling. She was sure they would discover every bad and semibad thing she had ever done.

Like how she became frustrated with Irvine's interminable stoplights and did not adhere religiously to the posted speeds. Like how she had once hurled her company-issued smartphone out her car window, on the day she quit the mortgage business in disgust. She was sure they'd stumble onto *something*.

Peters found a therapist. She described how police had discovered the drugs in her car, and how she had insisted over and over that they weren't hers. How police had not arrested her but still might, any day.

The therapist looked incredulous and said, "How did you get out of that? Nobody gets out of that."

It occurred to Peters that her own therapist might not believe her. She wondered how many other people, even her friends, harbored doubts. She thought, Would I believe me?

•

They had worked quietly for weeks, watching the Easters, learning their habits, and now the detectives were prepared to move. Early on the morning of March 4, 2011, a small army of Irvine police—nearly two dozen—gathered at the station to rehearse the plan. They would serve search warrants simultaneously at Kent Easter's Newport Beach office and at the couple's home.

Andreozzi and his team had debated how to get Kent Easter to talk. They had to get him alone, away from his colleagues. They would be foolish to underestimate his intelligence. But they thought that a man accustomed to winning with his brain might be undone by his faith in its powers.

So they would come on gently, playing dumb. Their edge was asymmetrical knowledge; he didn't know what they knew. The team followed Easter's Toyota Camry hybrid as he drove to work in Newport Beach. The vanity plate read UCLAJD1 in a Stanford University frame.

Easter had just pulled into the garage, into his reserved parking spot, when Andreozzi climbed out of his car and hailed him, and was joined moments later by another plainclothesman.

Their questions were vague: Was he aware of anything that had happened recently at Plaza Vista elementary?

At first Easter seemed happy to talk. He had a problem last year, he said. His son had been locked out of the school, and a school volunteer had berated him for being slow. He and his wife had filed complaints, but then moved on.

"We didn't want to press the issue," Easter said. "Bygones be bygones."

They mentioned the name Kelli Peters. Easter said he had never met her, didn't even know what she looked like.

As the questions grew more pointed, Andreozzi watched Easter cross his arms. He no longer seemed happy to see the detectives.

"Are you recording this, by the way?" Easter asked.

"Yeah," Andreozzi said.

Had he heard of anything happening to Peters lately? Had she been in trouble?

No.

Now Andreozzi's partner, Detective Wayne Brannon, said, "Got any idea what the heck we're talking about?"

"No."

Brannon told Easter he had been following him. He had seen him coming out of the dry cleaner's.

"You gotta ask yourself, as an educated man, why in the heck would I be following you around? 'Cause that's all I do. I work in criminal investigations. All I do is follow people around. I learn their little habits," Brannon said. "You gotta start asking yourself, 'Why are we standing in front of you, talking to you?'"

"I definitely am."

They told him to think back, about two and a half weeks ago. Was there any reason he would have been out in the small hours of the morning?

Now and then he ran out for diapers, Easter said, but odds are he was home.

Easter now looked very nervous, and when he was nervous he did what the caller had done. He began to stutter.

"I want you to use that big brain of yours, mouth closed, listen," Brannon told him. "At some point during this conversation you're going to have to make a big-boy decision, and that's gonna be on you."

In the age of computers and technology and cell phones, Brannon said, "Big Brother's always watching. We're absolutely not the smartest guys in the shed, OK? But we can follow the dots from one to the next to the next."

They knew, he said, that Easter's phone had been pinging in the middle of the night near Peters's apartment. And if there was DNA on the drugs in Peters's car, they would find it.

Brannon said, "I would hope and pray for your sake that there's a big light going off, big bells going off. Knowing what I just told you, is there anything that you would like to add to your statement to me, whether retracting or adding anything to your statement?"

"I would like to get a lawyer."

"That's the big-boy answer."

The search warrant crackled as Andreozzi pulled it out of his back pocket. In the center console of Easter's car were some diet pills. They were in a miniature plastic baggie. The label said EZY Dose Pill Pouch.

PART THREE: LIMBO

Jill Easter wasn't talking. She bounced a basketball in the driveway with her three-year-old daughter as Irvine police moved methodically through her house, snapping photos and jotting notes.

Inside, detectives found what seemed the well-appointed home of ordinary suburban parents. A garage cluttered with exercise equipment. Rooms with kids' sports trophies, an airplane mobile, a canopy bed decorated with Disney princesses.

In the master bedroom they found a copy of Easter's self-published novel, *Holding House*, written under the pen name Ava Bjork. It had just come out. She smiled glamorously from the back cover, with styled blond hair and arresting blue eyes. Like its author, the female protagonist was a Berkeley-educated lawyer who had found work at a Bay Area firm.

She was "a patient woman with a formidable intelligence," the novel explained, alluring to men but unlucky in love. To cope with life's stresses, she mixed wine with Xanax. When wronged, the heroine burned for revenge and applied her patient, formidable intelligence to the task of exacting it.

While Jill Easter waited unhappily for police to complete their search, a second team of Irvine cops had converged on a target a few miles away. This was her husband's fourteenth-floor law office, in a building overlooking Fashion Island in Newport Beach.

It was March 4, 2011. Detectives were looking for evidence that the Easters had planted marijuana and painkillers in a neighbor's car about two weeks earlier, the bizarre endgame of a year-old grudge that began at an Irvine elementary school.

Police couldn't just go into Kent Easter's office and rifle through his files; they were full of confidential information about his clients.

For the search, they relied on Paul Jensen, a personal injury lawyer who also served as an unpaid special master for the courts. He would take what looked relevant and leave the rest.

That morning, when Jensen showed up at the Irvine Police Department for the operational briefing, he counted a throng of cops—maybe fifteen or twenty—and thought it seemed like overkill. They were ready for Pablo Escobar. Kent Easter is a lawyer, he thought. He's not a Mafioso.

But now, as he went through Easter's papers, Jensen was happy the police were there in force, standing guard at the door. Some of the law firm's employees were raising a clamor, confronting the cops. Why are you here? What gives you the right? This is Newport Beach, not Irvine! Only after a cop threatened someone with arrest did things quiet down.

Neither of the Easters was arrested that day. The evidence seized included the couple's smartphones. Detectives believed their contents might clinch the case.

But the phones were soon locked up inside the chambers of an Orange County judge, where they would languish as legal arguments raged.

Easter's firm wanted his BlackBerry back because it held

sensitive client information. The Easters' criminal defense attorneys wanted evidence on both phones kept from police, citing attorney-client and spousal privileges. It was complicated enough to bring a case against two attorneys, even more so when they were married to each other.

•

At times the case approached the threshold of farce—a mash-up of Benny Hill, David Lynch, and *Desperate Housewives*.

Into the story, on the very morning the search warrants were served, stumbled a strapping off-duty firefighter—Jill Easter's married paramour.

Detectives were sitting in an unmarked car, waiting to approach the Easter house, when the firefighter came strolling up the block and spotted them. He took off, holding a phone to his ear.

Jill Easter emerged from her house in a negligee, by detectives' account, then noticed the cops herself, and hurried back inside.

Police stopped the firefighter as he pulled away in his pickup. His name was Glen Gomez. He drove an engine for a Los Angeles Fire Department station house, fifty miles north. He said he was in town to visit "a beautiful Swedish girl, her name is Jill."

Their affair had been going on for two and a half years. They arranged trysts, swapped explicit photos, and traded exuberantly pornographic texts, court records would show. She called him her "sex ninja," "Papi," and "Mr. Delicious." He called her his "sex goddess," "baby girl," and "Mrs. Delicious."

Gomez's phone records showed he hadn't been near the scene of the drug-planting, but detectives hoped to enlist his help.

They were tight-lipped with details, but told him that he was in the middle of something very serious, something that could hurt both his family and his career.

They kept saying, "She'll ruin you." He kept saying, "I love her."

Would he wear a wire? police asked.

On March 23, nearly three weeks after the warrants were served, he agreed. He wanted to show he had nothing to hide, and seemed to have a second motive: curiosity.

He met her in a park down the block from her house. She brought her two youngest children. She told them her male friend was the park ranger. She told them to go play. There was a playground with a sandbox, swings, slide, and seesaw.

As investigators listened in, Gomez, who had been given a loose script, told her cops had been asking him questions. He wanted to know what it was all about.

She was in some kind of trouble, she said, but wouldn't give him details.

"I really can't afford to have this type of investigation because my husband could lose his job," she said.

"I'm going to tell them the truth. I mean, it's not a crime to have a beautiful girlfriend," Gomez said. He said he thought they should keep their distance, for a while. "As much as I care for you and love you, it's probably not a smart thing for us to be, like, talking right now, because of what's going on and stuff."

He pressed her. "I just hope that you are who I think you are," he said. "And I'm pretty sure you are. I'm 99.999 percent positive. But when I have a detective calling me it makes you wonder a little bit, that's all."

Easter accused him of abandoning her. "I thought that if I ever had some trouble in my life or sadness that I would have someone to stand beside me, and I don't," she said. "It's a hard lesson to learn."

She continued to scold him. "I don't even know what I need," she said. "I need someone like you see in the movies to come in and help."

He persisted. Why were cops asking him questions?

"Do you think I know?" she replied. "I'm waiting for someone to help me. I'm losing everything here. I don't know."

"Well, if you haven't done anything wrong, then you should be fine."

Her tone was growing angrier and angrier. "I'm not going to be fine, do you understand me? Don't just put your head in the sand! This is the moment, this is when I needed someone and you turned your back on me! And I will not survive this!"

Soon after the conversation in the park, the firefighter told police, they broke up and she went "crazy." She showed up at his Long Beach home and told his wife about the affair, brandishing emails and photos.

She detailed the affair in a letter to the dance studio where his wife worked, Gomez told police. It was "cleverly written in the third person," according to a police report, "as if it was a close friend of Jill's who was writing it."

Irvine Police Detective Mark Andreozzi called Kelli Peters in late March 2011, more than a month after the drugs were discovered in her car outside Plaza Vista elementary, the school where she'd volunteered for years.

He couldn't tell her much, but he wanted to reassure her: The department now had strong evidence that the drugs had been planted, as she'd insisted all along.

He didn't reveal what the crime lab had just reported: Jill Easter's DNA was on the pot pipe and the Vicodin pills, though not on the Percocet. And Kent Easter's DNA was on all three.

Police insisted that Peters keep quiet even about the little she did know. Anything she said could derail the investigation. If word got back to the Easters, they might find some way to stop it cold. Now and then police told her, "You have no idea how much we want to get them."

Months went by, and they were nowhere close to making arrests. Jill Easter had hired Paul Meyer, an Orange County defense lawyer so formidable that judges turned to him when they were in trouble. Kent Easter had enlisted Thomas Bienert Jr., a former federal prosecutor with expertise in white-collar crime.

Detectives knew that just around the time of the drug-planting, Kent Easter's BlackBerry had been pinging off a tower near the crime scene, and that it had exchanged fifteen texts with his wife's iPhone during those predawn hours.

So far, however, defense arguments had thwarted police from

examining whatever incriminating messages the phones might contain.

Sitting in a windowless office, Jensen, the volunteer special master, combed through 20,000 emails on the BlackBerry, weeding out the thousands that seemed to fall under attorney-client and attorney work-product privilege.

What he was not qualified to do, he told the judge, was to screen the phones for spousal privilege, and with this chore still undone in late October 2011—more than eight months after the crime—he insisted he was done with the case. He had a practice to run. "I never in a million years thought it would be like this," Jensen said later. "I put in a Herculean amount of work."

The district attorney's office did further screening, and in November detectives got a stash of "non-privileged" Easter texts. To their chagrin, the most anticipated ones—the fifteen predawn texts—had been erased before the phones were seized.

At the Irvine Police Department, the frustration was climbing. The prosecutor, Deputy District Attorney Lynda Fernandez, seemed stuck in a holding pattern as the court weighed whether to release more evidence.

A year passed. The police investigation, including the embarrassing search of his office, had not harmed Kent Easter's career. His firm named him an equity partner, cutting him into a share of the profits.

•

For Kelli Peters, it was a time of self-consciousness and dread. In the mornings, she searched her car carefully for drugs. At Plaza

Vista elementary, where she still had a desk in the front office, people were always bringing her cakes and telling her she was in their prayers. Now and then she saw Jill Easter arrive, looking rushed, to pick up her son. Peters felt a chill and looked away.

Her daughter, Sydnie, who turned eleven that year, refused to sleep alone, fearing she would be abducted. At recess, Peters would find her sitting alone or wandering the yard, talking to herself. At the school's insistence, Peters sent her to the school therapist and came to regret it, because it meant Sydnie was being pulled out of class and made to feel even more like a spectacle.

Peters bought her a sketchbook to carry at school, and her daughter hid behind it, drawing superheroes and ponies. Peters asked other moms to please encourage their kids to play with her, but this made her daughter feel pitied, and eventually she was begging to leave the school.

Anxiety pervaded every hour. When Peters came home, she hurried to her door, afraid someone might be hiding in the hallway. Her husband would return from work to find her crying.

Peters slept fitfully, haunted by dreams in which Jill Easter was slashing her throat. In her waking hours she found her hands pulling her scarf protectively around her neck. She discovered a bald spot on her scalp. She got off Facebook. She snapped when people forgot to lock the doors.

At the big artificial lake where she took her dogs and where she had watched generations of Canada geese grow up, she now feared to walk alone. She made sure friends were with her, one on each side.

Her famously safe, master-planned city now seemed alive with hidden menace. As she walked among Irvine's tidy houses, she became fixated on how vulnerable they all seemed, with windows to climb through and sliding glass doors to break into. It made her grateful to live in an apartment, with one door in and out.

Often, her family would catch her talking to herself. She would be in the kitchen reliving her encounter with police at the school, pleading, explaining.

Please put the drugs away, she would mutter. *I don't want people to see them. . . .*

I have an enemy. . . . Her name is Jill Easter. . . .

I have an enemy. . . .

•

Some of the detectives were reading Jill Easter's self-published novel, searching for psychological clues.

She was adept at fashioning characters consumed by a primal need for payback.

The plot of *Holding House* followed a Berkeley-educated heroine, Libby, and her Berkeley-educated friends as they launch a "foolproof" crime: Kidnap a well-heeled target and hide out in Panama to await a wired ransom.

All goes awry, and Libby is spurned by her narcissistic lover and criminal confederate, the "chiseled and effortlessly handsome" Joe. She finds herself "churning over her one new mission in life—to make Joe pay for abandoning her."

She drains his bank account. She sets him up for a visa violation. She makes an anonymous call to cops. As they close in, he leaps to his death. Guilt consumes her.

It was possible to read Easter's novel as a cautionary tale about the self-immolating temptations of vengeance, the wisdom of avoiding beautiful narcissists, or the inevitable doom of "foolproof" criminal plots.

These were not the themes emphasized in marketing the book, as police learned when they discovered her online promotional page, which instead touted the seductions of lawbreaking:

"Ever dream about the perfect crime? It's in this book! As you read, you'll be wondering why no one has thought of it before. It's shockingly simple, twisted and 100% possible. Once you read about it, you'll be tempted to pull it off!"

PART FOUR: THE PROSECUTOR

The Orange County DA's Special Prosecutions unit dealt with crimes of particular sensitivity—high-profile cases involving doctors and cops, lawyers and politicians.

Christopher Duff, a career prosecutor in his early forties, joined the team in the spring of 2012. Among the files that landed on his desk was a bizarre caper involving a pair of married Irvine attorneys suspected of planting drugs in a neighbor's car.

Duff was struck by how thoroughly the Irvine police had investigated a crime in which the victim had suffered no physical harm. They had put twenty detectives on the case against Kent and Jill Easter at one time or another, and the lead investigator had spent six months on it exclusively.

Duff considered the possibilities. In so many places, he

thought, it would have gone differently. If the attempted frame-up had happened in one of the gang neighborhoods of Los Angeles where he used to prosecute shootings, rather than in a rich, placid city in Orange County . . . if the cop who found the stash of drugs in Kelli Peters's car had been a rookie, rather than a sharp-eyed veteran . . . if she had been slightly less believable . . .

It was easy to picture. Peters, the PTA president at her daughter's elementary school, would have left the campus in the back of a patrol car, a piercing sight for the teachers who loved her and relied on her, for the parents who had entrusted their kids to her for years. It would have stolen not just her freedom but her name.

When Duff met Peters, she seemed raw-nerved and brittle, the kind of person who would be traumatized by a trip through jail. "It would have broken Kelli Peters," he said. "I just know it."

He also knew jurors would find Peters sympathetic. She was never far from tears when she talked about the Easters' plot to destroy her, and the ways it had shaken her sense of security.

Duff was inheriting a case that had languished for more than a year, to the vocal frustration of Irvine cops. Duff's office had battled in court for access to the Easters' smartphones, whose contents were shielded by attorney privileges. What seemed to fuel the Easters' sense of superiority—their status as lawyers— was now protecting them from the consequences of their crime, Duff thought.

Looking over the evidence, the prosecutor decided he had enough. He had their DNA on the pot pipe and painkillers planted in their victim's car. He had motive and opportunity. He had incriminating smartphone pings. He had convicted killers on less.

•

The Easters expected a warning.

If charges were ever filed, their lawyers told them, the DA's office had assured them of advance notice.

This would allow the Easters to surrender at an appointed time, with bail already arranged, and they could be in and out of booking quickly. They would avoid the pinch of handcuffs, a luxury available to people with money and good lawyers.

But Irvine police showed little inclination to minimize the Easters' discomfort, and Duff said he was unaware of any surrender agreement.

In June 2012, police moved secretly under his direction. They obtained arrest warrants, careful not to record them in the public court computers.

•

Kent Easter had just dropped off two of his children at a tennis camp when the patrol car pulled him over near a busy intersection in Irvine. He was heading to work, to the Newport Beach office tower with his master-of-the-universe view on the fourteenth floor. He was in a suit, an equity partner, a high-dollar litigator. He had a deposition that day, and boxes of legal papers in the trunk.

Police called a tow truck for his Toyota Camry, handcuffed him, and drove him to the county jail in Santa Ana. He was standing in the intake courtyard when he saw his wife, who had been arrested at their house, arrive in a squad car.

The Easters were being charged with conspiring to plant drugs in Peters's car, the twisted culmination of a yearlong vendetta against the school volunteer. They were quickly out on bail, but their mug shots were all over the news.

No one had been killed, but something about the crime—the power and pettiness of the defendants, combined with the harmlessness of their victim—engendered a depth of indignation few cases matched. "Pure wickedness," said one online commentator. "One of the most malicious things I've ever heard," said another.

Orange County had long been dogged by images of rich and plastic people, the stereotypes fueled by the *Real Housewives* franchise with its rotating cast of socialites, their lives a whirl of feuds, shopping trips, personal trainers, lovers, plastic surgeons.

Now the Easters became symbols of this status-obsessed milieu at its most deranged, with an inexplicable crime that seemed to throb weirdly at the nexus of suburban psychosis and class privilege.

And it had happened in Irvine, no less—the county's model, master-planned city—inviting people to contemplate the ugliness that seethed behind closed doors in places that overpromised order and niceness and green.

•

Kent Easter was told to clear out his law office at Stradling Yocca Carlson & Rauth. A human-resources representative escorted him out of the Newport Beach building with his boxes, the detritus of a $400,000-a-year job.

It seemed inconceivable that he'd ever work for a top firm

again—none could risk the publicity—but he might salvage a semblance of a career.

As the months passed, however, Duff won felony indictments against the Easters and showed no willingness to let them plead to misdemeanors, which might have allowed them to remain lawyers. This had far sharper urgency for Kent Easter, the family breadwinner, than for Jill Easter, whose license had been inactive for years.

DNA from both Easters had turned up on the planted drugs, but the weight of the evidence was stronger against husband than against wife. It was Kent who had been captured on tape making a phony call to police, implicating Peters. And it was Kent's BlackBerry that had been pinging near Peters's car when the drugs were planted.

But it was Jill Easter who took the blame for planting the drugs, in a declaration filed with the court and quickly sealed.

It was not a confession in the normal sense. It could not be used against her. It was offered for a narrow purpose—as part of an ingenious defense motion to try the Easters separately.

Her admission of guilt provided a strong legal basis for doing so.

Kent Easter would naturally wish to put her on the stand in his own defense, but couldn't legally do so if they were put on trial together. He could if the trials were severed.

Superior Court Judge John Conley listened to the defense argument, and to the prosecutor's impassioned opposition.

If the judge decided to split the trials, it was easy to envision calamity for the state's case. The defense would push to have Jill Easter tried first, jurors wouldn't hear her confession, and the relatively thin evidence against her—coupled with the skill of her attorney, Paul Meyer—would give her a plausible chance at acquittal.

Then she would take the stand at her husband's trial, immune from the threat of jail. If she could testify credibly that she had planted the drugs, he would go free too. Game over.

It was a far-seeing strategy, equal parts cold logic and derring-do, but it had a flaw. First, the judge had to find Jill Easter's confession believable. He seemed to have doubts.

Motion denied. The Easters would have to stand trial together.

•

By fall 2013, Duff was making final preparations for trial, papering his home and office with yellow Post-it notes on which he would scribble ideas at all hours. Then his telephone rang. It was Meyer. Jill Easter would agree to plead guilty to a felony count of false imprisonment by fraud or deceit.

This would spare her the humiliation of sitting through a trial and would also allow her to testify for the husband on whom she still depended financially.

The sentence—to begin after his trial—was 120 days in county jail. She would serve less than half, plus a hundred hours at a Costa Mesa soup kitchen. She was promptly disbarred. Her Boalt Hall law degree was now useless.

•

The Central Justice Center in Santa Ana was a sad wreck of a building, with overcrowded elevators, graffiti-scratched bathrooms, and walls covered with fading portraits of former judges, retired or dead.

Into this setting, in November 2013, strode Kent Easter and his imposing defense team. It was headed by Thomas Bienert Jr., once Orange County's top federal prosecutor. Two years earlier, *Best Lawyers* magazine had named him the county's "White-Collar Lawyer of the Year."

In polish and pedigree, Bienert seemed more a creature of the federal courthouse down the block, a palace of domed ceilings, cherrywood paneling, and honey-hued travertine.

From the witness stand, Kelli Peters faced jurors and recounted her experience, shaking with tears. She described being detained by police when they found drugs in her car at Plaza Vista School.

When Bienert questioned Officer Charles Shaver about that day, the defense attorney sought to minimize her ordeal. She wasn't handcuffed, was she? No. Put in the squad car? No. Booked? No.

Duff counterattacked. To demonstrate how Peters had pleaded with Shaver not to arrest her, the prosecutor threw himself to his knees in front of the jury box, hands aloft beseechingly.

"She fell to her knees, crying, begging you, 'Please, please, please.' Correct?"

"Yes," Shaver said.

•

Having failed to fend off arrest, job loss, indictment, and trial, Kent Easter had one gambit left.

The successful litigator who had blazed through Stanford in three years would present himself as an emasculated patsy. His wife had berated him, deceived him, bludgeoned him with guilt.

"While Kent is a very good human being, he didn't have a backbone when it came to his wife," Bienert told jurors. "She wore the pants in the family. She pushed him around."

How this might explain away the evidence against him wouldn't be clear until the defendant himself took the stand.

Tall, composed, and well-groomed, Easter looked confident as he raised his right hand. He swore to tell the truth. Finally, he said, he would get the chance to explain.

PART FIVE: TRIAL

It was my wife, Kent Easter told jurors.

She had become obsessed with destroying the PTA mom, he said. She had planted the pot and painkillers in Kelli Peters's car. She had lured him into her criminal scheme. She was the reason he sat here today, his life a shambles, on trial for a felony.

Easter had taken the witness stand in his own defense, casting himself as a figure instantly familiar to aficionados of 1940s crime dramas: the hapless cuckold and sap, undone by a femme fatale and her noirish machinations.

It was a pitiable tale, but he was a hard man to warm up to. He had an air of bloodless detachment that came across as arrogance.

He had been a busy man, he explained, logging two hundred

billable hours a month for his big Newport Beach law firm, trying to appease a hectoring spouse who was never satisfied.

He knew that his wife, Jill, had been unfaithful to him, off and on, for years. "I felt that my job was to be a husband, to stay married," Easter testified. "Nobody in our family had ever gotten divorced."

As a glimpse into the toxic power dynamic of the marriage—as a window into his wife's obsessiveness—Easter's team presented Defense Exhibit L. It was an email she sent him in March 2010, he said, interrupting his workday.

The subject line: "Need to get serious." The theme: how to crush the lowly school volunteer who, she insisted, had deliberately locked their six-year-old son out of his elementary school a month before.

The email was a litany of demands. She wanted Kelli Peters's background checked. She wanted her arrested. She wanted her slapped with a restraining order. She wanted to sue Peters, the school, the school district, the school board, the public-schools foundation. She wanted action by tomorrow.

The email ended in bold capitals: WHY ARE WE LETTING THIS NO ONE ABUSE OUR SON AND THEN TRASH OUR FAMILY !!!!!!!!!!!!!!!!!!!!!!!!WHY!!!

There were 68 exclamation points, for anyone who cared to count.

"She thought I had let her down, that I had failed," Easter said. "I hadn't pushed hard enough on this."

As her obsession with Peters intensified, he tried to be the reasonable one, the moderating force. He had not known of her scheme to frame Peters, he insisted.

In telling this story, Kent Easter had to explain away a big problem: It was his BlackBerry that had been pinging near Peters's PT Cruiser in the predawn hours when the drugs were planted in a pouch behind the driver's seat. His wife's iPhone had been pinging at their Irvine home, a mile away.

Kent Easter was ready with an explanation: We swapped phones.

He had been at home, sleeping fitfully, sore from recent surgery. She had left her iPhone in their bedroom to charge and had taken his BlackBerry. He thought she was downstairs, tending to their sick daughter. Unbeknownst to him, she had slipped out to plant the drugs.

He was at work later that day, he said, when she called him to say she'd seen Peters popping pills and driving like a "madwoman" at Plaza Vista elementary in Irvine. She insisted that he call police, and he reluctantly agreed, afraid she would again belittle him as a failure.

To disguise himself, he gave police the first name that popped into his head, which happened to be "VJ Chandrasckhr," based on an Indian neighbor. He had then tried his untrained best to mimic the man's accent.

"It's incredibly uncomfortable to sit here and listen to something so ridiculous," Easter said after the call was played in court. "I feel stupid for having believed her and put my entire career and children in jeopardy."

To flesh out its portrayal of Jill Easter as an overbearing shrew with a talent for weaponizing guilt, the defense played a tape of her haranguing her former lover, a married Los Angeles city firefighter who had been wired up by police. She accused him of abandoning her as police zeroed in on her and her husband as suspects.

"Don't just put your head in the sand! This is the moment, this is when I needed someone and you turned your back on me!" she had cried. "And I will not survive this!"

It was a tone Kent Easter said he had heard before.

"That's the voice that I hear when I saw the 'need to get serious' email," he said. "That's the voice that plays in my mind. I mean, that's when she is upset about something and wants something."

•

Now it was Christopher Duff's turn to ask Easter a few questions, an opportunity the prosecutor relished.

Some prosecutors employed an aw-shucks persona, and some excelled at righteous indignation. Duff specialized in biting sarcasm. He had a stage actor's gift for outsize facial expressions, so jurors could read varieties of incredulity on his face from across the room.

The prosecutor stood in front of Kent Easter. He wanted to know why he remained married to Jill Easter, and in fact had been living with her until a month and a half earlier. How was this possible, considering all the ways she had betrayed him?

"Sir, this is the mother of my three children," Easter said. "And my wife."

Turning to the night of the drug-planting, Duff asked why Jill Easter would leave him her iPhone, whose passcode he claimed to possess, considering how easily he might have seen her trove of salacious exchanges with her latest lover.

"I mean, she has *Fifty Shades of Grey* on her cell phone, correct?"

"I don't know what you mean."

Duff was close enough to see that Easter, who had remained composed under his own attorney's friendly questioning, seemed increasingly nervous. Easter said it just didn't occur to him to look for her texts. "I had no idea they were in there, so I wouldn't have known to look there or not," Easter said.

"You knew your wife had already had one affair. You were concerned that she was out that night having another affair. And you had the one piece of evidence in your hand that could show you right then and there, correct?"

Duff now mocked the story of the smartphone swap. If his wife had really been sneaking around Peters's apartment complex in possession of his BlackBerry, wouldn't she have worried about it going off unexpectedly?

"And all of a sudden 'Who Let the Dogs Out' starts playing on your ringtone?" Duff said.

"That was not my ringtone," Easter said.

•

Everyone was waiting for Jill Easter to walk into the room.

She represented Kent Easter's best chance at acquittal, thought Irvine detective Mark Andreozzi, who sat beside the prosecutor.

The villain of her husband's narrative, she had already

pleaded guilty to her part in the crime. If she went to the witness stand and took the blame for everything—if she backed up his story and managed to come off as semi-credible—jurors might have reasonable doubt.

Duff expected the defense to call her. He was looking forward to the cross.

Instead, the defense rested.

They think they don't need her, Duff thought. They think they've won.

•

The defense's closing argument dwelled at length on Kent Easter's cuckolding and Jill Easter's supposed stratagems. It was a tale as superheated with intrigue and double crosses as a pulp-fiction plot—lust, concocted alibis, and frame-ups within frame-ups like Russian nesting dolls.

Her husband was her meal ticket, said defense attorney Thomas Bienert Jr., but the firefighter had her heart. On the very night she planted the drugs, the defense contended, she had found time to disappear for a tryst, which she recalled in a text to her lover the next morning: "Good morning you glorious man I am still swimming in romance."

Bienert portrayed her as an imaginative schemer. Hadn't she written a novel about "the perfect crime"? If the plot to frame the PTA mom unraveled, he said, Jill Easter had made sure that her husband's DNA would be on the planted drugs so that he would take the fall. Her calculation even extended to devising an alibi video featuring herself and her sick daughter, with a time stamp meant to show she was home at the time of the crime, the defense argued.

"If somebody was going to go down for this, it had to be Kent, not her," Bienert said. "He was expendable."

The charge was one count of false imprisonment by fraud or deceit. The jury could not reach a verdict. Eleven wanted to convict. One woman felt sorry for Kent Easter.

•

Again a jury was selected, again Kelli Peters cried, again Kent Easter told his lamentable story. And once more, ten months after the first trial, people watched and waited for Jill Easter's entrance. She had finished her two-month jail term. This time, the defense called her into the courtroom. But there was a complication. She pointed to her ears, claiming hearing loss. She wanted more than a sign-language interpreter. She wanted a screen on which to read lawyers' questions in real time.

At the prosecutor's table, they believed this a ruse to throw off the cross-examination. It would be harder to trap her. She'd get extra seconds to process questions.

The judge said she would have to make do with an interpreter like everyone else. The defense huddled, reconsidering the wisdom of putting her on the stand, and sent her home.

•

For Duff, there remained the challenge of trying to explain why the Easters wanted to ruin Kelli Peters in the first place. The provocation had seemed irrationally small. A school volunteer, Peters had inadvertently left the Easters' six-year-old son in the back recess yard for a few minutes one afternoon. Peters explained that the boy had been slow to line up after tennis class, which Jill Easter seemed to perceive as an insult to his intelligence.

"There's a whole show, *Orange County Housewives*, where all the housewives are crazy," Duff told jurors in his closing statement. "This is the twenty-first century, where everyone thinks their son should be the star quarterback, star shortstop, batting first, whatever it is. Whatever happened, whatever their son said, got these two very upset and it escalated."

As he had at the first trial, Duff emphasized that the Easters remained married. "How uncomfortable is it at the dinner table?" Duff asked. "'Jill, can you pass me the mashed potatoes, please?' 'Yeah, OK.' 'Don't frame me while you're passing the mashed potatoes, please, though.' Really? They're still together."

The most dramatic moments of the second trial came during Duff's final remarks to jurors. He noted that the location of cell phones is knowable in three ways—when they ping against the nearest tower during calls, when texts are exchanged, and when automatic "data checks" monitor the devices' health.

Until now, the data-check records—though put into evidence—had barely been mentioned. Irvine detectives had missed their significance during their investigation, as had Duff during the first trial. Preparing for this trial, however, Duff had pored over them carefully and discovered what he thought might destroy Kent Easter's alibi for good.

It had long been established, from the text pings, that Jill Easter's iPhone had been at the Easter home on the night in question.

For at least part of that night, however, the data checks indicated that her phone had also been near Peters's apartment. It had been pinging off the local tower intermittently from midnight to 8:00 a.m.

The Easters had executed the plot together while a babysitter watched their kids, the prosecutor argued. One had planted the drugs while the other acted as the lookout.

Even if the Easters had swapped phones, the records put Kent Easter at the scene.

"Guess where her cell phone is?" Duff said. "By the victim's house. Oops."

This seemed to catch the defense flat-footed. Because he had already finished his closing argument, it was too late for Bienert to try to convince jurors this was junk science. After the jury left the room, he railed against the prosecutor. He said he had been sandbagged.

Duff replied that Easter's team had had the phone records for years. Either the defense had not looked at the records, Duff said, "or was hoping that I didn't look at the records."

Judge Thomas Goethals saw no reason Duff couldn't save a good argument for the end. "It seems to me Mr. Duff made a strategic decision," he said.

The jury needed only two hours to decide. Guilty as charged.

Then came another surprise for the defense. The judge ordered Kent Easter taken into custody. Easter hadn't expected this. He had made no arrangements for his three kids, for his bills. The judge gave him a day to arrange his affairs, "out of concern for nothing but your children."

When he told his wife the news that day, Easter said later in court papers, she told him he should kill himself so she could collect on a $500,000 life insurance policy, and when he refused she made other desperate suggestions—an escape to Belize with the kids, or her own suicide.

He stayed up that night comforting her as he closed down his practice, he added, and the next morning he found the search term "how to kill yourself" on her iPad.

•

Easter had already been in jail for five weeks when he stood before Goethals for sentencing in October 2014. He faced up to three years in state prison. Goethals made no secret of his contempt for Easter, but noted that the prisons were full.

"In a perfect world, I would send you to prison largely as a statement of disgust for what you and your wife did," Goethals said. Instead, he sentenced him to 180 days in county jail, of which he would serve half, plus 100 hours of community service and three years' probation.

Easter did his time without the luxury of anonymity. Inmates recognized him from TV, and some thought he ought to be taken down. One day, he said, two of them knocked him down and bloodied his nose. He cleaned floors and toilets, and read *Game of Thrones* paperbacks.

More than once, inmates asked him for legal advice. Some of them he liked. He had been an ardent Republican with little sympathy for lawbreakers, but now he pondered the colossal waste of time and talent exacted by the system.

He had filed for divorce just before his second trial, and he was still serving his time when Jill Easter petitioned for custody of their three kids. Their dueling court filings provided as close a glimpse of their relationship as outsiders were ever likely to get.

She wrote of his "instability and irrational behavior" and described him as an angry workaholic and heavy drinker, prone to mood swings, who would isolate himself from his family by locking himself in the bathroom.

She said he blamed his drinking on his difficult relationship with his Catholic parents, who had rejected her as a non-Catholic. She said he had threatened to take the kids if she didn't plead guilty to the drug-planting.

"I am trapped in an endless cycle of lashing out at you—even after using you as a human shield," he wrote to her from jail, according to her court filings. "I am sick . . ."

Released from jail in December 2014, he complained in his own court papers that she wouldn't let him talk to their kids, wouldn't give him updates on the family cat, and wouldn't give him the airway machine he needed for his sleep apnea.

The criminal case had exacerbated their fights, he said in the filing, and she once pepper-sprayed his face in a rage. Helpless to stop her affairs, he said he needed a DNA test to prove his daughter was his.

He said she used the word "Orange" when she wanted him to stop talking about a subject, like finances, that made her too anxious. After her release from jail, he said, she became depressed, took antianxiety medication, and binged on Netflix for days.

Later, after they agreed to joint custody, he retracted his pepper-spray accusation.

"Moreover, Jill Easter has never been violent towards me or physically harmed me in any way," he wrote. "She was only ever loving and caring."

•

Duff, the prosecutor, thought justice had been served. But after two criminal trials, there remained an irreducible mystery at the heart of it—what had prompted the Easters to go to such astonishing lengths over a slight so small. "The story that hasn't been told is why these people did it," Duff said. "Everyone asks me, and I have no answer."

Rob Marcereau, an attorney whose Foothill Ranch law office was decorated with images of vintage motorbikes, shark fins, and bright green US currency, wanted answers himself. He represented Kelli Peters in her civil suit against the Easters.

He had waited patiently through the criminal trials, waited for Kent Easter to serve his time, waited for his crack at the man and his wallet. And now, in a December 2015 deposition, he faced Easter across a table.

Easter was now a convicted felon, disgraced, on probation, his law license suspended, his disbarment pending. Still the law threatened to exact a further price—monetary damages for Peters's emotional distress—and still he would not surrender an inch of ground or a ray of clarity.

"At some point in 2010 or 2011, did you and your wife hatch a plan to plant drugs in Kelli Peters's car and have her arrested?" asked Marcereau.

"I have testified at length about this in two proceedings, and my testimony is what it is," Kent Easter said.

Marcereau persisted: "I'm entitled to an answer."

Easter said: "I've answered that twice in criminal court."

"That means nothing," Marcereau said. "I need an answer, sir, or else I'll move to compel. I'll seek sanctions."

"OK. You can do that. I've answered it."

"You haven't answered it, sir."

Easter insisted he didn't know who planted the drugs.

"Did your wife ever tell you that she did it?"

"I can't answer that question due to spousal confidential communication."

Marcereau went at it again. "Sir, did you knowingly participate in a scheme with your wife to frame Kelli Peters?"

"No." He felt sorry for Kelli Peters, Easter said, but he had been through some terrible experiences himself. "I don't feel that she should have been as upset as she has been."

Marcereau asked, "So you think what you've gone through is worse than what you and your wife put Mrs. Peters through?"

"I know that."

Marcereau asked, "Don't you think you'd feel better if you just said, 'You know what? I did it. I screwed up. I regret it. I'm sorry'? Wouldn't that feel good just to say that?"

"Is this a therapy session or a deposition?"

"I would love to get some candor out of you after all of this," Marcereau said. "Can't you just admit what you did?"

PART SIX: RUIN

A tall, lanky man sat alone on a bench outside Courtroom 62. He was absorbed in the yellow legal pad balanced on his lap, silently mouthing what he had written there.

He was recognizable to many of the attorneys who passed through this third-floor wing of the Central Justice Center in Santa Ana. By now he was accustomed to the stares of curiosity and contempt. The white-shoe rainmakers in the $1,000 suits, the personal-injury guys hustling a living on slip-and-falls, the overworked public defenders—they knew his mug shot from the news.

Until recently Kent Easter had been one of them, a member of the tribe in good standing, a sworn Officer of the Court. He sat atop the roiling, competitive heap of Orange County's 17,000 practicing lawyers—a $400,000-a-year civil litigator, an equity partner in one of the county's biggest firms.

His career had been a trajectory of prestige schools and status gigs, from Stanford to UCLA Law to a big Silicon Valley firm, and finally to a fourteenth-floor office in a Newport Beach tower overlooking the Pacific.

This was before the arrests and the trials and the cameras, before his pedigree became a cudgel with which to flog him, before strangers were writing him letters urging him to kill himself. Now he sat alone in the din of the courthouse hallway, wearing ill-fitting pants and a homely purple sweater.

It was February 2016. His lips moved as he studied his legal pad. He was rehearsing a plea for mercy—his closing argument to jurors weighing his financial fate. Absent was the top-dollar legal talent that had flanked him through two criminal trials. Finally, representing himself, he would face his fellow Orange County citizens alone. He would paint a picture of his almost total ruin and beg them not to make it complete.

•

To Rob Marcereau, the attorney representing the plaintiff and her family, Kent Easter brought back memories of the William H. Macy character in *Fargo*—a man flailing to extricate himself from the web of his own doomed criminal scheme, losing more with each entangling lie. Here, as compensation for emotional distress, Kelli Peters wanted millions from him.

Some of Marcereau's lawyer buddies had told him the case was a long shot. Peters had suffered no physical injury and had kept her role as a school volunteer. But the more Easter tried to duck what he had done, Marcereau thought, the more the jurors would hate him.

Easter sat alone at the defense table, without his co-defendant and ex-wife, Jill. When Marcereau chatted with him during court breaks, he found him oddly affable—low-key, disarmingly polite, with a sense of humor—and had to remind himself he was the enemy.

"Kent Easter and his wife, Jill Easter, plotted and planned and schemed to destroy the life of Kelli Peters for a full year," Marcereau told jurors in his opening remarks. He detailed their futile campaign to oust her from her volunteer job at Plaza Vista elementary, and their ill-fated plot to disgrace her by planting drugs in her car.

When his turn came, Easter told jurors that Peters's tale of suffering was full of "exaggerations and embellishments." He said he took responsibility for what happened to her, though he did so only in the vaguest terms. And he added: "The fact that something very bad was done to a person does not give them a winning Powerball number."

Marcereau put Easter on the stand. Had he conspired with his wife to plant drugs in Peters's car?

"Very stupidly and very unfortunately, yes," Easter replied.

Marcereau pressed for specifics.

"Which one of you, you or your wife, actually planted the drugs in Mrs. Peters's car? Or was it both?"

"It was my wife."

That was in keeping with his failed defense during his criminal trials, in which he had cast her as the culprit.

She had not testified at those trials, and no one knew what she might say. When Easter put on his case now and called her to the stand—with a sign-language interpreter on hand for her claimed hearing loss—he did not seem angry at the woman he claimed had ruined him.

His tone seemed almost wistful, his gaze tender. She was now calling herself Ava Everheart, and so he began, "Good afternoon, Ms. Everheart."

"Good afternoon."

He began by acknowledging the damage he'd done to her name.

"I probably could have treated you a little better, couldn't I have?" he said.

"Yes."

"Despite all of that you have still been kind to me and haven't sought revenge, right?"

"No."

"I have known you since you were young. I don't know if you remember those days."

"Yes."

She was living with her parents in Newport Beach. Her father was an astrophysicist and inventor, but she did not mention this. She insisted she was not a child of privilege. She had worked three jobs to put herself through school.

She surveyed the courtroom and said, "I think I am the person that went to the best law school in this room, to be honest with you, and I am proud of that. Doesn't mean I am spoiled, or a bad person."

But now her reputation was ruined, she complained. She had done nearly two months in jail. She was disbarred, her law degree from Berkeley's Boalt Hall useless. "I lost everything. I mean everything," she said. "I am not a school terrorizer, as I have read about myself."

She wanted to dispel a misconception about her self-published crime thriller, *Holding House*, which Marcereau had invoked to illustrate her preoccupation with "the perfect crime."

"The point of the book is these people think they have the perfect crime, and then it gets really messed up," she said. "So the point is there is no perfect crime. You can't think of one in your head because you will always be fooled, and that is the point of the book."

Marcereau did not see much value in a lengthy cross-examination. He thought she had already buried herself.

"Ma'am, on February 16, 2011, you planted illegal drugs in Kelli Peters's car, true?"

"I pled guilty to that."

"Did you do it?"

"No."

"That is what I thought. No more questions."

It was time for Kent Easter to call his most important witness, and so he uttered one of the most melancholy sentences jurors would hear: "At this time I would just be calling myself."

He took the stand, wearing one of the unassuming sweaters that had seemed his sole wardrobe through the trial.

He turned to the jury box and explained that he was, at forty-one, a broken man. A UCLA Law grad who was sharing an apartment with his parents. His savings eviscerated by a quarter million dollars in legal fees. Barred even from driving for Uber or Lyft because of his felony conviction. Relying on acquaintances to throw him a little work. And still the sole breadwinner for his three kids, aged eight, ten, and twelve.

"All this education that I had is now completely useless to me, by and large," he said. "I have no expectation that I will be a lawyer ever again."

Marcereau was convinced Easter was hiding money, somewhere. Soon after his arrest, he pointed out, Easter had transferred ownership of his Irvine house to his father-in-law.

He told jurors not to be deceived. "You know, I think he has a good act. He comes in here wearing the same sweater three days in a row," Marcereau said. "He probably has a dozen tailored suits at home, and yet he is in here wearing the same sweater trying to tell you that he is poor. Don't believe it."

For Kelli Peters, the run-in with the Easters amounted to "the worst experience of her life," Marcereau said. Her daughter Sydnie, who was ten when the Easters tried to frame her mother, had refused to sleep alone for fear "the Easter monster" would abduct her, Marcereau said. She had grown isolated from her friends and had finally asked to change schools.

Even now, Kent Easter was still waffling on what he did, while his ex-wife showed "not an ounce of remorse," Marcereau said. He turned again to the crime novel. He reminded jurors that a promotional spot had appeared on YouTube, right around the time drugs were planted. It had featured a dramatic voice-over by Kent Easter: "If you knew how to commit a perfect crime, would you do it?"

"Kelli Peters is cowering in her house, crying with her daughter and her husband, scared out of her mind, worried she is going to be thrown in jail for God knows how long, and Kent and Jill Easter are toasting to the perfect crime," Marcereau said. "'We did it, honey.' Clink. The perfect crime."

Kent Easter sat in the hallway during the lunch break, clutching the legal pad on which he had scratched out his closing argument.

"I should never have hurt Kelli Peters," he told jurors when they returned. Still, he said, everybody had stood by her. The school had supported her. A policeman had detained her but had not arrested her, handcuffed her, pulled a gun on her, locked her in his squad car, or taken her to jail. The "polite and professional" cop had not even raised his voice.

Now came the abject plea for mercy. "I'm simply a parent of a young family that is broke," Easter said. "So I really come here already having lost everything I have except for my family, and I submit there is no further point to additional punishment."

His words were plaintive, but his tone nearly robotic. It was if he were talking about someone else, a character named Kent Easter that he did not particularly love.

Nor did jurors, who returned with a verdict of $5.7 million. He sat alone, looking stunned.

•

To celebrate the verdict, Kelli Peters's friends threw her a party. They had bought a heart-shaped piñata and decorated it with blown-up copies of the Easters' mug shots.

Someone gave Peters a stick. She held it tentatively, embarrassed, and administered some halfhearted thwacks. Her daughter, now fifteen, took the stick. The girl whose childhood had been blighted by the ordeal told her mother to step back. Some of the people in the room were laughing, and some of the same people were already beginning to cry.

She swung the stick full-force. PayDay and 100 Grand bars tumbled through the gash.

•

Four months after the verdict Easter was back in court, this time in a handsome dark suit, telling the trial judge, Michael Brenner, that the damages were excessive, that Peters's attorney had failed to show he had means to pay. "The case law is clear on this," he argued, rattling off legal citations.

Brenner thought the damages were just about right, the jury's reasoning sound. It was easy to imagine how they figured it, he said. They saw two "top of the heap" lawyers—"a couple of real legal smarties, sophisticated people"—who had used their legal acumen in an attempt to destroy a woman who lived in a little apartment, and who had quit her job to volunteer at her daughter's school.

The judge noted that Kent Easter could reapply for his law license after a five-year suspension.

Musing on his half century in the law, the judge called this "the most incomprehensible case I've ever seen," and said: "I can't figure out why you and your ex-wife did what you did."

The judge worked a rubber band with his fingers, gazing quizzically down at Kent Easter. He was struck by Easter's "flat affect" during trial, and reminded him that he'd never taken unambiguous responsibility for planting the drugs.

"Your position on this is always very vague," the judge said. "The jury could easily think, 'You know, Mr. Easter has a plan and what he's gonna do is keep it just as vague as he can.'"

He came right out and asked what everyone wanted to know: "Who dreamed up this idea?"

The judge let the question hang there, while Kent Easter, sitting nearly motionless, said nothing.

"It's just nuts," the judge continued, twisting the rubber band. "They're not exactly master criminals out of Boalt Hall and UCLA."

•

More than five years after the drug-planting, the upheavals ripple outward still. Kent Easter has filed for bankruptcy and appealed the civil verdict, so finding a way to get Kelli Peters her money has spawned another legal battle.

In that effort, Peters's lawyers recently sued Jill Easter's father, seventy-four-year-old Paul Bjorkholm, a retired scientist for EG&G Astrophysics who owns a $2 million Newport Beach home.

Summoned to answer their questions, Bjorkholm sat uneasily across from the lawyers amid the clamor of the busy third-floor cafeteria at the Santa Ana courthouse.

The lawyers grilled him about what happened in the summer of 2012, when—weeks after the Easters were arrested—they gave him their Irvine home.

The house was sold, and the $171,000 proceeds were split between Jill and Kent Easter, in trusts Bjorkholm had agreed to oversee.

That money rightfully belongs to Peters, the lawyers maintain. They are also asking for punitive damages against Bjorkholm, contending that because he participated in the home's fraudulent transfer, they may lay claim to his own assets.

During the questioning, Bjorkholm said he had been reluctant when Kent Easter asked him to become trustee so soon after the arrests. Nevertheless, he'd agreed to do it.

"At the time you were asked to do this, you were concerned that it might appear to be a fraud?" Marcereau asked.

"No, other people might think so," Bjorkholm said. "You're badgering me pretty hard, and I'm not happy with that."

Marcereau pressed for an answer. "Why did it seem odd to you?"

Kent Easter was sitting beside his former father-in-law, and now he did as a lawyer would. He interjected: "Objection, asked and answered."

Marcereau said, "You're not his attorney. You're not a lawyer."

Easter said, "I'm a party here. You're taking a record."

Marcereau's co-counsel, Roger Friedman, told Easter he could stay if he kept quiet, but threatened to get a court order if he interfered.

As if Easter needed reminding, he added, "You're not an attorney."

•

Ask Kent Easter about it today, and he answers in urbane, unfailingly polite tones that his criminal defense was a pack of lies and distortions, that he demonized his wife, that he pressured her into pleading guilty in the hope he might go free. Nor was he her dupe. "She was made out to be a cartoonish villainess," he says. "This master-planner ice queen from *Gone Girl*—it makes this great archetype. She writes these crime novels and planned this whole thing. But it's just absolutely not true."

For his trials, he says, he "embellished" one of the defense exhibits without his attorney's knowledge—the hectoring email in which his wife demanded that he "get serious" about destroying Peters. He says the all-caps last line, with its sixty-eight exclamation points, was his work, not hers. "To beef things up," he says.

It's hard to keep track of his shifting stories. In criminal court, he denied conspiring to plant the drugs and said his wife had done it alone. In civil court, he said he conspired with her but that she had done the actual planting. Today, he says, "She was not out there that night," but will not supply details. He worries about perjury charges for changing his story. He points to the county jail and says, "I don't want to go back over there." He acknowledges that the crime "was really not thought out very well," and adds: "I didn't expect that half the Irvine Police Department would be working on this."

He speaks of his ex-wife as if he still loves her. When he met her at their Silicon Valley firm in the mid-1990s, she was not like other women he met, laser-focused on a legal career. She was a hiker, a student of history, the owner of a pet bunny. She turned out to be a great mother who used flash cards with their kids and got them reading by age five. "All the best moments in my life have been with her," he says. "All the worst moments have been with her too."

He is scratching out a living, he says, doing odd law-related jobs and freelance writing.

Some time ago, he says, he met a woman and developed a romantic interest in her. He asked her out. They made plans. Then came the cancellation he half expected, expressed in four words:

"I just googled you."

●

One day this spring, Kelli Peters drove to Hollywood to tape a segment of the *Dr. Phil* show. She hoped to promote a book she was cowriting called *I'll Get You! Drugs, Lies, and the Terrorizing of a PTA Mom.*

She brought a mock-up of the cover, featuring herself in the cross-hairs of a rifle scope beneath Jill Easter's glaring mug-shot eyes.

Dr. Phil obliged by holding it aloft, which she hoped would bump up the advance sales. She needed the money. Her husband had leukemia and was out of work, and the Easters had not paid a penny of the civil judgment.

Entering the publicity circuit exacted a price, however. The producers had taped an interview with Jill Easter and filmed Peters as she watched, fighting nausea.

Easter was unrepentant. She accused Peters of having mistreated her son, leaving him "crying" and "dirty." Easter portrayed the presence of her genetic material on the planted drugs as innocent, mere "transfer DNA"—an explanation that elicited little more than ridicule.

It was not clear why Easter agreed to the interview; she came off so badly that the host asked, at one point, "What's wrong with this woman?"

•

For Peters, it is a relief, now that the Easters have left the neighborhood, even if—last she heard—they are just one city over, in Newport Beach.

She walks her dogs along Irvine's trim streets and watches

geese on the banks of the big, artificial lakes. She smiles at the same people she has been passing for years. She asks about their families, and pets.

It is friendly but dull. She misses beach cities. Maybe when her daughter graduates from high school, she says, she'll find a more exciting place.

Now and then, she runs into a member of the Police Department, the agency that saw through the lies and put twenty detectives on the case and saved her. They greet her like a friend, but act a little surprised to see her. Why hasn't she left town, considering all the bad memories?

"I feel safe here," she says.

THE EXILE

The fugitive shuffles to his computer and begins typing out his will. He is about to turn seventy-one, and it is time. "My life," he writes, "has been a wild and wicked ride. . . ."

All Pete O'Neal has amassed fits on two pages: A small brick home with a sheet-metal roof. A few road-beaten vehicles. A cluster of bunkhouses and classrooms he spent decades building, brick by scavenged brick, near the slopes of Mount Meru's volcanic cone. Everything will go to his wife of forty-two years, Charlotte, and to a few trusted workers.

He prints out the will late one Saturday morning and settles into his reclining chair to check the spelling. He signs his name.

Then, to guarantee its authenticity, he finds an ink pad, rolls his thumb across it, and affixes his thumbprint to the bottom of the page.

"I think that'll do it," he says.

When last he walked America's streets, O'Neal was a magnetic young man possessed of bottomless anger. He was an ex-con who'd found a kind of religion in late-'60s black nationalism, a vain, violent street hustler reborn in a Black Panther uniform of dark sunglasses, beret, and leather jacket. With pitiless, knife-sharp diction, he spoke of sending police to their graves.

This morning, he sits in his living room in Tanzania uncapping medicine bottles. A pill for high blood pressure. Another for the pain in his back and his bad knee. An aspirin to thin his blood. Time is catching him, like the lions that pursue him implacably through his nightmares, their leashes held by policemen.

He pushes through his screen door into the brisk morning air. A slightly stooped, thickset man with long, graying dreadlocks, he moves unsteadily down the irregular stone steps he built into the sloping dirt. He makes his way past the enormous avocado tree, past the horse barn with its single slow-footed tenant, Bullet, past the shaded dining pavilion.

His four-acre compound bustles with visitors, many of them preparing for a memorial service for Geronimo Pratt, a former Panther who died in his farmhouse down the road, his affairs untidy, his will unfinished, his death a sharp message to O'Neal not to put off the paperwork any longer.

Most of O'Neal's big dreams have faded over the years, or come to feel silly. Like beating the forty-two-year-old federal gun charges that caused him to flee the United States. Like the global socialist revolution that he was supposed to help lead. Like returning home to the streets of his Midwestern childhood. Like winning citizenship in his adopted African country, and the prize that's eluded him on two continents: the feeling of belonging somewhere.

This is what's left: the shell of a twenty-year-old Toyota Coaster bus that bulks before him in a clearing. It's a stripped-and-gutted twenty-nine-seater that he bought for $11,500 after years of squirreling away money. It came with dents, a cracked windshield, a peeling paint job, rotting floorboards, frayed seats.

Still, it seemed like a good deal until he found the engine had to be replaced, costing an additional $4,000. He's hired mechanics and craftsmen to rebuild the bus nearly from the chassis up, and a few of them are milling around now, telling him in Swahili of their progress.

He rarely leaves home anymore. Crowds jangle his nerves; traffic makes his hands shake. Yet nothing feels more urgent than readying this bus for an improbable three-hundred-mile trip to the edge of his adopted continent.

•

A group of American high school students, mostly white, is gathering in the dining pavilion. They've been coming by the busload for years, many drawn by the intrigue of staying with a former Panther. They pay him $30 a night for a bunk. The money—together with sporadic donations from sympathetic friends here and abroad—pays the bills.

The students pause before the poster featuring O'Neal as a fierce young militant, rifle in arms, Charlotte at his side. It's hard to reconcile that image with the grandfatherly host who greets them in Swahili as if they were old friends, booming, *"Karibu!"* Welcome!

He asks where they're from. A girl says Missouri, which happens to be his home state, and he hugs her theatrically. Everyone laughs. "All of you are welcome," he says, "even if you're from strange places."

He plants them before documentary footage about his life. It's easier than explaining the whole story himself. Where would he start? His childhood in segregated Kansas City, Missouri, where the amusement park admitted black kids once a year, a day so cherished that they went in their Sunday best? Should he start with the stabbings and shootings in the projects where he grew up?

"I lived in the streets," he says. "I didn't have time to be happy."

After one arrest, he was given a stark choice: reform school or the armed services. The Navy threw him out after he plunged a butcher knife into another sailor's chest over an insult, nearly killing him. He drifted in and out of lockup. He pimped girls in three states. He wore $300 Italian suits and a blond wave in his processed hair.

To the FBI, the Panthers were homegrown terrorists who romanticized lawbreaking with overheated Marxist rhetoric. To O'Neal, who founded the Kansas City chapter of the party in early 1969, it represented a lifeline out of an abyss of drugs and aimlessness. He blazed with purpose: End racism and class inequality, fast.

"I would like very much to shoot my way into the House of Representatives," he declared in a televised interview, angry at a congressman who was investigating the Panthers. Pressed to clarify, he added: "I mean it literally."

He stormed into a Senate subcommittee hearing in Washington, screaming accusations that the Kansas City police chief was funneling weapons to white supremacist groups.

Shortly afterward, a federal judge sentenced him to a four-year prison term on a conviction of transporting a shotgun across state lines. Out on bail, he decided to run. He and Charlotte fled in 1970 to Sweden, then to Algeria, and finally, in late 1972, to Tanzania, whose socialist government welcomed left-wing militants.

The O'Neals had $700. After a few years they bought a patch of inhospitable brush and volcanic rock in Imbaseni, a cobra-infested village of thatched-roof shacks in the country's remote northern interior. They were up before dawn, dancing with Al Jarreau on the tape deck, gathering locals for the day's work. Their two young African-born children, Malcolm and Stormy, carried bricks and water buckets.

Soon they had four walls, a roof, and little else. Plastic hung over the windows. No toilets. It was the back-to-Africa experience so many black Americans talked about, minus the option of escape. They learned to grow corn and raise chickens. He jarred pickle relish, smoked sausages, and bottled barbecue sauce for sale to local shops.

His temper was thunderous. When he heard something in Swahili that sounded offensive—such as *wa-negro*, a neutral description of black Americans implying no malice—he would scream, ready to fight.

"We were cowboys then," says Ikaweba Bunting, sixty-three, a Compton-raised college professor who arrived in Tanzania in the 1970s and stayed for years. "We were big and hard-walking and hard-talking, and ready to beat people up—the whole street culture."

Exile was supposed to be temporary. O'Neal corresponded with other Panthers and planned to return home to help lead the revolution. He watched from abroad as the party collapsed from infighting, arrests, and an FBI campaign of surveillance and sabotage. People stopped talking about revolution. Radicals found new lives.

O'Neal's exile became permanent. His fury abated. Some of it was age. Some of it was Tanzania, where strangers always materialized to push your Land Rover out of the mud, and where conflicts were resolved in community meetings in which everyone got to speak, interminably.

"It is so laid-back, so reasonable, that to be otherwise makes you look, even to yourself, like a damn fool," O'Neal says.

Around that first crude brick structure, the fugitive improvised a little island of hope. He built a small recording studio for musicians and a workshop for artists. He gathered cast-off computers and invited locals to come learn. He sank a well and opened the spigot to the village. It was, as he saw it, in the spirit of the free breakfast program he'd run as a Panther.

"He's had a chance to grow in a way that very few people get here," says his brother Brian O'Neal, fifty-eight, who lives in Kansas City.

Had he stayed in the States, Pete O'Neal believes, he'd be long dead from a shoot-out or street fight.

If exile saved him, it has also meant a life in which the sense of being a stranger never goes away.

"There's always a feeling of not being completely part of this culture. I know I am of a different tribe," he says. "People like me here, they love me, but I'm always other than."

Back in his house, he relaxes with a few shots of Jim Beam. He keeps a shotgun for snakes and a wall full of books. In mock-stentorian tones, he ridicules his early blood-soaked rhetoric. He puts a hand over his face, like an actor reminded of an embarrassing role, and says, "That was a man who was trying to find himself. He was trying to shed his skin, and emerge brand-new. I think he overstated and overacted."

For his radicalism itself, however, he won't apologize, even if—as he suspects—it is the one thing that might gain him safe entry back into the States.

"They will never convince me in my life," he says, "that what I was doing wasn't right."

•

A few years back, an ambition seized him. The village had scores of destitute children, orphans from dirt-floor shacks and subsistence farms. He collected donations and built a concrete-block bunkhouse down near his tomato and pepper garden.

He spread word that he had room for a few kids. More than one hundred appeared at his door, many shoeless. He had to send the majority away. The most desperate, a couple dozen, he informally adopted.

Now they roam his grounds in lively packs, playing four square on the basketball court. They sleep in rows under malaria nets. Volunteers and a few staff members watch over the children and give them English and computer classes.

They call him *Babu*. Grandfather.

How big is the ocean?

So big you can't see across it.

Really?

So big you can go for weeks and never see land.

He shows them a globe.

See how much more ocean there is than land?

So is it bigger than Tanzania?

•

The American high school students have questions, so he takes a seat before them. It's late, and he's weary, but this is his living. They want to know what country he belongs to, exactly.

He has no passport, he explains, and the Tanzanian government has rebuffed his efforts to become a citizen. "I'm not sure where the hell I belong at this particular point," he tells the students.

For years, he sought a way home. He found American lawyers willing to work for free to fight the gun charges. He would like to see his ninety-one-year-old mother in Kansas City one last time.

His longing for the States comes at funny moments, as when he sees shrimp sailing through the air in Red Lobster commercials. He still dreams about the Kansas City he knew as a child, the bakeries and the public swimming pool and the ladies with their hats. But the city seems wrong, somehow, becoming weirdly unrecognizable.

In other dreams, he finds himself fleeing from things he can't see or name, urging his wife, "Charlotte, you gotta run!"

He regards his complex of bunkhouses, workshops, and classrooms as "socialism in microcosm," he tells the students, though doctrinaire Marxism left him disillusioned. People, he concluded, are basically selfish.

Have his views on violence changed?

"I don't have the particular type of courage that would allow me to turn the other cheek."

One fresh-faced girl says she's been in Tanzania a week, and thinks it might be neat to move here. Does he recommend it?

Patiently, he replies: "It ain't that kind of party."

Of late, he tells the students, he's been haunted by the deaths of other exiled Panthers. One died in France last February, another in Zambia in October.

Then there was his close friend Elmer "Geronimo" Pratt, the Panthers' former field marshal, who spent twenty-seven years behind bars on a murder conviction before a California judge overturned it.

In 2002, Pratt bought a big farmhouse nearby with his false-imprisonment settlement, and O'Neal felt as though he'd rediscovered a lost brother. They drove through the village listening to Richard Pryor CDs, laughing until they wheezed and tears rolled down their cheeks.

Pratt was hospitalized with high blood pressure in May. He hated any confinement. He pulled out his IVs and went home. Days later, O'Neal found him on his side, dead in bed, just sixty-three. His memorial would be tomorrow.

"People are dropping, man," he tells the students. He doesn't say that his thoughts were circling his own mortality so relentlessly that he couldn't sleep last night, and climbed out of bed to tally up what he would leave behind.

•

Hundreds gather for Pratt's memorial service. O'Neal sits on the stage under the avocado tree and tells a few stories about their friendship: How Pratt always told him his toes were ugly. How they joked endlessly about who was the bigger hayseed.

Amid the prayers and the singing and the tributes, he manages to steal away for a few moments to inspect the bus. The seats are lined up in the dirt, ready to be scrubbed and resewn. The windows are taped up so the painting can begin. Panther colors: black and light blue.

•

He remembers discovering the ocean.

He was in his late teens, a heartland kid who believed his fearful precinct of Kansas City was the center of the world, its ugliness and bigotry a true picture of the world. It is why, to his mind, violent revolution looked logical and inevitable.

Then he arrived in California to report for duty in the Navy, and turned his head and saw the Pacific. His breath was caught short by the immensity of it, all that blue stretching out into other lands, other stories. It was the start of a decades-long lesson that the world is bigger, more complicated, and interesting than his little plot of bitter experience had led him to suspect.

His orphans have never left this inland region of cornfields and malarial swamps. They've never tasted salt water, or felt hot beach sand between their toes.

"They have no idea—no idea—what the ocean is," he says.

Nights and weekends, they pile into his living room and watch documentaries about sea life. He tells them about whales, giant squid, blind fish in the lightless deep. He regales them with shark stories.

Will they eat me?

If they're hungry enough, they'll try.

Because they don't like me?

No, it's the natural order of things.

Now and then he indulges in what he calls "Kansas City exaggeration," and even the majestic sea gets some burnishing. The sharks in his stories grow bigger than houses.

The kids study the TV. The sharks don't look that big.

OK. But they do have sharks bigger than that car.

•

The twenty-nine-seater is ready by late summer. The engine has been replaced, the dents in the body hammered out. The exterior has been sanded and smoothed, primed and painted, with a Panther emblem emblazoned beneath the big front window.

One day soon, he hopes to take the children southeast across the country to the Swahili Coast, with its coral reefs and pale sand and bright-painted old dhows. He planned to do it over Christmas, but a new pill regimen left him enervated. And money was short.

He'll need $2,000 for diesel fuel, food, tents. He hates to beg but believes the trip will be the culmination of every good instinct he's ever had—"The highest point in my life," he says—and he's calling in every favor.

His blood pressure, alarmingly high, keeps reminding him to be quick. "I could hear Geronimo say, 'We got a place reserved for you, come on down and keep me company.'" He told his friend no. Not yet.

In his sleep, the lions give chase. In the morning, he stands dreaming before the bus. They're running into the Indian Ocean, a man without a country surrounded by children who have barely seen theirs. He gives them the gift of an enlarged world, before his ends.

THE ROOKIE

The boy was first up the stairs, and he took them at a run, the way he did everything at eight years old. He was just home with his dad and kid sister, just in from feeding the ducks out back, and, minutes before soccer practice, he went bounding upstairs for his shin guards and cleats.

The lightbulb had burned out in the hallway, and through the dimness of his open door he didn't notice his older sister on the floor, stripped and butchered. Not until he flicked on his bedroom light.

For a second he stood there, taking it in, frozen in the doorway of the room he'd slept in since he was two, the room with race cars on the wallpaper. Then he was whirling, screaming for his dad, pounding down the steps so fast that he tumbled end over end.

It was January 20, 1988, just after 6:00 p.m. Jeremy Colhouer, who had been a grinning little boy with brown-golden curls, came to dread empty rooms, to peer at people from behind his mother's legs. He kept crawling into his parents' bed at night until a therapist advised them to lock him out. They listened to his screams, his small fists pounding on their bedroom door, until they decided that no shrink's advice was worth that price.

Detectives came by the house often, and then the fear melted a little. As long as the men with the badges were there, he knew, the monster wouldn't come back.

They gave his family composite sketches of the stranger seen on their block the afternoon fourteen-year-old Jennifer Colhouer was raped and murdered. Now fear had tangible features: a wide face, a pinched little mouth, big, predatory dark eyes.

Jeremy's parents hung these sketches on a tree and handed their eight-year-old a BB gun. Over and over, he squeezed off rounds, riddling that pinched face.

•

March 15, 1999. The newest road deputy at the Pasco County Sheriff's Office lugs a bulky box into his bedroom. He unpacks the thick, dark green slacks and light green shirt, the bulky leather gun belt and Kevlar vest, the silver, five-pointed badge and silver collar pins. One pin reads:

J. COLHOUER SERVING SINCE 1999.

He is not assigned to work this day, but he wants to feel the thirty-five pounds of extra weight, to stand in his new skin. It takes an hour, this first time, to get it all on. The gun belt feels huge, the slacks need hemming, but Jeremy Colhouer is giddy.

Finally, he thinks, I'm almost there.

By August he is there, his first day in his own patrol car, without a field training officer by his side, but his nerves aren't cooperating. He calms them by pulling someone over for a broken taillight and writing a warning. Ease into it. Okay. I can do this.

The youngest sworn patrol deputy on the Pasco force, clean-shaven and meticulously neat, appears too sweet-natured to arrest you. One guy looked at the cuffs on his wrists, looked at the deputy who put them there, and asked, "Do your parents know what you're doing to me?"

Ask Jeremy Colhouer why he wanted to be a cop, and he speaks about needing to give something back, of gratitude for those who helped solve his sister's murder—once his friends and idols, now his colleagues and bosses. He talks of his special empathy for crime victims, and saving other people's sisters.

Good answers all, but the answers of a mature twenty-year-old. The dream took shape, in fact, much earlier, before the traumatized second grader could have articulated anything so lofty.

"This is all he ever said he was going to do," his mother says. "He never wavered from that. As soon as she was killed, he started right away, 'I'm gonna be a cop, I'm gonna be a cop.'"

It may be that Jeremy Colhouer needed to be a cop as badly as he needed healing. The two had a lot to do with each other.

•

The kingdom of his childhood was the spacious sky-blue house at 70 Wayne Way. His father built it on a cul-de-sac in upscale Lake Padgett Estates, on a drowsy block of neat lawns and tidy sidewalks, a street untraveled by random evil.

At the lake out back, the kids played, Jennifer teaching Jeremy to swim, the two bounding down to the water with inner tubes and fishing poles and bread for the ducks. She called him Boo Bear.

A freshman at Land O' Lakes High School, Jennifer copied Bible verses in her journal and lectured her friends about keeping their virginity. She wanted to make a career of giving advice, as a counselor, and had just gotten her braces off, in time for the Sadie Hawkins dance.

A stranger passing through in a red Corvette caught Jennifer alone in the house after school and chased her upstairs to her little brother's bedroom. There she was raped and strangled. The killer grabbed an eleven-inch stainless steel knife from the kitchen and opened her from sternum to stomach.

That evening, she was supposed to babysit three-year-old sister Megan while Dad, Tom Colhouer, took Jeremy to soccer practice. About 6:15, Jeremy discovered his sister upstairs, among the scattered Christmas toys he'd unwrapped the month before.

The family never slept in that house again. In his nightmares, Jeremy kept returning to his childhood room. Awake, he went back only once.

Months later, his mother pulled him, crying, back up the

steps. His room had been stripped bare, carpet sliced out and furniture hauled away, toys bagged as evidence.

Cheryl Colhouer sat her son down, in a spot where light from the window fell onto him, and tried to heal his memory.

"I felt the only thing I could do was take him back in that room with it all cleared up, and maybe somehow we could change the thing in his head. I was trying to replace the one scene with the other one."

Jeremy offered to pay for Jennifer's funeral from his piggy bank. At school, for no reason other than that they could, kids taunted him: I'm glad it was your sister, not mine.

"I never in a million years thought he'd be normal," Cheryl says. "He was glued to me, almost like he was part of me."

Outside therapy, outside the family, Jeremy learned to keep what he had seen to himself. Teachers at Lake Myrtle Elementary School, including Laurie Howard, saw a freckled boy, always smiling, not much changed. "By fifth grade, I really couldn't tell anything had happened to him."

His mother saw someone else: The boy who came home from junior high to find that the house alarm wasn't working and, rather than go inside, waited nervously in the garage, for hours, until his parents came home. The eighth grader who, assigned to write about the worst day of his life, described the time he returned from a hunting trip without a deer.

Beset by dyslexia that made written tests difficult, Jeremy figured he wasn't built for college. Working as a bag boy at Winn-Dixie and behind the parts counter at an auto shop, he dreamed of the police academy, of foot chases and arrests and the heft of a gun belt.

Without knowing it, two Pasco sheriff's detectives had nudged him in that direction.

•

Gary Fairbanks and his partner, Fay Wilber, devoted months to trying to put a name to the pinched face glaring from the composite sketch. The detectives kept the Colhouer family abreast of leads.

They told them about Windy Gallagher, a sixteen-year-old nearly 1,000 miles away, in Griffith, Indiana, who had been raped and cut open three months before Jennifer. In the specifics of the savagery, they read the same killer's hand.

Six months after Jennifer's death, the detectives knocked on the door again. They had another name: Michael Lee Lockhart, a twenty-seven-year-old drifter captured in Beaumont, Texas, after he murdered a police officer.

Lockhart drove a red Corvette, and Officer Paul Hulsey Jr., pegging him as a drug dealer, followed the car to a motel. There Lockhart put a slug through the plates of Hulsey's bulletproof vest.

Lockhart had been in jail about four months when Fairbanks came across his picture in a police newsletter and placed it beside the composite. He saw the same man.

Cheryl finally could tell her son, They know who hurt your sister. But the boy's brain was crazy with questions: Do we know him? Can he get to me now? Can he get to us? No, she answered, he is locked up, "in Texas, away, away."

As Lockhart waged a legal war for nearly a decade, the Colhouers and the detectives grew close. "You try not to get too involved with a family" in a homicide case, says Wilber, whose family spent a Christmas with the Colhouers. "I guess they were different, because they're a damn good family."

Wilber says he gave them the composite sketches of the still-uncaught killer for Jeremy to shoot at, as therapy.

To a frightened little boy, Fairbanks and Wilber were more than the men who helped bring his sister's killer to justice. Against the fear that was drowning him, their presence was a lifeline.

"They were there, keeping things safe," Jeremy says. "Me and my mom talked about it. I probably felt that if I was a cop, I'd be able to protect my family and the people around me."

Jonathan Michaelis, a psychologist and expert in childhood trauma, says it's natural for a child who grows up with a real-life bogeyman to be drawn to the strength a police officer represents.

Comic book heroes are invincible. They wield the talismans that banish evil, the powers that whittle nightmares down to size. They are other people's safety. To a kid, here in the real world, a man who wears a five-pointed star might be the closest thing.

●

December 9, 1997. Mom, Dad, Jeremy, and Megan fly from Tampa to Texas, rent a car, and check in to a hotel near the state prison in Huntsville. Michael Lee Lockhart's legal saga is about to end at the point of a needle.

Jeremy Colhouer is eighteen. He desperately wants to witness the execution, to stand at his father's side and watch point-blank as the syringe sinks home, eyeball confirmation that his childhood ogre has been blasted off the earth. And something else: balance, symmetry. Witness a second death, payment for the first. "I saw my sister on the floor of my room. So this would be equal."

But at the prison, Jeremy learns that there isn't enough space in the witness room. Only his father will get to watch. Jeremy has to wait in another room with his mother and younger sister, with Wilber and Fairbanks, with families of Lockhart's other victims. Some cheer when word comes that Lockhart is gone. Jeremy's eyes pool with tears.

Flying home the next day, he seethes at being shut out. "He took that very hard," Cheryl says. "He said it's like he's not really dead."

Eight years earlier, on the day a Pasco jury said Lockhart should die for murdering Jennifer, Cheryl had faced him in a holding cell and asked, Why did you pick my daughter?

Just chance, Lockhart told her. He spotted Jennifer outside the house and posed as a real estate agent needing to use the phone; she invited him inside.

Cheryl didn't believe it—she had taught her daughter better than to let a stranger in the house—and considered the serial killer's story just one more cruelty. Yet with time, she came to forgive him. Let the anger own you, she says, and he wins again.

Jeremy recites his mother's lessons well: "He's winning if I tell him how angry I am. Then he's winning the situation." But forgiveness? That's where mother and son part ways.

"It won't happen for me. There's no forgiveness. After that, I don't think so."

Yet part of healing, part of what he learned growing up and in years of counseling, was that the role Lockhart forced upon him—the brother of a slain sister—need not define him.

"This had an effect on me, but it's not an image of me. It's not what I'm about. I should be judged by what I am, and not what happened to me."

•

December 11, 1998. Ceremonies are held for the twenty-three graduates of Police Academy Class 44 at Pasco-Hernando Community College. Jeremy Colhouer had not missed a day of the 672-hour training. When he crosses the stage for the handshake, his family screams.

His mom gives him a gift, a mug with little painted handcuffs. It reads: OFFICER COLHOUER.

At his swearing-in last June, Cheryl pins the sheriff's silver five-pointed star to her son's chest. She cries. Fairbanks and Wilber congratulate the beaming deputy, his shoulders now as tall as theirs.

They say they weren't aware how Jeremy regarded them all these years; they were just doing their duty. Fairbanks is now a major in administrative services, so Deputy Colhouer, on the road on the midnight shift, doesn't run into him much. Wilber, a lieutenant, supervises the rookie's platoon and makes sure no one has reason to believe he gets special treatment.

Deputy Colhouer wouldn't have it any other way. "He's my lieutenant, I'm a deputy, that's pretty much the way it is. I'm supposed to do what everybody else does."

The uniform goes on easily now; the gun belt feels more like a part of him.

People look at him differently when he wears it. It's not just the added weight on his five-foot-nine, 165-pound frame, the Kevlar shield that swells out the chest making him look bigger and older.

Jeremy Colhouer knows there are other ways the uniform transforms its wearer.

Not long ago, he was a teenager who liked action flicks, girls, and Ybor City, the speed and flash of his yellow Mustang. He's pretty much the same now, except in cop gear he's never invisible. Drive down the street, people stare. Walk into a store, people stare. He is Authority. He is other people's safety.

"You put on this vest and this big gun belt, and you walk into any building you want and it's amazing how people come to you for the answers."

His mother cried the first day he drove solo. She pictured him searching dark buildings, standing over a body.

"It scares me, of course, because I've already lost one child, and I do worry. But I'm a real bottom-line-type person, and the bottom line for me is, if he does die, then he's died doing something he loves."

Jeremy still lives with Mom, Dad, and Megan—now fifteen— in a roomy house in Land O' Lakes, only a few miles from Lake Padgett Estates. Coming home after the midnight shift, Jeremy always makes sure the front door is bolted. Not long ago, he found it unlocked and woke his parents at 4:00 a.m., demanding an explanation, irritated when all they could say, apologetically, was, We must have forgotten.

Like their old place on Wayne Way, the Colhouers' new home is a picture of suburban security, on a drowsy block of neat lawns and tidy sidewalks.

Except this time, visible from one end of the block to the other, there's a shiny green and white car parked in their driveway, with a big gold shield and the word SHERIFF on the side. Says Jeremy: "Anyone in their right mind wouldn't mess with a house with a police car at it."

It's a message he's been looking for a way to send since he was eight years old:

This family is protected.

BORDER WARRIOR

He senses them out there in the dark, making their moves, trying to outsmart him. He's planted on a hill in the cab of his mud-splattered, jacked-up truck, a greenish 1976 Silverado with roof-mounted motion sensors, holes in the floorboard, and a *Don't Tread on Me* sticker in the window. From the cab, he studies the valley below with night-vision goggles, Ruger revolver strapped to his ribs.

"I own the night, brother," says Max Kennedy, a lanky, sunburned man with a scraggly goatee and a voice like a fistful of desert gravel. In his fifty-three years, he says, he has driven a cab in Miami and ferried fur coats in New York, peddled marijuana and jewelry, played bass in a punk bank, and marched with 1960s radicals. He has been a Gingrich Republican and a pagan, a seeker of meaning in the Kabbalah and the sayings of Chairman Mao.

In his latest incarnation, he's a Minuteman staking out a small stretch of the US-Mexico border in the beautiful, inhospitable mountains of southeast San Diego County. Untethered to job or family, he's one of three or four hard-core members who camp out here full-time, trying to catch illegal immigrants as they cross.

But after fourteen months living "in exile from the United States," he might be the most ambivalent of border warriors. His relations with other Minutemen are uneasy, his faith in the mission fraying, his sense of the migrants' desperation increasingly keen. Plus, the desert has its privations. He misses women and chicken cutlets and good conversation.

"Emotionally, I'm burnt," he says. "My human side is beaten down."

Tonight, the desert is still and quiet. Scanning with goggles, he finds no sign of migrants hunkered in the cold, hilly brush, nor of the coyotes who smuggle them ingeniously through the thickets. But it's just 8:30 p.m., and Kennedy can wait all night. He has cigarettes to keep him calm, Coke to keep him alert, and a full belly. Earlier, he heated a dinner of chicken, mashed potatoes, and canned peas on his propane stove, eating alone in the truck's back seat, his plate on his lap.

He worked in the 1970s and '80s as an electronics technician, he says, but his job got sent overseas. That infuriated him. A couple of years ago he lost his job at a gas station in Cape Cod, Massachusetts, when the company changed hands, and he got angrier still. A lot of his friends were out of work too. He did not know what to do with his fury at President Bush, who struck him as the man to blame. Illegal immigrants were taking jobs from America's poor, he felt, and Bush was letting it happen—just as, he believed, the president let Hurricane Katrina wipe out the poor of New Orleans.

•

He soon found an idol in Jim Gilchrist, the retired Orange County accountant who cofounded the Minuteman Project citizen patrol. So he gave up his apartment in Cape Cod, crossed the country in a Greyhound, and in March 2006 joined the volunteer border watchers Bush has derided as "vigilantes."

The Minutemen gave him the old truck, which became both his bed and patrol vehicle. The job was simple—spot illegal crossers and let the Border Patrol sweep them up—but the terrain was hard. He learned how to navigate the network of steep, nameless, unpaved roads in the hills above Campo, to use the radio towers as lookout points and location markers.

The work combined a sandlot war game with angry idealism—an action-movie fantasy for a man who says he was kept out of the Army by phlebitis, a vein condition. He strapped on the gun for snakes and drug dealers, though he says he has never used it.

"I'm like the Rambo guy," explains Kennedy, who wears cotton work gloves with the fingers cut off. "I been livin' for this my whole life, looking forward to that Mad Max experience, and I found it."

For a while, he felt he'd discovered a sense of brotherhood and purpose, even if it meant sleeping in a cold truck and showering from a rubber bag. For a while, he felt history swirling out here amid the border dust.

Now, Kennedy can barely mention Gilchrist's name without wanting to scream. This year, Gilchrist's board of directors rebelled, alleging that thousands of dollars in Minuteman funds were missing. Gilchrist denied wrongdoing, but Kennedy now believes him a greedy, glory-hungry "poseur," more a politician than a man willing to log hard hours at the border.

The Minuteman Project, which split in two soon after it won national attention in 2005, fractured further. There are now hundreds of loosely affiliated cells nationwide, and the men who haunt the Campo border are a quarrelsome group. Unlike Kennedy, who scrabbles by on a few hundred dollars in donations a month, most others live on pensions, social security, or military benefits.

Home base is a patch of private land called Minuteman Village, just a dusty clearing with a few campers and old vehicles scattered around a big oak.

The titular head of the Campo Minutemen is Britt "Kingfish" Craig, fifty-eight, a one-eyed Vietnam vet from Orange County who continues to support Gilchrist, which made Kennedy quit his group in disgust and declare himself an "independent." For his part, Kingfish accuses Kennedy of "panhandling" to finance his border work, and says, "There's a tension with him, because he can't really afford to do it."

Another fixture is Howard "Ridgerunner" Smith, a fifty-six-year-old retired plumber from Simi Valley, a shaggy-haired former peacenik who doesn't talk much and keeps a Confederate flag in his camper's cracked, duct-taped window.

There's also a guy who calls himself CzechStan, a portly sixty-three-year-old widower and retired electrician who sleeps in a camper in Minuteman Village. Kennedy likes him but bickers with him constantly.

And there's Little Dog, a mysterious loner who lives on a solitary hill, a man others describe—even by the border's generous standards—as ornery, possibly crazy, and best avoided.

Once in a while Kennedy sees Gadget, a boisterous sixty-four-year-old former fireman who has camouflaged his perfectly nice Toyota Echo by spray-gluing on leafy branches and sand. Gadget, who goes home to San Diego after patrols, says, "I try to get my family out here, and they say, 'Tiger Woods tees off at 11,' 'The Chargers kick off at 12.'"

Most of the time, Kennedy says, he's alone out here. Apart from a zeal for tighter borders, he shares little philosophically with his confederates. A lot of Minutemen lean toward Republicanism and Christianity. Kennedy leans toward Buddhism and socialism, and still keeps Mao's Little Red Book in his dashboard.

"I'm the most isolated guy," Kennedy says.

•

Tonight, the moon is brilliant and nearly full. He can exploit the extra visibility. Proud of his prowess, he bows to no Minuteman on the border.

"I'm the best, brother," he says. "I won't deny it. You know why? I've got the wounds, inside and out. I been hit by bottles, rocks. I got calluses. I got sand in my lungs."

Covered with big granite boulders and a thick carpet of sage and cactus, with peaks that rise to 4,500 feet, the harsh and isolated terrain around Campo is easy to get lost in, easy to hide in. For maximum stealth, he's disconnected his brake lights.

A high school dropout from a poor Brooklyn neighborhood, Kennedy is a fount of fierce opinion who calls himself "the ghetto Mensa." His patter drifts from the greatness of Alexander Hamilton to the sexual practices of the ancient Egyptians to the appalling apathy of a society obsessed with *American Idol*—all those millions "sitting there on their couches, burping out low-fat KFC" while guys like him defend the border.

He never married, and although he has two kids, he knows little about them, which he calls "one of the biggest heartbreaks I have," a loneliness especially sharp around the holidays. He believes he might have made a mark on the world had affirmative action not thwarted his chances.

At 9:40 p.m., Kennedy is bumping through the dark mountains in his four-wheel-drive, navigating a network of steep, unlit dirt roads. Ahead, he spots an empty water bottle lying on its side at the edge of the road. He rolls to a stop and climbs out to inspect it. The bottle, which glows in the moonlight, is labeled *Ciel Purificada*. Coyotes fill these bottles with sand to pour over their clients' footprints.

But he thinks this one serves a different purpose: a directional arrow, a makeshift reflector. Kennedy has found many such ingenious markers—strings of cassette tape tied between bushes to catch the moonlight, bits of glass scattered like fairy-tale bread crumbs.

The bottle, he notices, has been arranged diagonally, pointing across the road to a spot where the brush slopes into a valley. He follows the pointer, crouches before a low bush with his flashlight and finds a small piece of white tape knotted around a branch: another marker. With it, he finds a footprint and a broken twig.

"That's his foot. The first guy has come through here. He's marked all this." Examining the print, he says, "That's a perfect fit, if I was a little short guy tying that tape."

A big pack of migrants is moving through tonight, he believes. He figures they will cross right here, dip into the gully, and climb out to safety on the roads beyond. If he positions himself on a nearby hill, he can catch them passing right beneath him.

•

And if he does? What then? He has come to doubt the Minuteman movement's practical relevance. Here he is with a bickering, ragtag cadre of men, patrolling a puny, nine-mile stretch of America's 2,000-mile southern border. Of every ten migrants he manages to spot, he says, eight will get away before the Border Patrol can reach the spot. The two who are captured just cross again.

He's not sure if he can blame them. In some ways, Kennedy, who ran away from home at fourteen and has been on his own ever since, says he feels a kinship with the migrants—more kinship, at least, than with many of the Minuteman Project's political and financial champions, the "Orange County Republican types."

"They have nice houses and they're rich, and they have no idea what other people live like," he says. "They kind of look down their nose at you."

In fact, he thinks of the migrants not as illegal immigrants but as economic refugees, and admires their cunning. But he figures someone has to stand up for all those Americans—the ones he's known his whole life—who can never seem to carve out more than a precarious toehold.

Running through the indefinable crazy quilt of his worldview is a belief in vast conspiracies—9/11 was orchestrated by US and Israeli intelligence, the moon landing was a hoax—and a conviction that forces of government and big business have their boot on humanity's neck.

So he'd like to strike a blow for the little guy, somehow. That, he says, explains why he's out here. But since he arrived, his sympathies have expanded in ways that surprised him. "Most of the people jumping the fence are pathetic," he says. "I see the poverty in their faces."

Off his truck rolls, rocking up and down, playing havoc with his bad back. He doesn't trust the medical establishment any more than he trusts the government and, even if he did, couldn't afford a doctor. "If I had $100, I look at that as ten days on the border, or half of a doctor's payment," he says. For his teeth, he visits a cheap dentist in Tecate, Mexico.

He survives on donations from the Huntington Beach–based California Coalition for Immigration Reform, getting by on as little as $150 a month, much of which goes for gas. There are few human voices to break the desert silence. On his little Grundig radio, he listens to audio of Fox News Channel in his truck. *The Simpsons* and *Family Guy* are highlights of his week, and he says he doesn't mind that he gets no picture.

"I'm not much on visual jokes," he says. "It's usually the lower IQ that gets visual jokes."

By 9:58 p.m. he's planted under Tower 139, where he figures he will be able to spot the migrants crossing right beneath him. He chain-smokes Skydancer cigarettes, which he gets tax-free at the local Indian casino. He keeps the lighted tips low, out of sight.

"They know Sunday night there's not much Border Patrol, so they think they got a free run," Kennedy says. He takes a swig of Coke. "It's like being a kid. It's hide-and-seek between me and the coyotes."

A voice comes on his walkie-talkie, which is jury-rigged with a piece of wiring to extend its range. The voice belongs to a new Minuteman on the border tonight who calls himself Northstar.

Kennedy hasn't met him and doesn't know whether to trust him. He might be a drug smuggler or a lunatic looking to bust some Mexican heads.

"We're down in La-something Canyon," Northstar says. "We got Mexican voices down in it."

"That's La Gloria Canyon. Let them go past. We're waiting for 'em," Kennedy says. "We found their path already. Hold your ground. Don't scare 'em too much."

Time ticks by. Overhead, power lines crackle. He waits, musing about some of the things he's seen. "It's usually the women who get caught, because they can't run like men can," he says. "And older people. They give up easier."

By 10:15 p.m., his hopes of catching the group have dwindled. He thinks coyotes have intercepted their radio transmissions, that other Minutemen, maybe this new guy Northstar, have killed the operation with excessive chatter. The migrants might be fleeing. He points into the dark eastward mountains. "They're probably heading that way."

Still, he waits. He scans the desert with his goggles. The desolation reminds him of dreams he used to have of nuclear annihilation. After the bombs fell, he sensed he would be one of the survivors. "This is like the postapocalyptic universe," he says. "It's a battlefield. Sometimes you can't think of a reason to go on."

He waits. Smokes. Scans. The temperature drops. He wants to participate in history. He wonders what it would have been like at Antietam or Gettysburg. He imagines he would feel right at home with Spartacus's army of rebel slaves.

"I know I should be somewhere else," he says, waiting for a sound, a flicker of movement, anything. "I just can't find that niche that I'll fall into perfectly."

A little after 11:00 p.m., a sound comes from the desert. "Cracklin' bushes, brother! Cracklin' bushes!" He seizes his night-vision goggles and scans. "Where are you? I definitely hear you." He puts his goggles down, disappointed. "Animal. Coyote. Four-legged."

By 11:30 p.m. it's clear that the operation is lost. The border-jumpers have evaded capture, at least for now—slipped into the east or back into Mexico. He turns the key in his truck and rolls down the hill. "It's really more of a protest than it is an operation," Kennedy says. "It's my only way to give Bush the finger."

•

At midnight he's keeping warm in CzechStan's camper in Minuteman Village. It's not long before Kennedy is railing about Gilchrist—just a politician living a comfortable Orange County life, he says, not a man you see at the border. And what about those missing funds?

CzechStan says that neither of them have seen the organization's books, so how can they judge?

"If you can't talk without screaming, you can't be leadership," he tells Kennedy.

"I don't want to be leadership."

"You get upset for nothing."

"Don't tell me what I know about my organization."

Soon, Kennedy is back in his truck, rolling out to another lookout. It's 1:00 a.m. He talks again about Alexander Hamilton, whom he considers a hero of freedom, and of Che Guevara, whom he considers a hero of the poor, and of the occupation of Iraq, which he considers a profit-driven assault on the world's powerless, and of his bone-deep, nearly uncontainable hatred of Bush. His brain teems with names, connections. He believes he can hold his own against a lot of college-educated types.

"And no one wants me!" he says.

He scans the desert. Nothing stirs.

Later that night, parked at Minuteman Village, he climbs into the back of his truck, unrolls a thin mattress over a rubber pad, and squeezes into a frayed nylon sleeping bag.

Sometimes, desert rats climb through the holes in his floorboard. The temperature has plunged nastily. He knows it will not deter the border crossers. He knows they will crouch in the cold mountains for hours, watching for their chance.

He pulls his sleeping bag up to his chest, leaving it unzipped despite the chill. He wants his arms free, in case he has to grope for the Ruger he keeps loaded on the wheel well.

Of late, he's been thinking of a change. Maybe going east. Maybe joining the antiwar movement. Maybe finding something else on the border. He has skills—electronics, mountaineering, survival. He's heard about a volunteer group called the Border Angels. They are vocal opponents of the Minutemen. They are the enemy. They supply water to immigrants who risk their lives in crossing. He wonders if they can use a man like him.

DIRTY JOHN

PART ONE: THE REAL THING

Their first date was at Houston's, a restaurant in Irvine, where he opened the door for her and put her napkin on her lap. Candles flickered along the polished-mahogany bar; jazz drifted from speakers; conversation purred.

Debra Newell had taken pains to look good. Her cornsilk-blond hair fell in waves over her shoulders. High black Gucci heels, designer jeans, Chanel bag. At fifty-nine, married and divorced four times, she had begun to worry that she was too old for another chance at love. Her four kids were grown, she ran a flourishing interior design firm, and she was looking for a man to share her success with.

Her date was fifty-five, six feet two, with hard-jawed good looks and a gym-sculpted frame. He looked a little weathered, and he dressed lazily—shorts and an ill-matching preppy shirt—but he might have once been an all-American quarterback on a trading card.

His name was John Meehan. He had thick, dark hair and a warm, friendly smile that invited trust. His eyes were hazel-green, with the quality of canceling out the whole of the world that wasn't her, their current focus.

It was October 2014. They had found each other on an over-fifty dating site, and she thought his profile—Christian, divorced, physician—seemed safe. She had been on three other recent dates, but the men were less handsome than their profile photos, and the talk was dull.

John was different. He showed keen interest in the details of her life and business. He didn't want to talk just about himself, even though his stories were riveting. He told her all about being an anesthesiologist in Iraq, where he'd just spent a year with Doctors Without Borders.

He said he had a couple of kids. That he owned houses in Newport Beach and Palm Springs. That he happened to worship at her church, Mariners. That he would love to meet her grandkids.

And he told her that she stopped his heart, she was so beautiful. She was just his type. Her last serious boyfriend had wounded her, in parting, when he said she wasn't.

John began caressing her back. She thought this was moving a little fast, but she decided to allow it. The intensity of his attention was flattering.

She brought John back to her penthouse, just up the block. They kissed. He wanted it to go further. "This feels incredible," he said, stretching out on her bed.

She thought, It's just a mattress.

She became uncomfortable. It turned into a fight. He just didn't want to leave, and she had to insist.

She went to bed thinking, Jerk.

She thought, Cross off another one.

•

The next day she was back at her office, a little sad, trying to lose herself in work. Over the thirty years that she had built Ambrosia Interior Design, it had been her refuge amid many romantic disappointments. Work was the realm in which her success was unqualified.

She designed model homes and clubhouses. She liked to hire single women and mothers because she could remember how it felt to be alone, with one child and another on the way, after her first marriage broke up.

When people walked into one of her exquisitely arranged rooms, they were invited to imagine their futures in them. She called them "approachable dreams." They were like glossy ads in upscale lifestyle magazines—purged of kids' toys and dirty dishes and other real-world complications.

In her big Irvine warehouse, among the vases and mirrors and other decorative bric-a-brac, stood shelves of color-coordinated hardback books—aqua, navy, gray, brown—because books made nice furniture in perfect homes. She hunted at weekend library sales. The titles didn't matter, as long as they omitted the words "sex" and "death."

Her perfect rooms were like the face you presented on dates, inviting people to fantasize about the piece that may complete their lives. If your eagerness or loneliness or desperation showed too soon, you were done. Maybe that had been John's mistake.

That day he called to say he was sorry. He knew he'd overstepped. He just wanted to spend every minute with her.

•

By the second or third date, he was telling her he loved her, that he wanted to marry her. She didn't mind his idiosyncrasies, like his habit of wearing his faded blue medical scrubs everywhere, even to a formal-dress cancer benefit she invited him to. Some people snickered, but she thought, Busy doctor.

"So you are the real thing," she texted him after one date.

"Best thing that will ever happen to you," he replied.

He began spending the night regularly at her Irvine penthouse. Her twenty-four-year-old daughter, Jacquelyn, who lived there with her, made it clear she thought he looked like a loser. Maybe even homeless.

She said she didn't like the way his eyes roamed around the place, among their velvet chairs and jewelry and fine art. Or the way he seemed so curious about the contents of her safe, where she kept her collection of Birkin and Cartier bags. Get this creep out of here, she told her mom.

Jacquelyn's reaction didn't shock Debra, since her taste in

men often exasperated her children. She thought they'd find something bad to say about anyone she dated. Her friends sometimes joked about her being a "bad picker." Where other people saw red flags, she saw a parade.

•

Soon Debra and John were quietly looking for a place together. They found a $6,500-a-month house on the boardwalk on Balboa Island in Newport Beach. She put down a year in advance. He didn't want his name on the lease. Tax problems, he said. They'd known each other five weeks.

Debra wasn't about to tell her kids that John would be moving in with her. She knew what they'd say—that she was moving too fast, acting with her heart, repeating old mistakes.

What her kids didn't see was how well he treated her. How he brought her coffee in the morning. Got her groceries. Took her Tesla and Range Rover in for maintenance. Carried her purse.

She was convinced that her kids would understand how wonderful he was once they got to know him. She thought that if any of her kids would give him a chance, it was Terra, her youngest.

•

The family's quietest, most docile member liked to daydream about the end of the world.

At twenty-three, Terra watched and rewatched every episode of *The Walking Dead*. She spoke of the series less as entertainment than as a primer on how to survive apocalyptic calamity.

She made careful note of why some characters lived and others perished. It had to do with vigilance and quick reflexes and the will to fight. "The world ends," she would say, "and those who are fit to survive will survive."

She was as nonconfrontational as her sister Jacquelyn was assertive. The first word people used to describe her was "sweet."

She was living in Las Vegas with her boyfriend, Jimmy, and studying to be a dog groomer. She knew her mom liked to take care of people, and that she saw the best in men, at times against all evidence. Sometimes they pretended to be sincere church-going Christians. Terra had seen her scared, screamed at, hit, taken for money.

She felt protective of her mom and wondered why a guy who sounded as good as John would still be single. Her skepticism only deepened when she and Jimmy drove out to Southern California and met him.

•

John towered over her by a full foot, and a coldness came off him. He barely made eye contact. He cut her questions short. As he helped Debra move into her new house, he huffed and strained and wrestled her queen mattress down the stairs single-handedly, a show of ludicrous machismo.

Terra's three dogs seemed anxious around John. She thought maybe they were picking up on her own unease.

She brooded on some questions. What kind of doctor had no car? Why had no one seen John's houses in Newport Beach and Palm Springs? Why did he seem to spend all day playing *Call of Duty* on the seventy-inch plasma TV her mom had bought?

•

Terra and her boyfriend moved into the spare bedroom of the new Balboa Island rental for a few days. This made it hard for Debra to maintain the illusion that John wasn't really living there, though she tried.

Terra discovered the truth the day before Thanksgiving, when she opened a closet and found a nursing certificate bearing John's name. Her mom said she was getting his certificates framed, but Terra knew, and she did something uncharacteristic. She confronted her loudly.

Here came John, instantly transformed by rage. Why was Terra snooping through his stuff? Why was she trying to steal Debra from him? Did she realize that kids should be smacked for this?

Terra screamed at her mother: "How could you let this guy talk to me like this?!"

Terra left, badly shaken, with the sickening feeling that her mother was choosing John over her.

•

"They're jealous."

That was John's explanation for her kids' hostility to him. They didn't want her to be happy. They just wanted her dead, so they could collect.

He had an explanation for why he had a nursing degree but called himself a doctor. He said he had a PhD, which earned him the title, plus advanced training in anesthesiology.

253

At the big Thanksgiving party the next day, it was impossible to ignore the sudden fissures in the family—impossible to ignore Terra's absence. But others were willing to give John a chance.

Debra's mother, Arlane, thought he dressed tackily, especially for Thanksgiving. But she made allowances for a busy professional. And he was so nice and courteous. "I think he's a great guy," she told Debra.

When Jacquelyn showed up, John asked for a private word with her. She announced that he was the devil, that anything he had to say he could say in public.

•

To John, this was more evidence that Debra's kids were spoiled and out of control. His words tugged at her anxieties.

She wanted a professional's objective advice. She found a therapist, who assessed the family dynamics and told Debra she needed to establish firmer boundaries with her children.

If they wanted to come over, they had to be invited. They couldn't yell at her. They couldn't try to run her life.

They couldn't sabotage her happiness—she had a right to it, just like anybody else. If John was the man she had chosen, it was her business.

"Absolutely," John said.

•

Their house on the boardwalk had floor-to-ceiling windows, and from the rooftop deck they could watch the sailboats and the great yachts slide over Newport Harbor. Water lapped against a ribbon of sand yards from their front door, and they could hear the tall, wind-rustled palms and the muted creaking of the boat docks.

They were living inside a postcard. They walked the island hand in hand. He doted on passing babies and dogs. He liked to play-wrestle her grandkids. He acted like a kid himself, vulnerable and sweet, and single-mindedly besotted with her.

He liked to pose shirtless and take selfies of his washboard abs. She smiled when he'd stop in front of a mirror and say, "Damn! I'm good-looking."

Wardrobe-wise, she thought he was kind of a mess, with his baggy pants and University of Arizona sweatshirts. He said his clothes had been stolen while he was in Iraq.

"Dress me," he told her. "I want to please you."

She took him to Brooks Brothers. She bought him shoes, dress shirts, slacks, a tweed sport coat, formfitting cashmere sweaters—deep burgundy, navy blue. He looked good in darker tones and pastels. It felt like having a new doll.

•

He kept begging her to marry him, and she kept resisting, until she couldn't. In early December, she was driving to Vegas on business, and he was tagging along. Why not drop by the courthouse?

The ceremony was in a plain room with a plant-covered trellis. He chuckled a little as he tried to get the ring on her finger.

They celebrated with lemon-drop martinis. They had known each other less than two months. No one had been invited to the wedding.

Debra would say, "I felt this was an opportunity to love again."

•

She kept it a secret as the weeks passed and Christmas approached. The family planned to have their traditional Christmas get-together at the Orange County home of Debra's eldest daughter, Nicole.

Jacquelyn refused to go. Terra was torn. She desperately wanted to spend the holiday with her little nieces and nephews, but she didn't even want to look at John.

Terra went to a therapist with her mom. They came to an understanding that Terra and John would keep their distance during the party.

The day came, and John bustled in with his arms full of presents for the children—dozens of presents Debra had bought. The kids surrounded him. Terra began crying hysterically. It became a scene.

"You promised he wouldn't hang out with the kids," Terra told her mom.

Terra's grandmother found her in the family room, trembling and crying.

"I just want to leave," Terra said. "I don't like him. There's something about him."

•

Terra knew what people were thinking: "There she goes again, being overemotional." She was the youngest in the family, her parents split up when she was young, and she'd been looked after by nannies during the years her mom built her business.

She knew some people still thought of her as the little girl who needed attention. It was sometimes a fight to be taken seriously, and she would question the intensity of her own feelings.

In early 2015, Terra was back home in Vegas, with Jimmy and their dogs. Terra wasn't talking to her mom. She just hoped John would go away.

•

Back in Orange County, Jacquelyn was thinking about John's fingernails. They were dirty.

She had spent time around doctors, during the time she worked in sales for a plastic surgeon. Their nails were meticulously clipped and scrubbed.

Plus, the doctors she had known did not go everywhere in their scrubs, as John did. She thought he looked like a man wearing a costume.

Something else was wrong with John's scrubs: the bottoms were frayed around the heels as if they belonged to a medical-office receptionist who ran errands in tennis shoes.

Other things unsettled Jacquelyn, like the slangy, misspelled texts she received from her mom's number that were clearly not from her. And the way her mom kept calling to complain that money was missing from her wallet. Had Jacquelyn dropped by her office to borrow some?

Jacquelyn told her to think about the loser she was dating. She thought her mom, so nice and trusting and naive, had no idea who he was.

Jacquelyn bought a magnetic tracker and put it on her mother's Tesla to monitor John's movements when he left the house. He said he traveled between clinics and operating rooms, doing anesthesiology work as needed, but who knew? Debra would not remember agreeing to the tracker, but Jacquelyn insisted she asked.

From her iPhone, Jacquelyn began studying the strange routes he took around Southern California, looking for patterns and clues. He went to doctors' offices in Irvine and Mission Viejo and San Diego, a warehouse, a post office, fast-food joints, Tesla charging portals.

Jacquelyn knew she had to be careful about what she told her mom—it could get back to John. She didn't want to be dismissed as a meddler. And none of what she found was necessarily incompatible with his story. These were fragments of a puzzle.

When she told Terra what she was doing, Terra asked, "What if he hurts her?"

•

In Debra Newell's family, the question carried a freight of unspoken dread, because the worst had happened before.

In 1984, her older sister, Cindi, had been trying to escape a husband she described as controlling and possessive. One day he pressed a handgun against the back of her neck and pulled the trigger.

It was the reason Debra hated firearms. It was the reason she refused to have one around, long after people began warning her that she needed one.

PART TWO: NEWLYWEDS

After church one Sunday, Debra Newell walked into the living room with her husband to find a woman she did not recognize.

The stranger sat trancelike before the big window that overlooked Newport Harbor, a thin, weathered woman in her late thirties or early forties. She had just used the shower; her curly blond hair was wet. She was dressed all in white; she had taken Debra's clothes.

She held a tiny Bible and sipped Ovaltine. She acted like she belonged there, though she wouldn't meet their eyes.

John pushed her head onto the countertop and pulled her arms behind her back. He ordered Debra to leave the house and call the police. Debra didn't want to press charges. She figured the woman was homeless, maybe a drug addict, and had climbed in through the third-floor skylight.

John denied knowing her, but Debra wondered. Had he said something to the woman before police took her away? Had he warned her not to reveal their connection? Had she been to the house before, and learned of its unlocked entrance?

John announced they needed to ramp up security. Even in a $6,500-a-month bayfront rental they couldn't be too careful about drifters. Soon the home bristled with cameras that he monitored on his smartphone. He also insisted on cameras at the Irvine office of her interior design firm. He just wanted her to be safe.

Is he watching me? Debra wondered.

And she thought: I can watch him, too.

•

She didn't know where he went all day, when he kissed her goodbye and disappeared in her Tesla. He never brought home a paycheck, but that was easily explained—as a freelance anesthesiologist who traveled between operating rooms, he was paid in cash by the uninsured.

One day, she pulled up the security footage and saw that John wasn't going off to work like he said. She watched him leave the house in his blue scrubs, return a little later, climb into bed, and go to sleep.

She debated whether to confront him. He could become so volatile when challenged, as he had with her children.

She decided to ask, but not in an accusatory tone that might upset him. Gently.

"The patient failed a treadmill test and they had to cancel the surgery," John explained instantly, nonchalance itself.

She didn't press him any further. Questions might puncture the dream.

•

Debra knew so little about her husband, beyond the way he made her feel. At fifty-nine, she'd never been happier with a man.

He ran her errands, the way her assistants usually did. Made sure her bills were paid. Sat beside her at doctors' appointments. Brought her bouquets of peonies, her favorite flower. Held her all night, breathing against her neck, his weight lifter's body draped over hers.

She wondered about the scars that crossed his abdomen and back, legs and ankles. He said he'd been in a chopper crash as a medic in the war zones of the Middle East, just before meeting her. He praised the accuracy of *American Sniper*, the film about a sharpshooter in Iraq.

During his time in the desert, he said, he had learned something about himself. Five or six times, he'd had to kill. It was easy, if you had to.

Ruthlessness was in his genes, he explained. He bragged that he was a blood relation of the notorious Mafia hit man who once ran Murder Inc. He didn't show a violent side himself, except the time he grabbed the shirt of a homeless guy who said something rude to Debra on a Seattle street. John screamed in his face, and Debra had to pull him away.

He told her she made him a better man. They attended Mariners, an evangelical megachurch in Irvine, with modern worship music, keyboards, and guitars. John always seemed excited to go.

He said he'd attended the church before he met her, though once he slipped up and called the pastor a priest. She thought it was because he'd been raised Catholic.

She watched him inject testosterone. He said this was for his kidneys. She watched him pop OxyContin. He said this was for his bad back.

Debra had been telling her nephew, Shad Vickers, all about the handsome doctor who seemed to live only for her, and when Shad met him he thought, A good, fun guy. He was impressed with John's confidence and tales of battlefield derring-do. Most of all, he was glad to see his aunt happy. She'd been looking for so long.

Shad and Debra had always been close. For years he had thought of her as a second mother. Their bond was forged by a shared experience of unhealable horror. When Shad was a boy in 1984, as his parents were splitting up, his father shot his mother to death and went to prison. The victim was Cindi, Debra's older sister.

Debra treated Shad like one of her own kids. She brought him on family vacations. She paid for his football and track leagues, which gave the traumatized boy some focus and release. She gave him a job in her furniture warehouse. She stuck with him during the years his rage and confusion were at their worst, during the brawls and scrapes with the law.

Now he was a single father in his forties with three daughters, gregarious and sweet-tempered, with a job at a trucking company, and he loved his aunt and hoped John would make her happy. Shad brought his kids over to the beachfront house, and John was great with them.

Shad knew some people in the family disliked John—Debra's daughter Jacquelyn had sized him up as a con man and been especially vocal in her contempt—but he was willing to give him a chance. He tried not to judge people too soon.

He did have some questions. Like why had he come into Debra's life with only a few old clothes? Why did he play video games all day long? Did doctors really jump out of helicopters with machine guns?

Then John said something that didn't sit right. It was at Debra's place in late February 2015, and John was making margaritas in the kitchen when Jacquelyn's name came up.

"I could take her out from a thousand yards," John said, and Shad would recall that Debra laughed, not taking it seriously.

Shad thought it wasn't a thing to joke about, even if you'd been to a war zone and had a war zone sense of humor. It seemed kind of sick, actually.

He began to fear for his aunt. So when he got word that some of Debra's kids had hired a private investigator to look into John's past—when he learned that a preliminary report had come back—he wanted to know everything.

He studied the report. John had a bankruptcy. A nursing license, not a doctor's license. Addresses in Arizona, Ohio, Indiana, Tennessee, and across California, including a recent one at a trailer park in the desert of Riverside County.

His curiosity gnawing at him, Shad called the trailer park. A woman answered. Shad thought up a lie, saying his mother had married John Meehan, and could she tell him anything about him? The woman said John had lived there. They'd had a relationship. He had disappeared. She hung up.

There was another address linked to John Meehan: 550 North Flower Street in Santa Ana. The Orange County jail.

●

Shad wanted to warn Debra without telling her too much. What if he was wrong? What if the man in the report was a different John Meehan?

In early March 2015, Shad called Debra and reminded her that he'd lost his mom, and he didn't want to lose her too. He said, "What if he isn't who he says he is? What if he isn't an anesthesiologist? What if I could prove to you he was in jail, and not Iraq?"

Her response would stay in his memory: "Even if it was true, I wouldn't care, because I love him."

And because she loved him, Debra relayed Shad's remarks right to John. And John decided that Shad was his enemy.

"Why don't you simply go away," John texted him. "You're not invited here. You come near and I call the cops. . . . Worry about your own miserable life and I'll worry about Debbie, who is a lot closer to me than you can ever imagine. You won't win this."

Shad replied: "You told my grandma and I that you are a doctor. Prove it. You told my grandma and I that you own two properties. Prove it. Once you prove those two, you are good in my book."

John: "I couldn't give a shit about being in your book."

Shad said he hoped his aunt would open her eyes and dump him.

John: "Boy, are you in for a big surprise."

Shad: "My mom is looking down on me making sure I don't give up on her sister and making sure I know her sister [knows] the truth about your lying ass."

John: "Good thing your mom ain't here. She'd be embarrassed."

Shad: "It's not a good thing. It's not good at all."

John: "You don't have an aunt anymore. Get it? . . . I ain't going nowhere and neither is she. Stay away from the house. Accidents do happen. Again, Deb wants nothing to do with you and if you were on fire I wouldn't piss on you to help you out."

Shad: "If I hear of you threatening my aunt or harming her, you will see me."

John: "Please show up. . . . And she ain't your aunt anymore. Just ask her."

John got a lot nastier. He insulted Shad's girlfriend and his little daughters.

John: "It isn't about me or what I've done. It's about you harassing her to the point where she fears for her life. . . . And by the way, we're married. That makes your threat my threat."

Shad: "I pray you're not married."

Now the whole family knew the secret.

Shad was a former football player, five feet ten, a burly 195 pounds. But John had four inches on Shad, and probably 25 pounds, and Shad had seen boxing gloves and a heavy punching bag in the garage. Shad thought John would be able to overpower him, if it came to that.

And there was a single-minded viciousness about John, a sense that he'd stop at nothing. For now, Shad decided to keep his distance.

•

The beginning of Debra's own disillusionment came in the mailbox, in the form of a letter from the county jail.

It was addressed to John, from a former jail mate saying hi. Debra tore it open and began reading, there in the walkway.

She stood there frozen for a minute or two, trying to make sense of it, and then she looked up. John was rushing toward her.

She realized that he had been watching her on camera—that maybe he'd been watching her more than she realized.

He snatched the letter out of her hand. She asked him what this meant. She told him she thought he'd been lying to her.

He demanded to know why she was looking at his mail. Didn't she know it was a felony?

John said his jailhouse correspondent was just a guy he was helping out—sending him care packages and a little money. He wouldn't admit he'd been in jail himself.

•

The next day, when John left on one of his mysterious errands, Debra walked into the home office they shared and began hunting. John was messy, and his papers were scattered everywhere.

Who exactly had she married?

The answer, she learned with apprehension that crept up on her and then came in a flood, lay in piles of documents he had made no effort to hide.

They told a story of a former nurse anesthetist who became hooked on surgical painkillers and lost his career. Of a con man who took nasty pleasure in the mechanics of a dark craft he had mastered, and who seemed obsessed with humiliating anyone who defied his will.

From 2005 to 2014—from about the time he got out of prison

in Michigan for drug theft to the time he met Debra Newell in California—he had seduced, swindled, and terrorized multiple women, many of whom he had met on dating sites while posing as a doctor, court records showed.

"You are my project for years to come," he wrote to a Porter Ranch woman after allegedly suggesting—in an anonymous letter—that he had raped her and taken photos while she was unconscious.

"This I promise. Do you think I joke? Every breath I take will be to ruin your surgically implanted life. Thanks for the pictures!" He described his planned campaign against her as "my masterpiece."

In another case, according to court records, a forty-eight-year-old Laguna Beach woman said she had been recovering from brain surgery at a San Diego hospital when she awoke to find Meehan standing over her bed. He said he was her anesthesiologist.

They dated. She said her family had millions. He suggested she transfer money into his account, to hide it from her estranged husband. She balked. He sent intimate photos of her to her family, and wrote: "You're in way over your head on this one. Make it happen and I walk away. If not, I will be your nightmare."

Police began investigating, and when they searched his Riverside County storage unit, they found a Colt .38 Special. Binoculars. GPS units. Ammunition. Heavy-duty cable ties. Syringes. A pocket saw. A bottle of cyanide powder. Eight cyanide capsules.

"A treacherous, cunning and very manipulative person who uses fear and intimidation as a means to control and coerce his victims," police called him.

As John Meehan awaited trial in the Orange County jail in late 2013, an inmate reported that he was offering $10,000 each for the murders of two Laguna Beach detectives, plus five other potential witnesses against him, including several ex-girlfriends and his ex-wife. His philosophy: "With no witnesses, there is no trial."

To the detectives, one of whom described him as "a ticking bomb, capable of unpredictable violence," the threat felt real enough to request a restraining order. But the jail informant refused to be a witness, no charges were filed for murder solicitation, and the restraining order was denied.

Meehan pleaded guilty in February 2014 to stalking the Laguna Beach woman and being a felon in possession of a firearm. He was out that summer, but jailed again for violating a restraining order against another woman he had threatened.

He walked out on October 8. He met Debra onlinc two days later. By the time they married in December 2014, three separate women around Southern California had standing restraining orders against him; in recent years, at least three others had requested them.

"He threatened to leak nude pictures of me if I did not give him money," wrote one woman.

"He was choking me, telling me if I tell the police anything else he'll kill me," wrote another.

"He told me once he was obsessed with me. And I am VERY afraid of him," wrote a third.

•

Debra thought, I am going to be killed like my sister.

She took Ativan for her nerves and called a lawyer, who told her to cut her husband out of her will, so he would derive no profit from murdering her.

She knew she needed to get out of the Balboa Island house, even if she lost $50,000 she'd paid on the yearlong lease. She had some time to maneuver, since John had gone to Hoag Hospital for back trouble and—because of vague complications that necessitated painkillers—had checked himself in.

Her family helped her pack. In John's possessions they found papers on which he'd scrawled gun names, codes, phone numbers, jail-inmate numbers, bank routing numbers.

He'd saved printouts from websites on which women posted warnings about scary and unfaithful men. Datingpsychos.com had devoted multiple pages to him:

He conned me out of money. . . . He is very persuasive. Emotionally needy . . . slick liar . . .

He grabbed me by the throat . . .

Do not let this man into your life . . .

Don't be fooled by his good looks and prince charming personality . . .

He is a parasite, a leech, an infection that festers on anyone he comes in contact with . . .

Trust your intuition, ladies. He is a pathologically rotten apple!

Stay away at all costs!

Classic psychopath . . .

PART THREE: FILTHY

He had lavished her with compliments, and now he savaged her looks. He had entered the marriage broke, and now he demanded half her wealth. He had been gentleness itself, and now he threatened her with "long-lost relatives" in the mob.

"Enough," Debra Newell texted him. "You are evil."

"Divide up the stuff and I never see you again," John Meehan texted back. "Your choice."

In March 2015, as Debra studied the paperwork detailing her husband's long record of women terrorized and laws broken, she learned that he had a nickname. It went back decades, to his brief time in law school at the University of Dayton.

Dirty John, classmates called him. Sometimes it was Filthy John Meehan, or just Filthy. But mostly Dirty John.

•

Ask John Meehan's sisters how he became the man who conned his way into Debra Newell's life—ask them where his story begins—and they point to their father.

Their Brooklyn-raised dad ran the Diamond Wheel Casino in

San Jose, and imparted to John a series of illicit skills, like how to pull off bogus lawsuits and insurance scams.

"How to lie," said one sister, Donna Meehan Stewart. "How to deceive."

Coupled with that was a cold-eyed ethos of leaving no slight unpunished. "If anybody did anything to John, my dad would tell us, 'You go there with a stick and take care of it,'" said Karen Douvillier, his other sister. "It's the Brooklyn mentality of you fight, you get even. If you want to get back at somebody, you don't get back at them, you get back at their family."

At Prospect High School in Saratoga, California, in the mid-1970s, John was a great-looking athlete, charismatic, a magnet for girls, an A student who swaggered with a sense of his superior intelligence. He learned that his gifts provided shortcuts.

"I think John thought he was smarter than everybody else, because everybody told him he was, but he had no common sense," Karen said. "He was taught to manipulate at a very early age.

"That's the fault of my parents, especially my dad. Because that's all my dad knew."

In family lore, the Meehans are related to Albert Anastasia, the 1950s-era New York mobster who ran Murder Inc. and was infamous for eliminating potential witnesses. Proof is elusive, but John enjoyed the dark glamour conferred by this supposed bloodline.

John Meehan's parents separated while he was in high school, and it was then, his sisters said, that rage and bitterness began to consume him. Mom had had an affair; Dad tried to win her back with violence; John became a child she'd had with a man she now loathed. He came to hate both parents.

John Meehan modeled himself after Sean Connery's James Bond, suave and beyond the law, and had a customized license plate that read "MEE 007." He liked the ladies, fast cars, and easy money. "He was a hustler," Karen said. "Whatever he had to do to get money, he would do."

To win legal settlements, he jumped in front of a Corvette and sprinkled broken glass in his Taco Bell order. Busted for selling cocaine, his sisters said, he testified against a friend and was forced to leave California as part of a plea deal.

He received a bachelor of arts degree from the University of Arizona in 1988, then moved east to attend the University of Dayton's law school that fall.

Kevin Horan, a classmate who lived with him in a house by the cemetery, said John did not stand out as a law student. He made an impression in other ways—for his laid-back, California-guy persona, and for the women he brought back to the house in unreasonable numbers.

His debauchery spawned the nickname Dirty John, though once bestowed it seemed to describe a lot of his behavior. Like the way he took money for roofing jobs he didn't complete. Like the way he rented his housemate a deathtrap truck with no brakes, and claimed not to know. Like the way he used fake names on the credit cards that filled the mailbox, a swindle he would boast about.

"He was basically this strange, lone-wolf guy that did all kinds of scandalous-type things, and it wasn't just with women," Horan said. "I'm like, 'That guy, you can't trust him for nothing. He's rotten top to bottom.'"

In the second year of law school, he disappeared. "Everyone's like, 'What happened to Dirty John?'" Horan said. They got an answer when his report card arrived. They held the envelope up to the light: Ds and Fs.

•

For his next con, John Meehan got married.

Tonia Sells, a nurse, was twenty-five. He was thirty-one, though he led her to believe he was twenty-six, just as he led her to believe his name was "Johnathan," not just John. He had shaved five years off his age and added five letters to his name.

"He would tell you story after story about, you know, that he just comes from this family that's just not him," Tonia said. "That he was able to escape them because other people stepped up into his life and helped make him a great person."

They were wed in November 1990 at St. Joseph Catholic Church in Dayton, her family church.

None of John's family had shown up, but he had an explanation: His dad was an alcoholic, his mom a pill-popper, and he didn't want them ruining the special day.

Tonia would keep a tape of the wedding that captured its strangeness. As the harpist plucked and the priest prayed, John sat in his tux fidgeting and smirking, like a boy in a grown-up's costume enjoying some fantastic private joke.

John was still wearing that glib, devil-may-care expression as his friend Phil gave a toast so brief and generic he might have just met him. It included the line, "If you talk to any of his friends, as far as the reaction to his wedding, you'll just find out they're completely shocked and baffled."

John's friends in attendance, some of them former law school classmates, had little to offer in the way of personal anecdote. There was a blank space where the stories should have been. The stories they did have weren't repeatable.

"Let me start by saying that John Meehan's, John Meehan's nickname is 'Filthy John Meehan,'" a guest said.

"Why? Why? Remember when you first heard that nickname?"

"Yes, I do, but it cannot be divulged on camera . . ."

After the wedding, watching this video, Tonia was surprised to learn the nickname of the man to whom she had just pledged her life. He laughed it off. It was nothing.

Tonia was a practicing nurse anesthetist, and John followed her into the profession.

They had two daughters, and she helped put him through nursing school at Wright State in Dayton and the Middle Tennessee School of Anesthesia.

He struck her as a playful father and a pleasant husband, and they rarely argued. He liked movies and playing basketball and dinner at home, and he studied a lot.

Ten years into the marriage—his degrees secure, his career launched—he wanted a divorce. Maybe, she thought later, her usefulness to him was over.

In July 2000, Tonia tracked down his mother, Dolores, a call John had always forbidden.

"I always knew you would call me," she said.

Dolores told her that John's real birthday was February 3, 1959. That his birth name was John, not Johnathan. That he had a drug charge in California.

For Tonia, it was hard to make sense of any of it. She had been enmeshed in a lie the whole time she had known him. She had had a normal upbringing in a good home, and had no yardstick with which to measure this.

"My first experience with evil," she called it.

Tonia searched the house they had shared in Springboro, Ohio, and found a hidden box containing the powerful surgical anesthetics Versed and fentanyl.

He had become hooked on drugs he was supposed to be giving patients; she knew there was no legitimate reason to have them. She felt guilty that she'd helped John get into her profession. She thought he was a danger to their kids and to patients. She informed police, who began an investigation. It was September 2000.

As suspicions of his drug theft circulated, John lost his job at Good Samaritan Hospital in Michigan and found work in Warsaw, Indiana, but fell under suspicion there too. He became convinced that Tonia had notified the state nursing board there, and she secretly recorded his increasingly menacing calls. He was furious that she had called his mother.

"Do you know why I have this big smile on my face?" he told her.

"Why, John?"

"Because, trust me, just trust me. That's why."

"Trust you what?"

"Just trust me."

"That doesn't make any sense."

"It don't have to. You'll understand it all."

"What, the Mafia's coming after me again? Or what?"

"When it happens, Tonia, and you see it in your eyes, remember it was me, OK?"

"Remember what, John?"

"Keep that in mind. It was me."

"Keep what in mind, John?"

He told her he would buy her a Cadillac if he was wrong. He wouldn't say what he might be wrong about.

"Tonia, you enjoy your time left on this earth, OK? Because that's what it's gonna come down to."

Tonia sounded relatively calm, as his remarks grew more frightening. Inside she was not.

"I got a big smile on my face," he said. "You know why? Because it's gonna get done."

"What's gonna get done? You're not making any sense."

"It don't have to. You will understand when the time comes. That's all I gotta say."

"Yeah, and who's gonna take care of your children?"

"I'll take care of them."

He told her he would be enjoying a Cuba Libre with a twenty-two-year-old when it happened—which she took to mean he would kill her or have her killed.

"If there's one thing that happens on this earth, it's gonna be you," he told her.

The court convicted him of menacing and gave him a suspended sentence.

•

Dennis Luken was an investigator with the drug task force of the Warren County Sheriff's Office in Ohio. He began looking into John Meehan in January 2002.

Hospital workers reported that they had seen Meehan bring a gun into the operating room and steal Demerol from a patient he pretended to medicate with it. Of all the criminals Luken studied, hunted, and arrested during a four-decade career in law enforcement, Meehan would occupy a singular place in his memory.

"The most devious, dangerous, deceptive person I ever met," Luken, now retired, would call him—a devil-tongued con man with the cold intelligence of a spy, a void where his soul should have been, and a desperate drug addiction that he would marshal his dark talents to feed.

Luken said he found emails showing John had sent drugs to his forty-four-year-old brother Daniel, who died of an overdose in Santa Cruz County in September 2000. He couldn't make a criminal case on that charge, but his investigation led to Meehan's guilty plea in 2002 to felony drug theft.

Meehan might still have salvaged his career. Instead of surrendering himself to begin a stint at an Ohio rehab clinic, he fled the state and stole an anesthesia kit. He checked into a Comfort Inn in Saginaw, Michigan, where police found him semiconscious, surrounded by drug vials.

The ambulance was rushing him to the hospital when he unbuckled his restraints, grabbed the drug kit, and jumped into the road. He fled into a nearby JCPenney, scrambled atop a cargo elevator and into the shaft, and kicked a cop in the face. They finally handcuffed him when he tumbled to the ground, covered in grease, and knocked himself unconscious.

Meehan spent seventeen months in a Michigan prison, but Luken doubted it would be his last insult to the law. "I knew this case was going to go on until either somebody killed him or he killed somebody," Luken said.

•

His house in Hamilton, Ohio, was ready for him, clean and land-scaped and rescued from foreclosure, when he emerged from prison in 2004.

His sister Donna did that for him. She covered his overdue child support and got his car out of impound and handed him a credit card. "There was nothing he would have had to do except to be a better person and go get help," Donna said.

His first night home, Donna saw him logged on to Match .com. She knew what it meant. He was looking for victims.

He followed Donna to California, where she gave him a spare bedroom at her Newport Beach house and a job at her real estate firm. She said he wouldn't show up for work. He kept going to the hospital for drugs, complaining of his back.

"He wasn't going to get better," Donna said. "He was going to do to me what he was doing to everybody else and just suck them dry."

He followed her to the Palm Springs area in 2007. He rented a house and did RV repairs. He was bitterly preoccupied by the past. He told her about visiting their hometown. The old neigh-borhoods. The family cemetery in Los Gatos.

"Did you go to Mom's grave?"

Yes, he replied. He had pissed on it.

Donna remembered how much John had hated their father, too—how, in the late 1990s, when their father was being consumed by cancer in a Southern California hospice bed, she left John alone with him briefly. And when she returned, their dad was dead.

She could never shake the feeling that John might have injected him with a fatal painkiller, because his slow death was delaying the insurance payout. There was no autopsy before the cremation, no proof.

•

The best glimpse into how John Meehan perceived himself—the best account of how he framed a life littered with self-made disasters—might be in a letter he wrote in June 2012, asking a friend to help him get his nursing license back.

In it, John cast himself as the brave, often-betrayed, long-suffering victim in his life's twisted narrative. He was the victim of his parents, who used him as a pawn in their divorce and treated him coldly. Of his ex-wife, who called police on him and kept his daughters from him. Of his mother, who fed damaging information about him to his ex. Of false accusations that he supplied prescription drugs that killed his brother. Of a herniated disk, which necessitated drugs to escape his pain and depression.

"To be honest with you, I was abusing this stuff not to get high or feel good but because it allowed me to sleep," he wrote. "My job—putting people to sleep."

He explained that he checked into the Saginaw hotel room with the intention of killing himself, and had taken a shower with the aim of leaving "a good-looking body." He injected himself with Versed and fentanyl, he said, but didn't get the fatal dose right—a farfetched claim for someone who put people to sleep for a living.

In state prison his suffering continued. "You don't even want to know what being in a Michigan prison is like. One guy came at me thinking I was going to be easy. They found him in the shower the next morning. I did what I had to do . . . several times. And they finally figured out I was not worth the effort of the trip to the ER. I learn fast, and always had that ability to turn it on when needed."

The letter had the trappings of a confession, but at heart it was a long snarl of self-justification. It was stingy with insights into what created its author.

•

In the end, he turned against his sister too.

When she asked him to remove his trailer from her RV lot in Cathedral City, he insisted the lot was his. He complained to the district attorney. He wrote to the Department of Real Estate.

In 2014, she got a court judgment against him for $90,000 she had lent him. "I knew I'd never see that money, but I did it to protect myself, because John left me alone after that," Donna said. "It was all I had. To me, that was stronger than a gun."

•

Debra Newell did not know all of this about her husband in March 2015. She hadn't talked to John's law school classmates, or his ex-wife, or the Ohio cop. Nor did she get a detailed history of his life and crimes from his sisters. But she did have a stack of documents outlining a history of arrests and restraining orders—more than enough to scare her.

His threatening texts, sent from his bed at Hoag Hospital, amplified her fear. Then, abruptly, his tone became conciliatory. Repentant.

"I still love you and simply can't live without you. I don't want this. I want us without anyone else," John wrote. "I am flawed. But I'm not so easy to give up on you. When I met you it was simply you. I helped you to get back on your feet and stood up for you."

He begged her to see him. He wanted to explain everything.

"I love and need you. Please."

PART FOUR: FORGIVENESS

The private investigator told Debra Newell how to make herself a difficult target. Change hotels every few nights. Study the crowd before she entered a room. Ditch her stylish clothes for bland ones. Get a wig to cover her conspicuous blond hair. Blend in.

She dreaded that she would meet the fate of her older sister, Cindi, dead thirty-one years earlier at the hands of her own husband. The deepest trauma in her family history seemed to be replaying, as if in a nightmare loop, and she feared her mother would have to bury a second daughter.

She had more than three hundred pages of documents she'd taken from her husband's home office, and during late winter and early spring of 2015 she pored over them, trying to determine the scope of his criminal past.

John kept texting her, pleading with her to visit him in the hospital. She wanted to look him in the eye and ask why he had lied to her. Also, she felt guilty about just abandoning him. "For better or for worse," she had pledged. So she went.

●

He had explanations.

He had hidden his criminal record because he knew she would never have given an ex-con a chance.

He had pretended to be an anesthesiologist because he had been so eager to impress her—she was such an impressive high-powered businesswoman herself.

He could explain why police had found cyanide capsules in his desert storage unit. He had multiple sclerosis, and kept the poison in case he needed a quick exit.

He could explain his cruel, threatening texts to her. It was the hospital drugs.

The restraining orders? Those were other John Meehans.

His arrest for stealing surgical drugs in the Midwest? His then wife was trying to frame him and get custody of the kids.

The claim that he solicited the murders of cops and witnesses from the Orange County jail? The fantasy of a jailhouse snitch.

His nickname, Dirty John? A mistake. He had no idea where that came from.

●

The idea of returning to him seemed crazy, and then less crazy, and finally a real possibility. He had her doubting what she had read—it seemed so at odds with the repentant, vulnerable John who kept writing to her in late March 2015.

"I will do whatever it takes to make your life easier," he wrote. "I can travel with you and be there for you. No more lonely nights and no more being alone. I am your husband. That means forever. There is nothing to debate. This is going to work. Forever means forever."

And: "When you are near me I want to protect you and be certain you are safe. It's a good feeling. It's just a bit odd feeling dependent on someone. Even married I never did. Bad habit I guess. I love you Deb. Nothing can take that away."

And: "God put me here for you. You can't see that?"

And: "I love you more than the entire world. Come with me to the four corners of the world."

John told her he needed her. He had multiple sclerosis, after all. She wouldn't abandon him to his illness, would she?

Debra made sure John understood that one day her children would inherit all her money. That was fine, John told her. All he needed was her. He liked to say that he would rather be with her, broke, living under a bridge, than living in a mansion without love.

•

She didn't tell her family. She knew they'd be furious. She didn't tell her employees. She knew they would look away. But she began sneaking away to see him. And she began quietly looking for another place with him. Their Balboa Island house was full of bad memories.

By June 2015 they were living in an apartment near the Irvine Spectrum shopping and entertainment center. He put up photos of their wedding and their travels. "He treated me so well," she would say. "It was as if I was the only thing on Earth."

To explain why Debra Newell returned to John Meehan, in the face of so much evidence, is not easy. He had deceived accomplished women before. A PR professional. A gynecologist. A nurse anesthetist who said it was not about the brain, and added, "The heart is a different organ."

Maybe part of the explanation lay elsewhere, in the peculiar dynamics of Debra Newell's family. It was a family steeped in Christian faith and the concept of forgiveness, even taken to extremes.

•

Debra's older sister, Cindi, was still in her teens when she married Billy Vickers. She was beautiful and vivacious and headstrong. He was a balding supermarket manager who loved football. They had two boys and lived in Garden Grove.

Cindi told her mother, Arlane Hart, that he had become possessive, that he wouldn't let her go shopping or wear a bikini to the beach—he feared another man might pick her up.

She met a professional football player in Palm Springs. She was flattered by the attention. He would send his limo by to pick her up. The marriage foundered. She wanted a divorce. Hart remembers her son-in-law saying, "I can't let her go."

On March 8, 1984, Cindi was writing out checks at the house they had just sold. Her husband pulled out a chrome-plated .25-caliber pistol with a black plastic handle. He stood behind her, raised the gun, and pressed it against the back of her neck.

He fired one bullet into her and another into his own stomach, just below the belly button. He called an emergency dispatcher and said, "I shot myself."

Later that day, Hart's doorbell rang. Police stood with their hats on their chests and told her the news. This is her description of what happened next:

"I lifted my hands toward heaven and I just said, 'God, you've gotta help me. I cannot do this alone. You've gotta help me, God. Help me, God.' I'd been a Christian since I was a little girl. I knew God personally. And all of a sudden I felt a sense of peace come over me, and it drifted down all through my body, and I breathed a deep breath and I looked at the policeman and I said, 'I'm gonna be OK.'"

Her eleven-year-old grandson, Shad, was in another room, watching TV. She told him that his dad had killed his mom. "He looked up at me right then and he said, 'You know, Abraham Lincoln didn't have a mother.' And I said, 'Yes. That's right. You're right, Shad, and look what he turned out to be.' He said, 'I know I can get through this, too, like you, Grandma.'"

Billy Vickers recovered from his self-inflicted wound and apologized to Hart for killing her daughter. She told him she still loved him. "And he said, 'How could you love me? How could you?' And I said, 'God has given that love to us for you. We love you, and we forgive you.' And he just sobbed and he cried."

Vickers was charged with first-degree murder and could have gone to prison for life. At a preliminary hearing, a witness named Carol Planchon testified that he came by her house to borrow her husband's gun about two weeks before the shooting. She joked, "Don't hold up a liquor store."

Planchon's husband testified that he never gave Vickers permission to take his gun and worried that Vickers would harm himself. He called Vickers repeatedly and asked to have it back, and Vickers replied, "I don't have it anymore. I got rid of it."

As the trial approached, the defense attorney, James Riddet, received a call that astonished him. The victim's mother wanted to testify on behalf of her daughter's killer. She didn't believe he had been in his right mind, and she loved him.

Her testimony stunned the prosecutor, Thomas Avdeef, who regarded it as a cold-blooded execution. As he interpreted it, the mother's testimony—and that of other family members whose names he doesn't recall—portrayed Cindi as having mistreated her husband.

"They threw her under the bus," Avdeef says. "I don't know the dynamics of the family. I could never understand that. Why say bad things about the victim?"

The defense attorney called on psychologists to make a case that Vickers had killed in a state of temporary unconsciousness. Jurors acquitted Vickers of murder but deadlocked on lesser charges. The prosecutor planned to retry the case, but then Vickers pleaded guilty to voluntary manslaughter.

In exchange, he got a five-year sentence. He got credit for time served, credit for good behavior, and he was out before

Christmas 1986. The consequence of forgiveness was this: Billy Vickers spent two years, nine months, and nine days in lockup for shooting his wife in the head. Vickers did not respond to requests for comment.

•

Debra disagrees with the prosecutor's interpretation of her mother's testimony. She says her parents taught her to see the good in people, always. Her dad was a youth pastor, her mom a piano teacher. They made it a point to take in troubled kids and give them another chance. They taught that it was important to see the good in everyone, even when it was hard. They believed that none of God's children was irredeemable, and enough love could work wonders.

Her sister's killer remarried and stayed in Orange County, not far from the scene of his crime. For years she'd see him in the bleachers at her nephews' football games and at family functions, and people were careful not to bring up Cindi.

Now and then Debra ran into him at Mariners church, and she'd say hello, she'd try to be polite, but she didn't want to be around him. Forgiveness might have brought her mother peace, Debra says, but she was never able to do it herself. Her inability to do so made her wonder if something was wrong with her, so deep did the idea run.

•

And now John was the soul of repentance. He wept in church. Debra thought it showed a real desire to change. The Father's

Day sermon seemed to hit him particularly hard. He said he missed his two daughters, who were being raised by their mother in another state, and thought about them every day.

He was still recovering from his hospital stay, trying to gain back the twenty pounds he'd lost, lifting weights, chugging protein shakes, frustrated at the slow pace of rebuilding his big frame.

Her kids thought it was lunacy that she had returned to John. And Meehan wanted her kids—particularly her oldest ones—out of her life. He blamed them for the troubles in the marriage, blamed them for hiring a private eye to probe his past, blamed them for temporarily turning his wife against him.

John's hatred for Debra's family did not seem to extend to Terra, Debra's youngest and quietest daughter, even though she had clashed with him. He found her the least troublesome of his stepdaughters.

So he didn't object when Debra drove out to Vegas to console Terra when she broke up with her boyfriend that summer. In the breakup, Terra got Cash, their miniature Australian shepherd.

Terra moved back to California and started applying for jobs. She found one as a kennel attendant and dog groomer. She loved the company of animals.

Terra feared and disliked John—he was the reason she sometimes carried a pocketknife. She said she was willing to sit down with him and try to work things out, believing he would never take her up on it.

Her sister Jacquelyn was upset with Terra for seeming to give John a chance.

"Terra's a lot more like my mom, where she wants to believe

the best in people rather than see any of the bad things," Jacquelyn would say. "I could probably be a little bit more like them, it would do me some good, but I just couldn't see anything good in him, just all bad."

Much of Debra's family was in disbelief. They pulled away from her. In some cases, they wouldn't let her see her grandkids. It was the price of having John in her life. Even her mother had trouble understanding why she stuck with him.

"It totally, totally wrecked the family for many months. The family was just torn apart. We didn't get together because of that," Hart said. "Everyone was talking about it. Why is Debbie staying with this guy?"

In the months to come, Hart would become terrified another daughter would be killed. "I kept praying, 'God, I don't want to lose another daughter. Not another one.' I just say, 'God, help, I didn't know how to pray.' Whatever God needed to do, I just wanted that man out of our lives."

Shad, the eleven-year-old who had lost his mother to his father's bullet, was now in his forties and estranged from the aunt he had cherished as a second mother.

When he tried to reach Debra, John menaced him with texts and emails. Shad tried to block his phone number, and John found him. Shad got off Facebook, and still John found him.

He thought, I'm done. If Debra wanted to be with John, she wouldn't see Shad or his daughters anymore.

Shad stopped trying to reach her. John left him alone.

●

Debra had cut John out of her will months back, for fear that he might kill her; and though she went to sleep beside him and woke up beside him, it was impossible to completely banish that fear.

He keep getting sick and needing to go to the ER. Maybe it's drugs, Debra thought. She couldn't be sure of anything anymore. She just wanted it to work. Her estrangement from her kids and grandkids was breaking her heart.

Her sister had been killed trying to flee a bad marriage. What was John capable of doing, if she tried?

"I realized," she would say, "that he's not going to be that easy to leave."

PART FIVE: ESCAPE

This couple is all wrong, the lawyer thought.

There sat the husband, John Meehan, glowering wrathfully as he plotted legal mayhem on his enemies.

There sat the wife, Debra Newell, soft-voiced and lovestruck and helplessly in his grip.

As he gazed across a conference room table at his newest clients in April 2015, attorney John Dzialo sensed that Debra was in danger.

The lawyer had not wanted to take this case, though Debra had paid an upfront $25,000 fee. His paralegal had been chilled, looking into Meehan's background. Extortion. Stalking. Harassment.

And now Meehan wanted the lawyer to prove that he had

been the victim, in case after case. His plan was a salvo of lawsuits. Against an ex-girlfriend whose accusations had put him in prison. Against cops. Against another woman he swore had cheated him.

Debra wanted help too. She wanted to fix her fractured relationship with her kids, who believed her husband only wanted her money. Could anything be done?

A postnup, Dzialo explained. If they got divorced, it would cut John off from Debra's money.

Meehan did not erupt, but he crossed his arms. He sank into his seat. His lips tightened. His eyes were hazel, but they filled with a fury so intense that Dzialo would recall them as "black as coal." Dzialo sensed a "seething cauldron" in the man's brain, a rage that looked as if it would split his forehead.

There are tales of encounters with religious personages so holy that their aura persists in memory, years later. It was like that for Dzialo, only inverted. Meeting Meehan would stay with him as a glimpse into some kind of human abyss.

"Scariest man I've met in my seventy years," he would say.

He took the case; maybe he could help her.

•

John Meehan didn't begin screaming until Dzialo called to say he had looked into his allegations and didn't see the basis for lawsuits.

"I'm done! You're fired!" Meehan yelled.

Dzialo had predicted this. He said he'd figure out his bill and return the remainder of the money.

Meehan demanded every penny. He would expose him as a

cheat. He would tell the bar. He would tell prosecutors. He would ruin him.

Dzialo had put some time into the case, he had bills to pay, and he hated the thought of surrendering to threats. No way. Then he remembered those bottomless-pit eyes and thought, This is a guy who would do anything. He cut the check.

It did not stop Meehan from complaining to the bar. Because he couldn't get through to Debra by phone, Dzialo drove out to her Irvine business and left her a note. What did she think of this? Soon Meehan was screaming through the phone:

"If you ever contact my wife again, you are going to regret it!"

•

John told her he wanted to die in her arms, that the world was a dark place without her. He got Debra's car washed, ran her errands, dropped off packages at the post office. He brought her flowers constantly.

It was strange to be in love with someone and fear him at the same time. She came home from work anxious about finding him with another woman. When they went to the dog park with their golden retriever, Murphy, she noticed a woman who kept smiling at her husband. Had they shared something?

She had wanted so badly for this, her fifth marriage, to work. It was hard to accept another failure. She didn't think she could endure another divorce. She thought, How can I keep getting this so wrong?

But the size of her mistake was dawning on her. And now she

was wearing a mask, trying to buy time, trying to figure out how to escape.

At times, John seemed to sense that something had changed. "You don't look at me the same way," he would say. "I know you're going to leave me."

She told him it was just his imagination. She was busy at work; she was stressed; she was sorry. To pacify him, she'd make him one of his favorite meals: pork roast with vegetables or jambalaya.

Sometimes they had the semblance of a normal domestic life. At night he'd watch TV while she sat reading beside him. He liked *Lockup*, the documentary series about life behind bars, and *Intervention*, the show about addiction—two subjects with which he had intimate experience.

His favorite show was MTV's *Ridiculousness*, which specialized in the mockery of people who did stupid things and got hurt. It always made John laugh.

•

In December 2015, for their one-year anniversary, he typed out a two-page love letter. It was a treacly bonbon with an arsenic center. It reminded her that between her family and her husband, there was room only for him.

One year . . . and forever means forever. It's been an interesting year to say the least. We've been through some hard times . . . complicated times. But at the end of the day

*I have you to myself. No family and no issues that we can't
work out. I love you. You have the kindest, most forgiving
heart I have ever known . . .*

*I want to grow old with you. Hear you breath[e] in
the middle of the night. Feel you reach for me when there
is nothing else between us. I can't imagine living without
you . . . and your absolutely nutty family. I hope to get over
what they did . . .*

*You are simply the best person I have ever known with
the biggest heart imaginable. I wish I was more like you
. . . I wish I knew you when we were both younger. I can
only imagine how ditzy you must have been and how you
could have made me laugh until I couldn't see straight. It
would have been a dream to have a child with you . . .*

*I love you. I love the way you smell and the way you
drift off to la-la land while I'm talking to you. I love the
feel of you. And needless to say . . . making love to you is
about as close to a religious experience that I have EVER
had . . .*

*I hope I am a better husband than the others. I hope
I am a good man and that you are proud to hold my
hand. I hope you look at me the same way you do now but
in twenty years . . . I hope you love me and we grow old
together. I hope . . .*

She was no longer thinking about forever. She was hiding
money. She took $2,000 from every paycheck and gave it to a
daughter or a friend. She didn't want him to have access to all her

money, for fear he'd take it. And she didn't want him to know she was still giving money to her kids.

He didn't even want her seeing her kids, particularly Jacquelyn, who had been so vocal in her contempt for him. One day he caught Debra sneaking away to see her and said he'd throw Jacquelyn in the ocean if it happened again.

When he discovered that Debra had been paying for Jacquelyn's real estate classes, he called the school to malign her. He sent Jacquelyn lewd messages. She sent him a googled image of a pile of feces.

"Mommy wants nothing to do with you and that will kill you," he texted her.

And: "Jumping off a tall building would make me smile. Head first will work."

•

This is sick, Debra thought. In March 2016—after a year and three months of marriage, after threats and lies and the blind, desperate hope that everything would turn out if she just loved hard enough, after taking him back when everyone said it defied all sense—she decided it was over.

She withdrew $120,000 from her bank account, hoping he wouldn't notice. She had $30,000 stashed in the bottom drawer in a closet—banded stacks of hundred-dollar bills—but he found it and dropped it in front of her.

She told him it was hers. He said, Everything yours is mine.

He told her to hit him. He would make sure she never got up again. She grabbed some makeup, just one shoe, and left.

They had been dividing their time between Orange County and Henderson, Nevada, where she had bought a house in the hope of keeping John away from her children.

Now she and Jacquelyn hurried out there to pack her stuff into a moving truck. Debra put tape over the camera lenses, in case John was watching.

She found a family-law attorney, Michael R. O'Neil, who filed to annul the marriage in April 2016. If Debra had glimpsed a frightening side of him during their first separation, John now seemed a creature of pure malignancy.

"You get your family," he wrote. "I got the dog. I got the better deal."

He demanded money. He would drain her accounts through the divorce courts if she fought him.

"For once in your holier than thou life, listen to me," he wrote. "You are going to have to pay both sides. Which could easily take a year."

And: "We had a good run except for your family. There is no trust. But the last thing I want to do is break you."

He sent her a photo of himself with a provocatively posed ex-girlfriend, taunting her. He threatened to ruin her.

"Make yourself available or I ruin a family. There are children involved, Deb. This is bigger than you," he wrote. "You're selfish to allow this. You'll never forgive yourself but I am doing it."

He called her a crook on Yelp. He had once coaxed naked photos out of her, and now he posted them to her nephew's Facebook page. He texted her that he knew where she was when she picked up her grandchild.

He lectured her. "You don't know how to live. Sex is not love. Get help."

He accused her of assaulting him. "It's pathetic it's come to this point, but you leave me with no options after your storm of lies."

"Storm of lies!" she replied. "Wow. You are the expert in that area."

He had entered their marriage with only a few boxes, mostly old clothes, and now he accused her of stealing $120,000 in cash and gold coins from him.

He complained that he shouldn't have to live on the $558 monthly disability checks he received for his bad back. He demanded $7,000 a month in spousal support and $75,000 in attorney's fees.

"It doesn't matter that paying support isn't what a 'real' man demands. It's what the court feels is equitable. That's all that matters. Think Deb. There is no alternative to this unless you start thinking. That, or you will eventually get bled dry," he wrote. "Be smart Deb. You have no idea of the mistakes you made. Be smart and you'll save a fortune."

•

He had posed as her soul mate, the answer to her longings after four failed marriages, and now he used her past as a barb.

"You think I'm going to allow your family to continue. Look in the mirror. Five times and still making the same mistakes," he wrote. "Now you're getting yours. Pray Deb. Pray hard."

He had turned himself into a churchgoing Christian and wept during sermons, knowing God mattered to her, and now he used her faith as a cudgel.

"Everyone is a better Christian than you," he wrote. "Paybacks are costly and a bitch."

He had rhapsodized endlessly about her beauty and promised she would never know loneliness again, and now turned her vulnerabilities into points of attack.

"You lying old bag," he wrote. "You'll grow old alone."

He sent her a list of her clients—builders who used her interior design business—and threatened to call them twice a day.

"I don't trust anything you say," she replied. "You're evil."

"Face it Deb, I'm smarter than you."

"Stop! Don't contact me again or I will go to the police!"

•

She began wearing a wig, living and working out of hotels, checking in under the names of her assistants. In a request for a restraining order, her lawyer laid out John Meehan's long, ugly history. How the Indiana nursing board had yanked his license and called him "a clear and immediate danger to the public."

How he'd jumped out of a moving ambulance in Michigan. How he'd swindled multiple women and done prison time and been slapped with restraining orders. How Laguna Beach police, who had also asked for a restraining order against him, had found cyanide capsules in his belongings.

An Orange County judge decided there was no immediate

threat to Debra's safety. Her husband lived in another state; he had never physically harmed her.

•

If there was any chance of trying again, Debra undermined it when she visited John at the Henderson house soon afterward. She thought she could talk him into an annulment. She suggested they might even try to start fresh, afterward, with no lies—it was the only thing she could think of to say.

He looked terrible. He said he had terminal cancer. He wouldn't hear of it. Hadn't she promised "Till death do us part"? How could she leave him to die alone?

Trying to buy time, she wrote him a $10,000 check to rehab the Henderson house and told him he could stay there while they figured things out. She slept on a mattress on the floor that night.

"I'm dying Deb. Slowly dying. Please just come up with something so we can move on," he texted her when she got back to California. "I'm doing horrible without you. I need you."

O'Neil knew what a judge would say. How scared of him could she be?

•

O'Neil thought, Just a sick son of a bitch. He believed his threats were probably idle. He thought this until June 11, 2016, when Debra's $64,000 sport-model Jaguar XF disappeared from in front of her Irvine office.

Grainy surveillance footage showed John, in jeans, crouched behind the bushes, watching the car that morning. And it showed him coming back about an hour later wearing gloves and a painter's uniform to steal it.

The car turned up a block away, reeking of gas, with fire damage to the seat and doors. As arson, it was a display of incompetence. The windows were rolled up, the doors closed, so the fire had extinguished itself for lack of oxygen.

June passed, then July. Now it was the third week of August, and Irvine police still hadn't charged him.

Debra was living with Jacquelyn at the Carlyle Apartments in Irvine, near the airport. Jacquelyn liked that there were security cameras.

Debra had cut John off. She wasn't taking his calls or texts. She and her kids were looking after John's golden retriever, Murphy, which he'd left at a pound. And she had the Buick Enclave he'd been using, which had been impounded after he ran it into a gate.

●

On Friday, August 19, 2016, Terra was working at Rebel Run, a Newport Beach dog kennel. A man called with what sounded like a French accent.

The man made it sound as though they had met at some point, and wanted to know if she would be working tomorrow; he wanted to bring in his Rhodesian ridgebacks for her to groom.

She did not recognize the voice, or remember having met him, or think too much about the fact that most of the grooming requests came from women, not men. She told the stranger her work schedule. Yes, she would be there tomorrow until about 5:00 p.m.

•

Around 11:30 that night, Jacquelyn was returning from dinner with a male friend when she saw John in a car, in the dark, waiting outside her apartment gate.

She saw him reflected in the glow of his smartphone, and they locked eyes. John ducked his head. She told her friend, "Follow him!"

Jacquelyn watched John head onto the 405 Freeway. John had smashed or removed the lights on his car, as if to improve his ability to move furtively in the dark.

Jacquelyn believed John was there to kill her or her mom. That he had been hoping to catch one of them alone, an easy target, and the presence of her male friend scared John off.

Debra was skeptical of her daughter's account about seeing John. She thought the guy probably had just looked like John, that Jacquelyn was overreacting. They didn't call police.

Jacquelyn wanted to know: What if he goes after Terra? Debra didn't share this fear; a psychologist had told her the danger was to her, not to her children. Plus, what had Terra ever done to him? She thought he even seemed to like her, sort of.

But Jacquelyn told her friend to drive to the Coronados, the sprawling apartment complex in next-door Newport Beach where Terra was living.

Jacquelyn circled her sister's apartment complex. She checked her sister's door at Apartment W304, to make sure it was locked. She listened for the reassuring jingle of the collar of her sister's cat. She didn't want to wake her.

She called Terra at 6:00 a.m. and said, "John's in the area. He's in a white Camry."

In the dark, Jacquelyn had misidentified the car John was driving. Terra would be watching for the wrong one.

PART SIX: TERRA

John Meehan bragged frequently about his supposed ties to organized crime, and claimed to trace his bloodline to the prolific East Coast hit man who had run Murder Inc. itself. It had the ring of empty boasting from a man who lived by lies.

What is believable is that he approved of the mob's way of doing business, particularly when it came to dealing with enemies. Over and over, he spoke approvingly of a cold-blooded ethos: A dead enemy couldn't suffer, so you went after their loved ones. You went after their families.

•

Terra Newell was twenty-five. Everyone described her as "sweet." Her voice, a soft singsong, forced people to lean in. As a kid, the smallest on the team, she was so uncompetitive in softball games that she didn't bother swinging at pitches.

Terra was a child of the upscale Orange County suburbs but

adored country music, and she liked the songs about drinking beer, having a good time, and loving God. It had started with a high school crush on a boy from Oklahoma, in the same way her current obsession with *The Walking Dead* had started with her ex-boyfriend Jimmy.

Like the company of dogs, music made her forget her anxiety. For years, Terra had lived with a vague sense of dread. When she was around six, she woke up screaming, believing that someone had climbed through her bedroom window to snatch her. Her parents didn't call police.

Her mother thought maybe it was a dream, the function of Terra's distress over what was happening in the house. Her parents were fighting a lot, and were soon divorced. Terra had frequent nightmares at that age. She'd see dark shapes and become convinced they were ghosts or aliens.

Over the years, she said, she wondered whether she was a little bit crazy. In therapy she questioned whether the abduction memory was a real one, but became convinced it had actually happened.

When she was a teenager, a guy she'd been dating flipped out and rammed a car into her leg; she said he was on meth. She got a tattoo on her foot that said "Psalms 23"—the Lord is my shepherd—with a heart she'd seen in a Taylor Swift video.

•

Early on, even before John became her stepfather, Terra sensed he was dangerous. She had sobbed uncontrollably at a Christmas gathering, saying, "There's just something wrong about him. I don't like him." But not everyone felt what she felt; for the longest time, her mother certainly didn't.

She sensed that John was somehow watching her. She liked to have friends crash at her Newport Beach apartment so she would not be alone.

Once she had a dream that John was attacking her, and she had to stab him to save herself. She wrote out a note and put it in her drawer. If anything happened to her, it said, she wanted Jimmy to get Cash, the miniature Australian shepherd.

She was not a brawler and had no martial arts background except for a long-ago self-defense class in PE. She did, however, study television violence with uncommon intensity.

In *The Walking Dead*, she absorbed the first axiom of combat with zombies: They will keep trying to kill you until you destroy the head, by blade or screwdriver, machete or gun. She regarded the show as a fount of survival tricks. When a favorite character extricated himself from a bad spot by biting into an attacker's jugular, she thought, My teeth are a weapon.

More than technique, she said, she took a certain mind-set from the show: "Kill or be killed."

•

Keep your pocketknife handy, her sister Jacquelyn warned her on the morning of Saturday, August 20, 2016. She had spotted John in town last night.

Terra acknowledged the warning, but her mind was elsewhere. She and a girlfriend had $100 lawn-seat tickets to see

Jason Aldean, one of her favorite country acts, who would perform that night at Irvine Meadows.

She put on her rain boots and drove to work at the Newport Beach dog kennel. She greeted the Labs and terriers and Dobermans and poodle mixes. She unlocked the cages. She carried the big bag of dried, high-protein pellets to the bowls. She hosed out the cages and the concrete dog runs. She had strong, round shoulders, strengthened by years of working with large, aggressive dogs.

The French-sounding guy who was supposed to bring in his Rhodesian ridgebacks never showed, but she didn't think much of it. She left work in her Toyota Prius just after 5:00 p.m. for the three-mile drive home. Cash was in the back seat. It was still full daylight.

•

John Meehan had removed the license plate from the gray 2016 Dodge Dart he had rented.

Inside the car, he had his passport, a vial of injectable testosterone, and what police called a "kidnap kit."

An Oakley backpack.

Camouflage duct tape.

Cable ties.

A set of kitchen knives.

•

Terra pulled up to the Coronados, the sprawling block-long complex where she lived. It was not Newport Beach's choicest zip code. People who lived there said it was common to overhear domestic fights and common to look the other way.

Now she drove up the ramp and through the sliding gate to the elevated outdoor parking lot. She always parked in the same stall, SR 423. She saw the Dodge Dart backed into a nearby stall, a man fidgeting in the trunk with a tire iron. She brushed it off, even when Cash growled. She was eager to get to the concert.

She had Mace in her car, pepper spray in her purse, a pocketknife in her apartment, and no weapon in her hands when she climbed out of the car.

•

He had been formidably big, six feet two and 230 pounds of steroidal muscle, a survivor of jail or prison cells in at least three states. He had lost serious weight—he was down to 163—but Terra was still a foot shorter and 33 pounds lighter. He had the element of surprise. He had a long silver knife, concealed inside a Del Taco bag. It bore no resemblance to a fair fight.

•

She was crossing behind her car with Cash, and suddenly John Meehan's arm was enwrapping her waist, his eyes cold. "Do you remember me?" he said.

He clapped his hand over her mouth. She bit down. She screamed. Cash lunged for his ankles.

Meehan jabbed at Terra with the taco bag. She realized there was a knife inside. She threw up her forearm to protect her chest. Her arm opened. They wrestled. They tumbled to the pavement.

•

Blond, small-boned Skylar Sepulveda, fourteen, who didn't know Terra but looked as though she could have been her little sister, had just pedaled home on her beach cruiser from junior-lifeguard training at the Balboa Pier.

She was in apartment T302, wearing only a T-shirt-covered swimsuit, when she heard the screaming and went to the window that overlooked the parking lot. She saw Terra struggling on her back, and Meehan above her, the knife raised over his head.

Skylar told her mom to call police, grabbed her beach towel, and said, "I gotta go."

Barefoot, she rushed out the door, rushed down the apartment stairs, rushed toward the parking-lot stairs.

Scores of balconies overlooked the lot, and she saw people standing on them, grown men and women, just watching. She saw others walking their dogs, as if the bloodcurdling screams weren't splitting the air.

"Going on with their daily lives," she would recall. She saw some people get into their cars. She felt what she called "total disgust with people."

Skylar—a girl with wrists so thin a grown man could have encircled them with one hand—did not pause long enough to worry that the attacker might turn the knife on her when she got to the scene. She just knew she would blame herself if something awful happened that she could have stopped.

•

Now John Meehan's long silver knife was free of the taco bag, and he was striking downward.

The rain boots Terra wore that day were her sturdy pair, with thick tread.

She was on her back, pedal-kicking, trying to save herself, when she clipped his knife hand.

The blade flew from his grip.

It fell to the pavement.

It fell with the handle pointed toward her.

It fell inches from her right hand.

She was right-handed. She didn't think. She began flailing, looking for targets. She connected, again and again.

His shoulder. His shoulder blade. His triceps. His shoulder blade. His upper back. His shoulder blade. His upper back. Between his shoulder blades. His forearm. His triceps. His shoulder. His chest.

His left eye—and through it—into his brain.

•

When she reached the top of the steps, Skylar Sepulveda found John Meehan facedown, bleeding and convulsing. Terra was crawling away, shaking, screaming about how he had stalked her and tortured her family.

Skylar could see exposed muscle in a gash on Terra's forearm, like a surgeon's incision. Skylar wrapped it with a beach towel and tried to calm her down. She asked her questions: "What is your birthday?" It happened they had the same July birthday. Terra was terrified that her attacker would get up and come at her again. Someone else had arrived and was checking on him.

"He can't get up," Skylar said. "He can't hurt you."

Terra picked up her cell phone and called her mom. "I'm really, really sorry," she said. "I think I killed your husband."

John Meehan was not breathing when the police arrived, and had no pulse. They administered CPR, and soon his pulse was back, and he began to take small, short breaths as they rushed him away in an ambulance.

In another ambulance, Terra Newell asked if she would be done in time to get to the Jason Aldean concert, and they said no, but they turned on some country music. They let Cash ride with her.

•

Shad Vickers thought of how many times John had done evil and escaped the law, and how if anyone might rise from the dead to hurt them again, it was him. Even now, he seemed larger than he was, like a horror-movie villain.

Meehan's sister Donna heard the news and didn't rule out the possibility of some trick. Her brother knew every kind.

His other sister, Karen, was summoned to the Santa Ana hospital where he lay unconscious with thirteen stab wounds. She had long ago come to accept that her brother would die unnaturally. Maybe of an overdose, maybe in a confrontation. Not like this.

Debra Newell did not want to be responsible for pulling the

plug. She let Karen, a nurse, decide. Karen looked at the brain scans and gave the OK. A transplant team tried to harvest his organs, but years of drug use had ravaged them.

John Meehan—drug addict, failed law student, disgraced nurse anesthetist, fake doctor, prolific grifter, blackhearted Lothario, and terror of uncountable women—was declared dead at age fifty-seven on August 24, 2016, four days after he had attacked Terra Newell.

Debra was numb. She and Karen were led to a room in a Santa Ana funeral home where his body lay in a long, plain cardboard box. They watched the lid go on the box and the box go in the oven. The door closed, he turned into black smoke, and that was all. There was no memorial service.

•

News of Meehan's death made the local papers, with scant details. "I just wanted to hear he is really dead," said an ex-girlfriend who called police, then cried in relief.

People were trying to reckon the improbability of the outcome. "Impossible," said Shad. "The last person on Earth I'd ever think would send John to hell would be Terra."

Detectives told the prosecutor, Matt Murphy, that it looked like a clear-cut case of self-defense. In such scenarios, the killer usually wound up on the run, the victim dead, dumped off a freeway or in the desert.

Blind luck, the gift of adrenaline, Meehan's drug-weakened condition, Terra's instinctive refusal to comply with his script—all of them had helped to save her.

"Ninety-nine times out of a hundred, the nice person is the one that is dead," Murphy said. "Every once in a while, good guys win."

•

She was not going to take any chances, and so her last strike had been through the eye.

"I guess that was my zombie kill," Terra said. "You need to kill their brain. That's what I did."

Had she killed a man loved by someone, somewhere? This bothered her. Then Donna came by with flowers and told her, "You did a good thing." Her brother had hardly known his daughters. He was as isolated a man as ever lived.

Terra went back to the dog kennel, but barking triggered memories of the attack, and she had to quit. Sometimes she'd see a man roughly John's age, and she'd struggle to breathe. For a while she smoked pot to get to sleep, but it made her paranoid and irritable. So she gave it up, but then nightmares flooded her sleep.

She found a therapist, who helped her build a place in her mind where she could go when things felt overwhelming. She thought of a lake in Montana where she used to go with her dad. She put dragonflies in the picture, and, as her protector, her dog.

•

Debra Newell still struggles with guilt that she brought John into her family's life.

She's close with her kids again. She recently bought her daughters stun guns, pepper spray, and rape whistles. They talk every day, sometimes just to say "I love you." She doesn't need a boyfriend or a husband, a year later, and said she has no desire to date. She works constantly.

She said she feels she's over John. At the Nevada house where he'd been living, she found a clutter of drug vials and syringes. She found some two hundred women on the laptop he used, some of them described with references to their anatomy. She found that he was flirting on three dating sites on the day they were married.

She has concluded that he was some kind of sociopath. But for months she tormented herself, trying to figure out what was real. On her side, the love was genuine and deep, and it was hard to imagine that he had been lying every second, every minute, every day.

Not long after the attack, she took out her iPad and called up footage of their Las Vegas wedding. She watched as they exchanged rings and he smiled down at her tenderly.

She turned away from the screen. She had a catch in her throat, and a question.

"Doesn't he look happy?"

THE DESERTER'S SON

There they are in the black-and-white snapshot, the deserter and his firstborn son: Big Al and Little Al Moreno, the man who ran from war and the Marine who is running to it.

In the photo, it's October 1968. The son is graduating from boot camp, about to head to Vietnam. He's twenty-two, bolt-straight in his uniform. On one side, his mom squeezes against him. On the other, his father keeps his distance, wearing a trapped half-smile, his big workman's hands hanging awkwardly at his sides. As his son stands tall, he seems to shrivel. He cannot bring himself to embrace his son, to touch his uniform.

The son keeps the photo in his living room, to remind him. He's looking at it right now, on a sunny afternoon in May. Without that picture and all it represents, what he is about to do makes no sense at all. Moving briskly around his apartment, he gathers up his wallet and car keys. Under his arm, he tucks a manila folder containing his military records. He heads downstairs to his car, where he studies directions to the military recruiting station in Lakewood, not far from his home.

It doesn't show, but he's nervous. He doesn't know how they will respond to a sixty-year-old former Marine asking to be sent to Iraq. He wonders if they will snicker at him, finding his motives as quaintly unfathomable as everyone else. Not many men show up asking, nearly forty years after surviving one war, to plunge into another. Not many come looking to atone for someone else's crime, one that happened sixty-two years ago, and which everyone else—the government, his siblings, everyone—believes was paid for long ago.

Al Moreno is a Newport Beach private eye and a former Los Angeles police officer. He is divorced and lives alone. Since the day in his teens he learned of it, he has been tormented by his father's desertion from the Navy on February 14, 1944.

For almost two decades, Moreno has been trying, in any way he knows how, to close the gap between the bodies in that snapshot. He's written to presidents, to congressmen, to the Justice Department, to anyone who might listen. What he wants is simple: a posthumous pardon for his father, who died destitute in 1977, nearly three decades after the Navy released him from the brig with a dishonorable discharge.

"He died a broken man both physically and mentally," Moreno says. "He saw himself as a total failure."

Though his father failed his country, Moreno has argued in letter after letter, he also worked tirelessly to raise twelve children. And three of them—Al and his two oldest brothers, Artie and Tony—volunteered for the military and shipped off to South Vietnam. "I don't know how many families can actually say, 'We sent three boys to war.'" In a man's final ledger, shouldn't that count for something?

"There is a historic tradition where a father's sin can be cleansed, in his stead, by his sons," Moreno wrote in a letter to the first President Bush.

Though some historic figures, such as Robert E. Lee, have received posthumous pardons, the Justice Department's pardon attorney rebuffed Moreno, explaining that such pardons were not "established practice."

Years went by, and he kept trying. Local politicians expressed sympathy but said there was little they could do. The staffs of President Clinton and the second President Bush sent polite brush-offs.

He has been waging the campaign for so long that many of his friends and much of his family think he's delusional, a man chasing a mirage. "It doesn't mean squat to anybody," he says. "They look at you sort of cross-eyed." He can't seem to make people understand what he calls "the curse and the taint in the family blood" caused by his father's desertion, a curse that no one else can see, but which feels as real to him as a scar might be across his face.

Even his brothers, the fellow Vietnam vets, support the general goal of a pardon but don't quite understand what possesses Moreno. "If my brother thinks he can rectify history, that's great," says Artie, fifty-nine, an employee for Sequoia National Park. "But what is, is."

Moreno's oldest sister, Irene, who cares nothing for a pardon, recalls that her mother and some of her brothers, including Al, used the desertion against her father in family disputes. The term "yellow-belly" became a surefire argument-clincher, the ultimate cudgel. "It tortured my dad," she says. "I think that's one of the reasons he's doing this—to make up for his cruelty to Dad."

Moreno acknowledges that his relationship with his father was a volatile, sometimes violent one—they scuffled for years until Big Al found himself overmatched by his growing son—but he insists he's waging his campaign out of love and duty, not guilt.

If Moreno looks long enough at the enormous framed reproduction of Michelangelo's *Last Judgment* he keeps on his living room wall, he sees a reflection of his father in the sea of writhing bodies. A lifelong Roman Catholic, he knows the hellscape intimately. It is the day of reckoning, and the killers and traitors are thrashing about in darkness. To begin to grasp Moreno's obsession, look through his eyes at the tormented figures on his wall. Hell has a place for cowards.

•

Right now he's on the 605 Freeway, heading north to meet the Marines. It's just before 2:00 p.m. and traffic is light, so the drive shouldn't take more than twenty minutes. He drives carefully, obeying the speed limit, a sensible sexagenarian. And yet here he is, racing toward war all over again, like he did when he was an angry kid from South-Central with a hundred street fights behind him.

He remains as puzzled now as then about why his dad ran the opposite way. He has chased answers his whole life, hunting down and collecting family anecdotes, a few brittle letters, old military records.

He knows this much. His father, a high school dropout who grew up to Mexican-born parents in the San Fernando Valley, was working for an optical company in Bell when he decided to enlist as an apprentice seaman in November 1943. He was twenty-four years old. He promised the Navy two years.

On Valentine's Day in 1944, just eight weeks after joining the service, he failed to return from a brief period of leave to his post at the US Naval Training Center in San Diego. The Navy posted a straggler's reward and sold off his effects.

As the war roiled, Big Al drove a cab in Tijuana, sneaking back now and then to Los Angeles, where his wife, Trinidad, was living with her parents and receiving support from the American Red Cross.

On March 4, 1947, apparently tired of running, he surrendered at the naval base at Terminal Island. He and his wife already had a daughter, Irene. They also had Al, who was a year old and called by his nickname, Corky. In the brig awaiting his fate, Big Al wrote a letter to his wife.

Sweets,

I just got a letter from you. That makes 3 this week boy it's sure swell hearing from you often. . . . Honey give my regards to your folks for me and kiss the kids for me and tell Irene her father loves her. Of course you can tell Corky the same thing only he doesn't understand. . . . As for you well I don't have to tell you Honey. Boy I sure wish I were home with you and the kids. Someday maybe eh honey?

        I love you sweets and a million kisses to you.

Six days after writing the letter, Big Al was court-martialed. For desertion, the Navy sentenced him to six years' imprisonment, though he would serve only two and a half. They let him go home in September 1949, a thirty-year-old man with a dishonorable discharge and $25 in his pocket.

Little Al was three years old, watching a strikingly handsome man with thick forearms lug an olive-drab duffel bag through the door. Years later, he would remember the sweetness in his father's face, remember thinking, "Wow, that's my daddy." How could anyone say blood was an abstraction, a figment of the imagination, considering the raptures of love he felt that day?

Big Al got work hauling furniture, and he was strong enough to hoist huge appliances single-handed onto a dolly, lug a sofa bed up a flight of stairs, twirl a couple of kids on each arm. He worked sick or well, rattling across the Southland in his bobtail truck. "Of anything he could salvage to show his manly worth, it was his work," Moreno says. "He worked like three men. That's the kind of soldier he would have been."

Mostly, he managed to keep the lights and water on in their little house in South-Central, where they lived on flour tortillas and fifty-pound bags of rice and pinto beans. A dyed-in-the-wool conservative, an admirer of Richard Nixon and John Wayne, Big Al smoked a couple of packs of Pall Mall a day and spent weeknights drinking Eastside or Brew 102. Weekends, he drank scotch, unbuckled his belt and started lashing.

It would be a mistake to forget how tender Big Al could be—a man who made a place at the family table for local children even poorer than the Morenos, who sang show tunes to his girls, who scavenged golf clubs from a thrift shop and made a backyard putting course for his family out of tin cans. His youngest daughter, Cristina, remembers him simply as "an angel here on Earth."

But when Moreno thinks of his father, he remembers his rage, his drinking, how often he hit him and his brothers. It was the obliterating fury, as he sees it, of a man raised in a Chicano culture of machismo who could neither face himself in the mirror nor put his anguish into words.

"If you look at the core of his personality, he was a very proud man. His spirit was destroyed and there was no way to go back and rectify it," Moreno says. "That's the cruelest part about it."

When his boss sacked him in the late 1960s, Big Al tried to make it as an independent driver, buying a crumbling flatbed truck that his older boys helped him start in the morning. He had little education or business sense. Those were the years the Morenos ate string beans and tomato sauce. At the market, his daughter Teresa remembers, Big Al's pride prevented him from bringing the family food stamps to the cashier. She would do it while he waited in the car, hiding.

•

As he pulls off the freeway, cutting west down Del Amo Boulevard, just a few blocks away from the recruiter's station, Moreno wonders how he's going to tell it. He hasn't made an appointment. He'll have to make his pitch succinct and try not to seem crazy. All they'll care about is whether a sixty-year-old can hack the modern-day Corps.

He's sure they'll see that he's different the minute he walks through the door. They'll see a lean, flat-bellied man who still runs thirty miles a week and attacks the weight stacks at Gold's Gym. They'll see the hard posture and muscle-coiled arms. To be on the safe side, he's bringing a photo of himself, shirtless and ripped after a rock-climbing workout, for the recruiter to pass on to his superiors.

He's not some wide-eyed kid, innocent of war save through the movies. He was that boy once, growing up in the wake of World War II, playing in foxholes, thrilling to *The Sands of Iwo Jima* and *Guadalcanal Diary*.

Naturally, he wondered why every other kid's dad seemed to have war medals, but not his. In their big extended family, no one ever said a word about what Big Al did during the war.

Moreno was in junior high when he finally thought to ask his mom. She cried and said, "He left." It felt like a sledgehammer between the eyes.

Soon after, his father approached him in the backyard. It was a beautiful day, and their peach tree was full of blossoms. The effort it took his father to speak looked excruciating. He did not volunteer details or explanations.

Moreno would not remember the words they exchanged. But years later he can remember the expression on his father's face, his eyes saying, The punishment goes on and on. Saying, Don't become me.

It should have brought them closer, that meeting, but it did something else. His secret exposed, his oldest son's admiration for him capsized in an instant, Big Al retreated further into booze and work and silence.

Things were different for Moreno, too, his father's blood in his veins feeling less like a gift and more like a disease.

•

He was not like his brothers, who joined the Army for the usual reasons poor boys sign up. Artie was drinking too much and going nowhere and wanted to get out of Dodge. Tony didn't want to go to college and figured he'd be drafted anyway. They both came home with Purple Hearts.

When Al Moreno Jr. joined the Marines in 1968, he had his own reasons. Now and then, huddled with his buddies in a jungle tent, he would speak of the secret his family never breathed. Explain why he strapped on two two-hundred-round bandoleers instead of one, six grenades instead of two. Explain why, despite a congenital hip condition that supplied a ready-made excuse to stay home, he had fought to get here, exactly where no one else wanted to be. Explain that he longed to do something insanely courageous, to win the Medal of Honor.

In early 1969, Moreno shot and killed three Vietnamese soldiers in the Son Ga mountains. Soon after, when he complained of hip pain, X-rays revealed a bone deformity, and the Marines sent him home. His failure to finish his tour haunted him, but he could never speak of it to his father. Nor could he tell him what he saw in Vietnam, about "screaming, yelling, pain, blood like you didn't know a person had that much blood."

Back home, after repeated medical rejections, the LAPD gave him a uniform. In March 1977, he was on patrol in Hollywood when he was ordered to head to Martin Luther King Jr. Hospital. His fifty-eight-year-old father had arrived there a few hours earlier, suffering a heart attack, and was dead by the time Moreno arrived.

There had been no final words, no deathbed reconciliation. The gulf between them, preserved in that black-and-white snapshot at Moreno's boot camp graduation, now looked as if it might yawn forever.

•

As a policeman, for a time, Moreno thrived. He led the gang unit in recovering guns. But in 1982, the LAPD stripped him of his badge for an off-duty fight and for roughing up a murder suspect.

He came to understand his father's sense of shame and failure in a new way. More than once, he put his gun in his mouth. He saw his own face in *The Last Judgment*—in the demon-clawed figure whose eyes glimpse no reprieve from despair.

He began working as a private investigator, a profession that has proved lean or lucrative, depending on the year, though rarely as exciting as he'd like.

At this particular moment he's pulling off Del Amo Boulevard into the Lakewood Center Mall, scanning for the recruiter's station. There it is, right across from the Arby's.

As he walks up, he's wearing creased khakis and a tight-fitting short-sleeve shirt emblazoned with a Marines emblem. He has prevailed before when a more reasonable man would have relented. Fighting his nerves, he opens the door.

•

For years, Moreno has tried to put himself inside his dad's head during those years underground, as war filled every inch of the nation's air. Though it all, Moreno was convinced of this much: "By no stretch of the imagination did Dad desert because he thought he was gonna be wounded or killed."

Once, Moreno remembers, he was riding with his father when a truck cut them off, sending Little Al's head into the gearshift. A husky hillbilly climbed out with a wrench. Dad knocked him cold with a left hook and took his boy for a malt. That was not the behavior of a gutless man.

"*Mijo*, your dad is not a coward," an aunt told him once. "He was just afraid his mom was gonna die of a heart attack from the stress of going to war."

That was the best explanation the family could give him: that Big Al's mother had him in some kind of sick guilt vise. That was the only story, however incomplete and unsatisfactory, that made sense.

One recent day, a reporter to whom he told his story decided to hunt down the one public record Al Moreno had never thought to look for: his dad's court-martial transcript. He was not prepared for what it said.

The court-martial convened at 11:18 a.m. Wednesday, April 23, 1947, at the naval base in San Diego.

"Not guilty, sir," Al Moreno Sr. pleaded to the desertion charge.

When his lawyer asked him about his physical condition during his recruit training, he replied: "Well, I got a bad back and I kept going over to the sick bay every day, but the doctors wouldn't listen to me." He continued: "Any kind of work I do, or exercise, I just can't stand it, and I can't sleep at night. My legs hurt me."

His back pain resulted from an old car crash, he said, and while he was on leave in February 1944 he decided he couldn't take any more.

"And what did you do?"

"Well, I just didn't come back."

He didn't work for about a year and a half, hiding. Then he started driving the cab in Tijuana, pulling in $60 to $70 a week and sending most back to his wife.

He crossed the border into California once or twice a week, and occasionally supplied a border patrolman with tips on drug dealers.

Asked why he didn't return sooner, he said: "I always did want to, but I don't know what got into me."

He added: "It was always on my conscience. It was driving me crazy all the time." His wife and his mom urged him to return to the Navy, he said, but he "just couldn't pick up enough nerve."

Moreno Sr. had no valid reason for leaving the Navy, the prosecutor concluded, arguing that he had "fooled around a year and a half" before deciding to flee to Tijuana. He turned himself in, the lawyer said, only "to get it over with."

Reading the transcript nearly sixty years later, the son felt physically sick, then apoplectic with fury. He had never heard his father say anything about back problems—nor, he learned when he called her, had his sister Irene. Back problems? From a man who hauled heavy furniture uncomplainingly for decades?

Moreno didn't know what to do with the knowledge. As he saw it, instead of owning up, instead of asking the court to throw the book at him, his father had tried to duck responsibility with his "not guilty" plea.

"For a year and a half before the war ended, every single day, twenty-four hours a day, he was a new coward. Every day he had a chance to turn it around," he says. "And I'm talking about my dad, who I love."

He began to reconsider the wisdom of his decades-long campaign. It suddenly seemed so pointless. Did his dad even deserve a pardon? "I've learned that anger can chew you up," Moreno says. "It just takes too much juice out of you. Probably I do put too much energy into this whole thing. It has affected my life."

He concluded that his father had lied about having a bad back—not because he was afraid of war, but because of that demented maternal spell. It was still the only explanation that made sense.

When his fury abated, he decided he should persevere in trying to win a pardon for his father. Because even if the old man didn't deserve it, the family did.

•

The Armed Forces Career Center is mostly empty. Staff Sergeant Matthew Klepsa, the youngish recruiter who greets him with a firm handshake, hasn't had a walk-in all day. Moreno notices a pull-up bar and asks Klepsa how many he can do.

"Fifteen, sir."

"I can do twice what you can."

Good-naturedly, the recruiter replies: "I believe you, sir."

Moreno feels the impulse to jump on that bar right now and pump out a few. But he knows it would be unseemly, that he must take pains not to seem unhinged. He gives Klepsa his military records and tells him he has an unusual request.

"I want to get back in the Corps," he says. "I work out seven days a week."

"I can see that, sir."

"I just turned sixty in November."

"You don't look sixty, sir."

"I am willing to sign any kind of waiver. I am willing to take any kind of physical agility test. My blood pressure is 119 over 78."

From his folder, Moreno takes out the pumped-up muscle shot of himself. "This is a little cheesy, a little distasteful," he says, extending the photo. "I want you to take this." He adds, "It would be a very positive thing for the Corps."

Now the tricky part. Moreno's voice goes quieter, and he says, "There's one last very personal part of this." He explains that he's here because his dad ran away from World War II.

"He shamed the blood of our family," Moreno says. "Dad had a year and nine months to go. And I want to make up the year and nine months for my pop."

The recruiter nods somberly.

"It's a very profound emotional disgrace to my family," Moreno says.

The recruiter nods again. He explains that the matter is above his head.

Moreno begs him to kick it up a pay grade, to give him a chance.

"I can pass it up," the recruiter says. "It's definitely not something we see every day."

"It's just a win-win situation," Moreno says. "Go the extra yard for me, man."

Moreno leaves feeling giddy. He feels as if he got through to the recruiter, who at least didn't laugh at him.

"Today may be the day that changes my life," he says. "This is my last shot."

A few days later, Moreno gets a call from a gunnery sergeant. It's not that they don't believe he can pull his weight, the sergeant says. The trouble is the precedent they would set by allowing a sixty-year-old to join up.

Moreno argues back, pressing the point that his presence would be a PR bonanza for the Marines. He invokes his thirty miles of running a week, his hundreds of sit-ups a day. The sergeant patiently explains that men his age are more prone to injury, which makes them liabilities.

Moreno hangs up the phone. He doesn't know how to argue with that logic.

"I'm just gonna live with it," he says finally. "You've got to live with the pain. It's not gonna go away. That's just the way it is."

A few months pass. He goes on with his life, a bachelor entering his seventh decade in a one-bedroom apartment hung with Marine emblems. He does private eye work. He takes daredevil rock-climbing trips. He watches war documentaries, studies news from the Iraq war, thinks of all the Americans who went and the one who didn't.

Near him, always, a black-and-white snapshot stares. A father. A son.

Sitting at his desk one afternoon, he finds himself opening a folder. Fishing out the recruiter's business card. Grabbing the phone.

"This is Al Moreno," he says to the voice on the other end, asking if they might reconsider.

HOW SHE FOUND HIM

She arrived in Los Angeles with $600 in borrowed cash, a failing heart, and arthritis in both knees. She spoke no English. She had not seen her firstborn son, Tuan, in the twenty years since he fled Vietnam for the United States as a teenager.

Judging from the letters he sent home, he had prospered here. He was repairing watches, living in Santa Ana. Inexplicably, four years ago, his letters had stopped coming. Now, Hai Nguyen had crossed the ocean herself, hoping to find her son before she died.

She had one lead, the address in Santa Ana. She took a cab there from the airport. She went to the door to find that her son was long gone, leaving no clue behind. She shuffled away with her single suitcase, not knowing what to do next. He could be anywhere. She had no grasp of America's immensity, though a friend who knew the country tried to warn her: It would be like finding a needle at the bottom of the sea.

Where would she start looking, in a country of 300 million strangers? Still, how could she go to her grave without trying?

So, in September, a tiny fifty-seven-year-old woman began stubbornly pushing a pair of green worn-out plastic flip-flops along the sidewalks and strip malls and alleys of Southern California, past street signs she couldn't read and storefronts she couldn't fathom. She didn't have long—just a few months before her visa expired in January, maybe less before her legs buckled or her heart quit or her cancer returned. Or her money ran out.

She had a husky voice and thick, rough hands. Her skin was the deep brown of the Vietnamese poor who spend their lives in the sun. She printed fliers with Tuan's face and stuffed them in the hands of street people and business owners and anyone who might listen.

She found her way to Little Saigon in Westminster, the country's largest Vietnamese American enclave. There, people sympathized. They gave her couches to sleep on, bowls of soup. In their own flight from starvation and violence, many had said goodbye to their families in Vietnam, often forever. Parents cleft from children was one of the community's defining stories. So was arrival in the States with little save hope.

But in other ways she was hardly familiar, this worn-looking woman who had single-mindedly chased hope 8,000 miles, knowing so little, and having no time to count the odds.

•

He was sixteen when she sent him to the boat. For his passage out of Vietnam, the price was two bars of gold that she spent a year buying on layaway. It was 1986, and Ho Chi Minh City was a desperate place. Everyone she knew was starving.

She knew Tuan's escape would be risky. Once before, the scrawny, gap-toothed boy had tried to flee the country only to be seized by police and thrown into jail for six months, to return home even more haggard and emaciated than before.

Now, around midnight at a big marketplace, she handed him to the boat captain who would smuggle him away. She had packed her son a bag with three changes of clothes, sweet rice, moon cakes, and lemon bars. She could tell him nothing about America—not what it looked like, not its language or customs, not its size or landmarks. She knew it only as a mythical country over the sea where people had opportunity and plump cheeks. America was, in one popular phrase, the Jungle of Money.

But it was inconceivably far, and many died on the way. She tried to hold her tears, not wanting to scare Tuan or make him hesitate. Existence had been a day-to-day struggle since 1973, when her husband, a Vietnamese army soldier, died fighting the Communists.

Orphaned of his father as a toddler, Tuan would now face life without his mother, a misfortune that a Vietnamese proverb found even more profound.

Lose your father, you can still eat a poor meal of rice with fish, the proverb went. Lose a mother, you lick the leaves littering the streets. It conjured the crumbs clinging to cast-off leaves used to pack food.

But as she saw it, there was no choice. On the night they said goodbye, it was raining lightly. She kissed him and told him, I love you. Write. She watched him go. He seemed eager.

She did not know if she would see him again. She had two other children to take care of, a son and a daughter. To feed them, she peddled grain from her bicycle and fruit at the market. There was no money to send them away, too, or she would have.

•

Soon Tuan's letters started arriving. He wrote of many days at sea, of running out of food and water and then being rescued by a commercial fishing boat that took them to Malaysia. Of how he found his way to the United States, to Minnesota, which was so cold he moved on to Denver, then farther west, to Southern California.

His letters came steadily for years. He wrote that he was doing well, learning to repair watches. He said nothing to worry her. He sent a picture of himself, smiling. His muscles were thick. His cheeks were full. America had been good.

In Vietnam, where a mother's worth is largely defined by the accomplishments of her kids, to say "I have a son in America" conferred instant pride and status. Everyone understood that fate had smiled on the family.

In 2001, doctors diagnosed Nguyen with ovarian cancer and

gave her two months to live, a prediction she was able to defy with chemotherapy and surgery. Tuan sent $500 and spoke of visiting. Then his letters stopped coming. Twice, medical bills forced her to move to smaller quarters, so she thought perhaps his letters were getting lost.

A year passed without word from him, and another, then a third and a fourth. Her cancer seemed to be in remission, but her overall health was poor. She had developed a heart condition, osteoporosis, arthritis. She knew she was dying, and her final wish was to see him.

She gathered her savings, which had been meant to buy her burial plot. Her younger son, who worked as an ambulance driver, and her daughter, who sold clothes out of a small shop, scraped together loans. Finally she had $1,400, enough for a ticket to California. It was her first time on a plane outside the country. Crossing the ocean, she couldn't eat or sleep.

•

She was not in America long before her money ran out. She had covered mile after mile on foot, stuffed fliers into hundreds of hands, and still there was no sign of him. At wit's end, she pleaded with *Nguoi Viet*, the country's largest Vietnamese-language paper, based in Little Saigon. It published her story and a five-year-old picture of Tuan, the one of him smiling with full cheeks. Soon, local radio picked it up. Donations started pouring in, as well as tips.

One led her to the Westminster Police Department, where she learned two things that shocked her, upending her image of the solid, prosperous life Tuan had lived in the States. At some point, she learned, her son had been incarcerated for robbery. At another point, he had stayed at the Los Angeles Mission. That meant he had been homeless, the orphaned beggar from the proverb.

The possibility of a plummet so extreme had not occurred to her. The Vietnamese had flourished in the United States, and the community had a reputation for taking care of its own. What had happened to her son?

She took a cab to the mission, but he wasn't there. She printed and distributed more fliers, this time offering a $1,000 reward. It was money she didn't have, but she was desperate.

She got word that a man who looked like her son dug up recyclables in the trash cans at John Wayne Airport. For a week, she went there every day, waiting. No luck.

She had reconciled herself to the possibility that she would find him dead. But even that, she reasoned, would be some consolation, better than not knowing.

Chasing every lead, she took cabs to the Asian Garden Mall and Chinatown and across the San Gabriel Valley. She searched homeless shelters and alleys, parks and strip malls. All through the land of promise, to her astonishment, the concrete was littered with human shapes crouched under reeking blankets.

She went from shape to shape, slowly lifting the blankets off ragged, hollow-eyed faces that smelled of beer, off men with tangled hair and dirty hands. They cursed in words she couldn't understand and yanked their blankets back, many of them, sinking back into their covers. Some just looked at her in bewilderment.

She looked into dozens of hopeless faces. There were other mothers' sons, but not hers.

Sorry, she said, over and over. Sorry. Sorry. Sorry. It was one of the few English words she had learned.

She shuffled forward long after her knees burned with pain and her breath came short. When it got too bad, she would sit down on a bus bench and rest. She thought of giving up, taking a plane home to die without him. Then she would get up and keep walking.

Finally, in November, there came an improbable call from a restaurateur in San Jose, a woman named Huong Le who had seen Nguyen's story on Vietnamese-language television. She said Tuan had been living behind her restaurant for the last couple of months at the Lion Plaza shopping center on King Boulevard. He slept on the sidewalk on a patch of cardboard.

On November 19, a woman moved by her story offered her a ride from Orange County to San Jose. It was about noon when she found the restaurant. Her son wasn't there, but restaurant employees said they had been taking care of him. When he was hungry, he'd knock lightly on the rear kitchen door and they would pass him beef noodles and rice, bread and pork. He rarely spoke, they said, and often stood completely immobile. But they found him polite, unthreatening.

Look for his blanket, they told Nguyen. It's blue and yellow fleece. We gave it to him.

After three hours of searching, there in a parking lot across the street, she spotted the blanket. It was just another filthy shape, curled upon a sheet of blue vinyl against some bushes, beside cast-off rolls of iron fencing and rusted steel bars. From the blanket protruded one shoe with a gashed sole. On the ground were take-out containers filled with rotting Vietnamese food.

She had been searching in the United States for three months, lifting blankets off men and women who had somehow fallen into its sewers. Now she knelt and lifted one more.

•

Right away she knew it was him, even through his thick, tangled beard and his long, unkempt hair. He was sleeping, curled in a fetal position, and she startled him awake. She knelt, looking closer. She recognized his overbite, his eyes that were so much like his father's, the scar on his left brow he got as a kid, jumping on a bed with his brother.

She was shaking. Looking at him, she couldn't speak. When words came, she told him through her tears who she was and that she had come across the world to find him.

You have the wrong person, he said. You're not my mother. My mother is sick in Vietnam and ready to die.

She begged him to let her hug him, but he refused. His only possessions were his blanket, a windbreaker, a pocketknife, and sixty-nine cents.

Why would you want to hug a homeless man? he said. Wouldn't you be ashamed?

She planted herself on the pavement, refusing to budge. Afraid he would run away, she grabbed his collar and held him. He kept saying, Let go of me, woman. But she had not flown 8,000 miles and walked for three months to go home without him.

She talked the restaurant into calling the police, hoping they would hold him.

They took him to the Santa Clara Valley Medical Center for observation in the psychiatric unit. They shaved him and cleaned him and gave him a room.

She came every day, to sit with him. He said little. Mostly he sat slouched forward, staring at the floor, his hands folded in his lap. He seemed to recognize her but would not acknowledge it. Perhaps he just could not grasp the improbability of a poor woman from Vietnam coming to find him in a land so large.

When he did speak, he told of having been chased by men who meant to harm him. She did not know what it meant, whether it was a real memory or part of what doctors called his mental illness. They had diagnosed him with an unspecific psychotic disorder.

There were details of his time in the United States that she didn't ask about. So she would not learn that in 1995, he and several other men had burst into an Arcadia home and used a rope to tie up a man and his wife before making off with their cash and jewelry. That police had labeled him a gang member. That a judge had sentenced him to ten years in state prison, though he was released in five. That he went to prison three more times on parole violations, finally going free in January.

I'm nobody, he kept saying. You don't want anything to do with me.

Hoping to break through, she brought him photos of his brother and sister back in Vietnam, of aunts and nieces and nephews. She spoke of taking him home to Vietnam. She did not dwell on whether such a trip was even possible. She had to return in January, when her visa expired. It was not clear whether authorities would let him go too.

For now, though, she had arranged a place for them to stay, at the Cao Dai Temple in San Jose, when the hospital released him.

She ran her hand up and down his back and promised she wouldn't leave him. She would take care of him from now on. She told him that it didn't matter to her, whatever had happened, whatever he'd done. She blamed herself for sending him across the world with no one to watch over him.

Five days had passed since she rescued him from the streets, and all he would call her is "aunt," a generic Vietnamese term for an older woman, not necessarily of blood relation. Now, he spoke a word she had not heard him utter in twenty years.

Mother.

THE OLD MEN AND THE SEA

Like the other old men at this Costa Mesa boatyard, where the hulls of peeling sloops and half-made cutters rot on their wooden posts, Karl Markvart can't be certain he'll live long enough to reach the water.

Again and again, he's watched the boatbuilders around him lose their race to the sea, their unfinished vessels hauled off to the junkyard to make room for another boat, another mad dreamer.

At sixty-nine, Markvart knows it's dangerous to dwell on the size of the task before him, all the work that remains on the thirty-two-foot Dreadnought cutter that is now his home and that he expects, with luck, will one day be his tomb.

He's one of the few regulars at the Boatyard Storage, which sits two miles from the nearest harbor. Piece by piece, Markvart has been building his cutter since buying the fiberglass shell for $9,000 thirty-four years ago, but the boat has been with him— shimmering in his imagination—for nearly twice that long.

As a boy in Prague who'd never seen the sea, he found an adventure book in his tiny neighborhood library. It told of two kids who slip their parents and brave the wild oceans on a sailboat named *Little Cloud*. The accompanying illustration showed a boat with a single mast, three sails, and a stern nearly identical to the bow. He memorized the picture and the names of the parts.

Long after he forgot the book's name, it scudded through his dreams, that magical boat, begging to be built. "From ten years old," says Markvart, whose English is broken, "I had a sailboat back of my head."

Since then, he's sailed in the Adriatic and the Mediterranean and the Pacific, but never on his own craft.

Behind the boatyard's barbed wire fence, set back from Placentia Avenue in a nondescript industrial area, Markvart's boat, a single-mast double-ender modeled after the classic shape in the picture, is inching toward completion.

Every morning, he descends the twelve wooden steps from his boat's deck to his workstation below, where the ground is littered with fine metal scraps and shavings. There, using surplus metal foraged from machine shops, he builds the boat's hundreds of metal fittings, including the complicated stainless-steel blocks that will adjust the sails. He cuts the metal sheets with a hacksaw, drills them in a twenty-five-year-old press, smooths them and stamps them with his initials.

"When you are an old man in rough seas, alone, you have to have everything well-made," says Markvart, a stout, round-faced man with thinning white hair, a slight stoop, and an ironworker's thick, strong hands. "You cannot go to the store and buy fittings like I'm making. It's junk, and high price tag."

Markvart, a retired aerospace engineer, makes his $320 rent at the boatyard with social security and a little savings. In the boat's galley, he cooks cheap, simple meals of potatoes or pilaf, and a boatyard neighbor lets him visit his nearby house for a shower when he needs one. While others work from blueprints, Markvart's finished boat exists only in his head. He's already completed many of the big jobs, like laying 7,000 pounds of lead and rebar ballast into the keel.

"It's like building Mount Rushmore," Markvart says. "It takes a lifetime to finish it."

The circulation in his left leg is bad, but if his strength keeps up, Markvart figures he can launch in three years. He'll head to San Francisco Bay, to Oregon, then up to Alaska and British Columbia, and then who knows? He'll make salmon fillets, adjust his sails, listen to the BBC on his shortwave, and try to stay awake through the night, to steer clear of the big boats that can't see him.

Other boatbuilders nurse visions of "going to Tahiti and chasing girls," he says. "They're between sixty to seventy, and they still dream what they will do in the South Pacific, and their boats will never be finished."

Though he has a gregarious manner, his social links are fewer by the year. Most of his friends and relatives are dead. "I had cell phone for two months, and I had to ask someone just to call me to see if it works," he says. "I see these other guys, and they're retired, and they have wives. They can't do what they want. I'm free."

When he was married himself, to a woman eighteen years his junior, he was able to devote just two hours to his boat on Sundays. She thought the boat stupid. The marriage lasted seven years.

"Once I leave this yard and get on water, I plan to stay on water. And if something happens on high seas, so what? It's much better than to die in traffic accident, or under surgeon's knife," he says. "If something happens like heart attack and boat is not finished, I don't need it anymore." He laughs. "It's easy to die for a man who has lot of things to do and has to do it on little money."

He knows the solitude of the open water drives some people crazy, but he insists he won't be lonely out there where "you have just the water trembling." Adrift, he figures he'll do fine with the companionship of his movies and his medallion of Saint Christopher, the saint of travelers, affixed to his life vest.

He has a plan, should incurable illness come at sea. He has worked it out in his mind. He'll open the boat's through-hull valves and let the ocean in. "That will be my home," he says. "I can take it with me to the other world."

•

His whole life, he's been planning escapes. His father was a prosperous Prague capitalist, which made his family a target of the postwar communist government. In his teens, Markvart was captured trying to sneak into West Berlin and conscripted into the Czech army.

He fled again in 1967, this time taking the train in wide, looping patterns until he reached the border between Yugoslavia and Italy. He hid in the high grass, he says, and sneaked into Italy past border guards while they were distracted by their noon meal. A year later he was in the United States.

His boat is crowded with VHS tapes, and among his favorites is *Night Crossing*, the 1982 film about two East German families who secretly improvise a balloon to carry them to freedom across the Berlin Wall. He'll watch just about anything with a dramatic getaway in it.

One year soon, he's going to make his own final jailbreak.

The boat's name is already engraved on the hull: STARA-LASKA. In Czech, that translates as "old love."

•

On this gravel lot, the ocean breeze blows past ranks of sailboats and speedboats new and old, past water-ready beauties bright with paint and woebegone craft whose owners pay the rent every year but never come. With 110 rental slots and a long waiting list, it's one of the few do-it-yourself boatyards in Southern California, even if doing it yourself swallows your savings and every spare minute.

Manager Maria Chan says sailboats are overwhelmingly a male obsession, and from what she's seen, a frequent cause of divorce. "Either the husband has to give up the boat or has to give up the wife," she says.

She remembers a man in his eighties who came regularly to visit his fifty-foot sailboat but lacked the strength or the will to build out the bare hull. For years, she says, "he just sat on the boat dreaming and didn't do anything." A couple years ago, he died alone at home, and she had his boat hauled to the junkyard.

Then, one morning last year, she opened up the boatyard to find another old boatbuilder stiff at his workstation, his TV running. He'd been dead a couple days, and no one had missed him.

"All these loner people," she says. "No wife, no children."

Markvart is in that category. She gives him a 50-50 chance of making the water.

She's less optimistic about Larry Myers, an eighty-one-year-old widower who drives from Anaheim every morning to work on his forty-four-foot ketch. He's hanging on heroically at a workstation not far from Markvart, taking his stand against time. He recently installed Burmese teak on the deck, strip by strip, despite a World War II mortar wound in the shoulder.

Myers, who has seen enough of the globe to suit him—including North Africa and Italy during the war—is in no rush. "I hope I launch at ninety. Better yet, I hope I launch at ninety-five," says Myers, whose goals for the boat are modest. "This is gonna be a party boat. We'll go to Catalina Island and have coffee, cake, and cookies."

It's a gray day in late fall, and Myers is taking a cigarette break on the steps below his boat. Here comes Markvart, wandering over to say hello. Myers admires Markvart's craftsmanship but ribs him about his frugality. "If he can get something for nothing, he's happy," Myers likes to say. "If not, he wants to pay ninety-nine cents for it."

Before long, the two are musing about mortality. Maybe it's the color of the sky, or maybe death is the most logical subject for those who find themselves sharing a windy corner of its anteroom.

"If you get old and you have some project to do every day, you live forever," Markvart says.

"You want to know what the most fatal disease of all is?" Myers says. "The most fatal disease is life itself."

This elicits one of Markvart's favorite stories, that of a workaholic couple he knew who wasted a lifetime grabbing money with both hands and then died—a heart attack for him, a stroke for her—without children.

Myers feels Markvart hasn't exactly grasped his point, and clarifies: "Everybody dies, period."

"Fatal diseases," replies Markvart, who is known to worry about toxic airborne substances, including fiberglass particles from other boatbuilders carried into his shed by the wind. He tries not to complain too loudly, because there are so few places for a man to build a boat, and doesn't want to stir up trouble.

"Karl, I'm just saying you die," Myers continues. "It doesn't matter. You could be going down the freeway and get killed. And if you have to worry about dying, you may as well die."

"I was very close to death the last time I went to Europe," Markvart says, describing how a box of flowers and soil nearly fell on him during a 2001 visit to Czechoslovakia. "I was just a half second from certain death."

"Hey, Karl, you want me to tell you how many close calls I've had in life?" Myers says, launching into the story of how a German mortar shell killed the soldier beside him in Italy.

It's less a conversation than a duel of alternating monologues. For his part, Markvart invokes his own memories of the war, describing how an Allied bombing raid nearly flattened his home in Prague. "The house next to us, there was nothing but crater," Markvart says. "I was five years old."

Their exchange has exhausted itself. Myers walks carefully up the wobbly steps to his boat. Markvart walks back across the gravel to his own. As always, there's work to be done, steel scraps to measure and hack and press into perfect, shiny fittings.

Markvart knows it's perilous to think too much about the day he's aiming for, when he finally lowers his boat into the Pacific. He knows it's smarter to focus on one task at a time. But when the day comes, Markvart doubts anybody will show up to see him off, because he hasn't spent a lifetime collecting friends, which is one of the reasons it will be easy to leave.

He will not bother breaking a champagne bottle, since he thinks of the ritual as a rich man's theatrics, and he's not building the perfect boat only to risk chipping it pointlessly. He will just motor out of the harbor and into the open ocean. His final plot executed, his final escape launched, he will angle his sails and point his boat north. It won't be a dramatic sight, just a stooped, smiling old man with strong hands, and a little time left, giving himself over to a boy's picture and the wind.

ACKNOWLEDGMENTS

Thanks to the *Los Angeles Times* and the *Tampa Bay Times* for permission to reprint these stories, and to the editors, colleagues, friends, and family who helped in ways large and small: Jesse Wilson, Andrew Conn, Matt Snyder, Will Fischbach, Rick Loomis, Tom Lake, Tom French, Kelley Benham French, Barry Siegel, Jamal Thalji, Chuck Natanson, Dana Parsons, Evan Wright, Erik Rangno, Mark Johnson, Miles Corwin, Erika Hiyasaki, William Friedkin, Sherry Lansing, Mike Wilson, Mike Sager, Mike Moscardini, Mike Anton, Richard Suckle, Richard Bockman, Bill Stevens, Iris Yokoi, Marc Duvoisin, Davan Maharaj, Scott Kraft, Steve Marble, Steve Clow, Steve Padilla, Shelby Grad, John

ACKNOWLEDGMENTS

Barry, John Canalis, Tom Curwen, Mary Cooney, Millie Quan, Elaine Martino, Melanie Long, Karlee Long, Joe Mozingo, Kim Murphy, Kent Wilson, Roger Smith, Hannah Fry, Brady Dennis, Bill Varian, Graham Brink, Sue Horton, Mike Brassfield, Anne and Mark Albracht, Mai Tran, Bill Lobdell, Ashley Powers, Emily Foxhall, Danny Wein, Urban Hamid, Sean Manning, Sean Cook, Sean Keefe, Chris Argentieri, Seth Jaret, Cameron Jackson, Hernan Lopez, Karen Lowe, Lydia Wills, Cullen Conly, Phil Patterson, Luke Speed, Ellen Goldsmith-Vein and the team at Gotham, Carol Bagley, Jennifer Reed, Joe Rubio, Marlene Briones, Omar Briones, my parents, and especially: Jennifer, Julia, Sophia, and Olivia.

ABOUT THE AUTHOR

Christopher Goffard is a two-time Pulitzer Prize finalist for Feature Writing. He has worked at the *St. Petersburg Times* and the *Los Angeles Times*, where he shared in the 2011 Pulitzer Prize for Public Service. Goffard is also the author of *You Will See Fire: A Search for Justice in Kenya* and *Snitch Jacket*, a finalist for the Edgar Allan Poe Award for Best First Novel.